TECHNOLOGICAL SHORTCUTS
TO SOCIAL CHANGE

Technological
Shortcuts
to
Social
Change

AMITAI ETZIONI
and
RICHARD REMP

RUSSELL SAGE FOUNDATION
New York

PUBLICATIONS OF RUSSELL SAGE FOUNDATION

Russell Sage Foundation was established in 1907 by Mrs. Russell Sage for the improvement of social and living conditions in the United States. In carrying out its purpose the Foundation conducts research under the direction of members of the staff or in close collaboration with other institutions, and supports programs designed to develop and demonstrate productive working relations between social scientists and other professional groups. As an integral part of its operation, the Foundation from time to time publishes books or pamphlets resulting from these activities. Publication under the imprint of the Foundation does not necessarily imply agreement by the Foundation, its Trustees, or its staff with the interpretations or conclusions of the authors.

Russell Sage Foundation
230 Park Avenue, New York, N.Y. 10017

© 1973 by Russell Sage Foundation. All rights reserved.

Library of Congress Catalog Card Number: 72–83834

Standard Book Number: 87154–236–6

Printed in the United States of America by Connecticut Printers, Inc.,
  Hartford, Connecticut

CONTENTS

ACKNOWLEDGMENTS

The study was supported by Russell Sage Foundation, initially carried out under the auspices of the Bureau of Applied Social Research, and completed at the Center for Policy Research. The authors are indebted for research assistance to Astrida Butners and William Johnson for Chapter 2 on Antabuse, and to Nancy Gertner for Chapter 4 on gun control. Chapter 3 on drinking drivers and pages 33–48 of Chapter 1 on Methadone were written by Lily Hoffman. A fifth case study, on the Intra-Uterine Device (IUD), will appear as a separate report, prepared by Sarajane Heidt, a research associate of the Center for Policy Research.

INTRODUCTION

We started the research project reported here with one question in mind: can new technologies be used to reduce significantly the costs and pains of needed social changes and to accelerate their pace? Recognizing that remedial social change is usually slow, expensive, and tortuous, we examined six "cases," not so much in order to study these particular ones, but rather to gain an insight into the opportunities and limitations of technological shortcuts. The cases examined include two medical ones (methadone for heroin addiction, antabuse for alcoholism); an educational one (instructional television—ITV); one dealing with violent crimes (gun control); one dealing with highway safety (the breath test), and one dealing with the population explosion (IUD).[1]

We came up with two *partial* answers. One pertains to the conditions under which shortcuts can be effected, since the general answer has turned out to be not a matter of "yes" or "no," but rather one of degrees and specifications (*i.e.*, all shortcuts which "work" are much more effective for some subpopulations than for others). Second, we learned something about a question we had not thought about asking: under what conditions, and to what extent, can one answer such questions as ours regarding the efficacy of a social solution? It was not only that we were hampered again and again by our own shortcomings, *i.e.*, our limited capacity to gather, absorb, and analyze information from a large variety of sources and disciplines, but that we saw the great difficulties of those we observed—experts, political leaders, "think tanks," governments—in making informed, relative, rational choices.

This book is, hence, at one and the same time, a substantive treatment of one issue—the uses of technology to solve social problems—and a treatment of the conditions the "actors" facing the same question encounter when they try to solve it for themselves.

---

[1] The report on the IUD (Intra-Uterine Device) is being completed by Sarajane Heidt and will be published independently. This part of the study is supported by the Population Council. As there are several fine summary works on instructional television, we return to this case only in the Conclusion. See the Conclusion, p. 179 also for references to these works.

TECHNOLOGIES

We mean by technology a set or system of tools, techniques, and the knowledge their use requires.

Technologies extend or replace human capacity. Of those we deal with here, the use of machines for teaching instead of actual instructors (ITV) is the clearest example.

Merrill defines our subject as:

Technologies are bodies of skills, knowledge, and procedures for making, using, and doing useful things. They are techniques, means for accomplishing recognized purposes.[2]

Webster defines technology as follows:

1. The terminology of a particular subject: technical language 2a: the science of the application of knowledge to practical purposes: applied science [the great American achievement has been . . . less in science itself than in∼ and engineering—Max Lerner] *b* (1): the application of scientific knowledge to practical purposes in a particular field [studies are also made of polymeric materials to dental∼—*Report: Nat'l Bureau of Standards*] (2): a technical method of achieving a practical purpose [a∼ for extracting petroleum from shale] 3: the totality of the means employed by a people to provide itself with the objects of material culture.[3]

However, as Merrill notes, "There are techniques for every conceivable human activity and purpose. The concept of technology centers on processes that are primarily biological and physical rather than on psychological or social processes."[4]

In contrast to science, especially fundamental research, technology focuses more on objects, less on symbols; more on service and applied objectives, less on discovering fundamental generalities. Most commonly, we think about technologies as extending our capacities, usually in terms of our muscles (historically most machines have served this purpose); and more recently as means of aiding our nervous system, our preceptive and integrative capacities (with communications equipment and computers).

In 1966 Alvin M. Weinberg, then Director of the Oak Ridge National Laboratory, inquired,

In view of the simplicity of technological engineering, and the complexity of

---

[2] Robert S. Merrill, "The Study of Technology," *Encyclopedia of Social Sciences,* Vol. 15, p. 577.

[3] *Webster's Third New International Dictionary of the English Language Unabridged* (G. and C. Neiman, Co., 1961).

[4] Merrill, *op. cit.,* p. 577.

social engineering, to what extent can social problems be circumvented by reducing them to technological problems? Can we identify Quick Technological Fixes for profound and almost infinitely complicated social problems, "fixes" that are within the grasp of modern technology, and which would either eliminate the original social problem without requiring a change in the individual's social attitudes, or would so alter the problem as to make its resolution more feasible?[5]

Specifically, the question of the feasibility and effectiveness of technological shortcuts is that of the ability to use technologies significantly in handling the kind of domestic problems the society now faces. Can the teaching of the disadvantaged, for instance, be turned over to machines; or the treatment of drug addicts? Few would question that some marginal aspects of these problems can be so handled; say, a slide projector as a teaching aid. But what about the core of teaching? Social work? Mental health? Crime control? How much help can we gain here?

In trying to answer this question, it seemed useful to us to separate two kinds of domestic problems. Some are manifestly "technological," in the realm of objects, and we see little reason even to question that technological development would make a difference. The problem of limiting atmospheric pollution by eliminating the most harmful components from the emissions of automobiles and industrial plants, for instance, is primarily a technological problem requiring a technological solution.

The second kind of domestic problem, concerned with the realm of *human* action, is basically located in people, not in objects (*e.g.,* alcoholism, drug addiction, lack of education). These problems seem to require handling by a person, a teacher, a nurse, a psychotherapist. Can *technology* help *here* in a *significant* way, we ask?

We chose the technologies to be studied in terms of their relevance to the problems our society faces, particularly alcoholism, drug addiction, crime control, population control, the overloading of educational systems, and highway safety. It is not surprising that we found ourselves dealing more often with biological techniques than with physical ones, as this is the area in which involvement with human beings is most direct, and where science is currently making much progress.

Accordingly, three of the technological solutions studied are "medical" in one sense or another: methadone (to curb heroin addiction), antabuse (to fight alcoholism), and IUD to curb population growth. All have to be introduced into the human body; two are drugs; and one is a tool. *All do not treat the personality or require its restructuring.* This is the source of the

---

[5] Alvin M. Weinberg, "Can Technology Replace Social Engineering?" *The University of Chicago Magazine,* Vol. LIX, No. 1 (October 1966), pp. 6–7.

potential economy provided by these "shortcuts." While it is not agreed what are the sources of addiction or of preferences regarding family size—whether they rest in early childhood, peers, group influence, or subcultural values— it is widely recognized that it is very difficult to change a large number of personalities in a calculated and useful way. (As this is an essential point in our discussion, we shall return to it below.) As very large numbers of people are involved in the relevant domestic problems (*e.g.,* 9 million alcoholics in the United States[6]), if a "mechanical" insertion could solve or significantly reduce any of these domestic problems, the economy would obviously be enormous. The image of treating polio or Parkinson's disease with and without a drug is indicative of the economies suggested. Unfortunately this is not "as simple" as it sounds, but then nothing is.

One of the examined technologies, instructional television (ITV), is clearly analogous to other uses of technology, only it replaces not animal or human muscles, but the entire physical presence of a teacher. Additionally as ITV never tires, gets angry, rarely breaks down, does not mind repeating a lesson a number of times, and can teach the same lesson to ten, a hundred or a million people, the potential economy is obviously large. But can it handle a significant part of the teacher's human, personal interaction with students?

We also deal with automobile safety which is in part "pure" engineering and in part is a "medical" technological problem.

Crime control involves a manner of solving problems which may well become more common—the treatment consists of removing an existing technology rather than introducing a new one.

The second general issue, which we were aware of but did not plan to study here,[7] was the way information about the value of a technology is generated, assessed, and used. This question can hardly be separated from ours as almost never is there a clear answer if a technology "works" or not, and the decision if it "works" is much affected by the societal context in which knowledge is produced, communicated and used. Thus we found it necessary to give considerable attention to this issue.

---

[6] *New York Times,* February 19, 1972.

[7] See Amitai Etzioni, *The Active Society* (New York: The Free Press, 1968), chapters 6–9 for a previous discussion.

1

METHADONE:
A SHORTCUT
FOR THE TREATMENT
OF HEROIN ADDICTION?

INTRODUCTION

Methadone is a long-acting narcotic which, given in sufficient doses, is reported to block the euphorigenic effects of heroin and other opiates. The drug has long been used in small doses or rapidly decreasing doses for withdrawal treatment of drug addicts. Only recently, prolonged, relatively high-dosage maintenance on methadone has been medically attempted in order to keep people off heroin, as distinct from just getting them to break the habit of using it.[1]

The pioneering work with methadone as a maintenance drug was conducted by Dr. Vincent Dole and Dr. Marie Nyswander. The program was launched at Rockefeller University with a grant from the New York City Health Research Council and later continued at Beth Israel Medical Center under other grants. By mid-1972, methadone maintenance programs were operating in most of the major cities in the United States.

---

[1] The use of methadone as a therapy for heroin addiction is discussed in Nat Hentoff, *A Doctor Among the Addicts* (New York: Rand McNally and Co., 1968), and Gertrude Samuels, "Methadone—Fighting Fire With Fire," *New York Times*, October 15, 1967. For a comparative description of a methadone treatment program and seven other therapy programs, see Judith Calof, *A Study of Voluntary Treatment Programs for Narcotic Addicts*, 2 pts. (New York: Community Service Society of New York, 1969). For a review of the medical and legal controversy surrounding methadone maintenance see Paul D. Gewirtz, "Methadone Maintenance for Heroin Addicts," *The Yale Law Review*, Vol. 78, No. 7 (June 1969), pp. 1175–1211. An examination of the nature and effects of the effort to control addiction through legal penalties, which has prevailed in the United States since the 1920s, is provided by Alfred R. Lindesmith, *The Addict and the Law* (Bloomington, Indiana: Indiana University Press, 1964).

Methadone has its advocates and its critics. Drs. Dole and Nyswander, and Dr. Frances Gearing, who conducted an evaluation of their findings[2] hold that methadone maintenance is an effective means of returning a heroin addict to a relatively normal life-style; persons on methadone are reported to hold jobs, study, and support their families, including hundreds who did not do so when they were on heroin. The reasons given by methadone's proponents for the drug's efficiency relate to several characteristics that seem to distinguish it from heroin: methadone is longer acting, and the patient does not continually require larger doses in order to avoid withdrawal symptoms.[3] Since the effects of methadone last up to thirty hours, rather than the four to six hours characteristic of heroin, it can be administered daily on an out-patient basis under close observation at hospitals or clinics. From a psychological viewpoint, the methadone "high" is said to be stable, not to fluctuate as a heroin "high" reputedly does. The drug's proponents also suggest that the dosage required to block the effects of heroin and avoid withdrawal symptoms remains stable and apparently has no debilitating effects. There are no reports that methadone has the physiologically harmful effects heroin is alleged to have. A patient can be maintained on methadone for long periods of time, perhaps indefinitely.

The methadone maintenance program has aroused considerable criticism, much of it based on the idea that addiction to heroin is frequently a consequence of an individual's pre-existing psychological disorder. From this perspective methadone maintenance seems merely to replace one means of avoiding, or masking, the fundamental difficulty with another. For example, Dr. Robert Baird, Director of the Haven Clinic for narcotic addicts in Harlem, has described the use of methadone as being like "giving the alcoholic in the Bowery bourbon instead of whiskey in an attempt to get him off his alcoholism."[4] Similarly an ex-addict and staff member of Synanon, a therapeutic community for addicts, asked "what has happened to him [the methadone patient] psychologically as he sucks on this orange juice and methadone? Does he magically no longer have the emotional nature of a drug addict? I would contend that he remains an addictive personality unless something else takes place."[5]

---

[2] Frances R. Gearing, "Evaluation of Methadone Maintenance Treatment for Heroin Addiction: A Progress Report," mimeographed (New York: School of Public Health and Administrative Medicine, Columbia University, November, 1969).

[3] Vincent P. Dole and Marie E. Nyswander, "Rehabilitation of Heroin Addicts After Blockade with Methadone," *New York State Journal of Medicine,* Vol. 66 (August 1, 1966), p. 2015.

[4] *New York Times,* February 16, 1966.

[5] Lewis Yablonsky, "Stoned on Methadone," *The New Republic,* Vol. 155 (August 13, 1966), p. 14.

In view of the rise in illegal drug use that has occurred in the United States in the last two decades, the possible development of a means of forestalling many heroin addicts from committing crimes in order to support their habits, and possibly dying of overdoses, and of permitting them instead to lead relatively normal, productive lives (even though still addicted to narcotics) calls for careful examination. This is particularly so because the proposed procedure is quite drastic—the maintenance of a large population on narcotics, possibly for the rest of their lives. Such a step is held to be desirable only because the apparent alternative—high and rising rates of heroin-induced deaths and crimes—seems worse.

We will initially review the procedures and reported results of the Dole-Nyswander project itself, then examine the results of other comparable methadone maintenance projects, and the findings of an independent evaluation of the Dole-Nyswander project. Finally, we will consider some of the processes by which the methadone maintenance program began to attract support to its means of handling heroin addiction.

We will be concerned initially with the methadone program's "effectiveness" in a broad sense—clarifying whether methadone maintenance achieves the results its supporters claim. Subsequently, we will begin to specify the interpretation of "effectiveness" by raising the question of the mechanisms by which the Dole-Nyswander program achieves its results—inferentially, the question of costs, or efficiency.

THE MAINTENANCE PROGRAM: AN OVERVIEW

Volunteer patients were initially admitted to the Dole-Nyswander Methadone Maintenance Treatment Project (MMTP) in accordance with the following criteria, which were intended to ensure that only "real" addicts would be included:

1. Minimum age at twenty years old;
2. A primary addiction to heroin for at least five years;
3. A history of previous arrests and convictions;
4. A history of previous failures to "kick the habit";
5. Residence in New York City;
6. No evidence of overt major psychiatric or medical problems;
7. Willingness to sign an informed consent form for participation in a long-term medical treatment.[6]

More recently, as the program has expanded, the entrance requirements re-

---

[6] Gearing, *op. cit.*, p. 2.

lating to the applicant's having a previous history of arrests and convictions has been dropped, the period of prior addiction has been reduced to two years, and the age limit has been lowered to eighteen.

The Dole-Nyswander methadone program itself was initially set up in three phases.[7] The first phase was a six-week period of hospitalization. It was in the hospital that the addicts were introduced to oral methadone and their doses gradually increased from small doses (10 to 20 mg. per day) to a level high enough to block the effects of heroin (80 to 100 mg. per day). The drug was first given in divided doses, morning and night, which were gradually increased and decreased respectively until there was one morning dose only. This was designed to reassure the patient that he was being adequately medicated.[8] In the hospital patients were also given extensive medical checkups and care. Near the end of the hospital stay, the patient began to work with a counselor to find a suitable place to live after discharge from the hospital. Recently, however, the MMTP has started inducting the majority of its patients on an ambulatory basis, without an initial hospitalization. Phase two begins with the transition from in-patient to out-patient. The patient returns to the clinic daily for his methadone while he begins seeking a job with the help of a program counselor, or continuing his education. The third phase is reached when the patient is considered a "functioning, self-supporting individual in the community"[9] for a year. His methadone medication is continuing, possibly at a more convenient clinic.

The question about why withdrawal of methadone does not take place at this point, or when it is planned, is answered by Dr. Nyswander in the following manner:

> Our feeling is that it is too soon to attempt it. These people have long been losers in life. They have wasted years of their youth and of their prime because of their addiction. They have now spent up to three years making up the deficit and achieving personal and social stability. If, as we believe, the underlying problem is metabolic, removal of methadone could be disastrous to these individuals. We are not yet ready to take this risk.[10]

In 1969 when the methadone program was being examined by the Bureau of Narcotics and Dangerous Drugs, Dr. Dole is reported to have indicated that

---

[7] Vincent P. Dole and Marie Nyswander, "A Medical Treatment for Diacetylmorphine (Heroin) Addiction: A Clinical Trial with Methadone Hydrochloride," *Journal of the American Medical Association* (JAMA), Vol. 193 (August 23, 1965), pp. 646–650.

[8] Marie Nyswander, "From Drug Addict to Patient," *The Bulletin* (NYSDE), Vol. 9 (May, 1967), p. 7.

[9] Marie Nyswander, "The Methadone Treatment of Heroin Addiction," *Hospital Practice,* Vol. 2, No. 4 (April, 1967), reprint.

[10] *Ibid.,* p. 4.

"so far as he is concerned . . . administration of the drug can go on indefinitely. 'It is totally refractive in its action; there is no pharmacological action. . . . I think that is a separate question. It is not a part of whether these maintenance programs are useful in their present form.' "[11]

The primary objectives of the MMTP are those of ending the patient's dependence upon heroin and facilitating his return to a relatively normal and active style of life. As a means of checking the patient's abstinence, urine samples are collected frequently and analyzed for indications of heroin use.[12] Records are also kept of each patient's employment, attendance at school, and of arrests and convictions.

The results of the MMTP have been reported in a series of articles by Drs. Dole and Nyswander. The program has been generally presented as very successful, with all of the patients who remained in the program (80 percent) stopping heroin use, and most of these patients (approximately 75 percent) becoming self-supporting citizens by the end of the second year of treatment.[13] Although Drs. Dole and Nyswander presented encouraging reports about the operation of the MMTP frequently at scientific meetings and in medical journals, the project did not receive widespread support from public authorities dealing with addicts for nearly three years, by which time the procedure had been examined and replicated by several independent investigators.

In April of 1965, in an article discussing the medical treatment of drug addiction, Dr. Dole observed that "it is now possible to stabilize the pharmacologic state of an addict by a long-acting synthetic agent; in proper dosage this removes the desperation of drug-seeking and the constant threat of abstinence symptoms, without producing euphoria or excessive sedation." He went on to suggest that social rehabilitation rather than abstinence from narcotics should be the initial goal of the medical treatment of addicts and observed that "a stabilized addict should be more open to new interests."[14]

---

[11] "Program Developer Comments on Bureau Study," *Journal of the American Medical Association,* Vol. 208, No. 2 (April 14, 1969), p. 256. The suggestion that methadone is "entirely refractive" in its action is disputed by W. R. Martin, "Commentary on the Second National Conference on Methadone Treatment," *International Journal of the Addictions,* Vol. 5 (1970), p. 550.

[12] Vincent P. Dole, *et al.,* "Detection of Narcotic Drugs, Tranquilizers, Amphetamines, and Barbiturates in Urine," *Journal of the American Medical Association,* Vol. 198, No. 4 (October 24, 1966).

[13] Marie Nyswander, "Methadone Treatment of Heroin Addicts," *The Bulletin, American Psychiatric Association, The New York State District Branches,* Vol. 9, No. 5 (January, 1967), p. 7.

[14] Vincent P. Dole, "In the Course of Professional Practice," *New York State Journal of Medicine,* Vol. 65, No. 7 (April 1, 1965), p. 289.

In August of 1965, in the methadone program's first major report in a medical journal, Drs. Dole and Nyswander discussed the progress of twenty-two patients over a fifteen-month period.[15] The authors report that stabilizing the patients on methadone had "two useful effects: (1) relief of narcotic hunger, and (2) induction of sufficient tolerance to block the euphoric effect of an average illegal dose of diacetylmorphine. With this medication, and a comprehensive program of rehabilitation, patients have shown marked improvement; they have returned to school, obtained jobs, and have become reconciled with their families."[16]

A table detailing the progress of the twenty-two patients indicated that eleven of the twelve patients who have been in the program for at least three months were employed or in school (See Table 1). The first patient listed is a truck driver with an eighth-grade education whose "present activity" is preparing for college. The report also noted that, although there had been rare and sporadic instances of heroin use, in general the patients had no desire for heroin and "have stopped dreaming about drugs, and seldom talk about drugs when together."[17] The patients' mental and neuromuscular functions were reported to be unaffected (aside from a problem with constipation) and "as measured by social performance, these patients have ceased to be addicts."[18] Drs. Dole and Nyswander have reported few side effects of extended maintenance on the drug; however, the possibility that large numbers of people may use the drug throughout a major portion of their lives suggests the relevance of continuing attention to this question.

The next step was to increase the population using the drug. In August 1966, Drs. Dole and Nyswander published a report on the progress of the 120 patients admitted to the MMTP during the first twenty-six months of its operation.[19] It was reported that while thirteen, or 11 percent, of the admitted patients had been dropped from the program—some for reasons unrelated to the use of heroin—none of the remaining 107 patients had become readdicted to heroin. "Before entering the program all patients had been involved in illegal activities, and most had spent a considerable amount of time in jail. . . . The records of these patients after stabilization on methadone would compare favorably with any comparable group of nonaddicted

---

[15] Dole and Nyswander, "A Medical Treatment for Diacetylmorphine (Heroin) Addiction," pp. 646–650.

[16] *Ibid.*, p. 646.

[17] *Ibid.*, p. 649. The report does not indicate how the subjects of the patients' conversations were ascertained.

[18] *Ibid.*, p. 646. No formal measures of "social performance" are reported.

[19] *Idem.*, "Rehabilitation of Heroin Addicts After Blockade with Methadone," pp. 2011–2017.

individuals of the same age and cultural distribution. The blockade treatment, therefore, has virtually eliminated criminal activity."[20]

The data presented to document this interpretation are unfortunately limited. Two comparisons of rates of illegal action are implied: between the program's patients before and during treatment, and between the patients during treatment and a comparable group of nonaddicted individuals. While the report offers some information on the patients' current level of illegal activities (one patient has been convicted of a narcotics charge; "other patients" have been convicted of non-narcotic charges), it does not present comparable data for the other side of either of the two implied comparisons. A chart presented earlier in the report does indicate the number of times the patients were arrested prior to treatment, but no data on these convictions are provided for comparison with convictions of patients during treatment. Similarly, no data are provided or referred to, which indicate rates of conviction or illegal activities of any "comparable group of non-addicted individuals. Nevertheless other sources have indicated that arrests decrease sharply as the number of years patients are in the program rises. They fall from 20 percent in the year before admission to 6 percent during the first year, 3 percent the second year and 2 percent the third year of observation.[21] These indications of reduced criminality have contributed significantly to the growth of support for the program. Additionally 71 percent of the seventy-nine patients who had been in the program for three months or longer were reported to be engaged in "socially useful activities" (58 percent were indicated to have jobs, 9 percent to be attending school, and 4 percent to be combining the two activities). It was suggested in conclusion that "at a conservative estimate the program has already saved the community 3 million dollars," exclusive of the savings associated with the reduced load on hospitals, courts, jails, and the welfare system.[22]

INDEPENDENT CORROBORATION

Two sorts of data generated somewhat independently of the MMTP itself illuminate the effectiveness of the Dole and Nyswander approach to

---

[20] *Ibid.*, p. 2016. The Dole reports include many such ideological statements, without any data. One reason seems to be that the program was under attack from law enforcement authorities, who viewed methadone as just another narcotic, and some medical authorities, who took a similar position. Interviews we conducted with Dole clearly indicated his sense of being persecuted, and his desire for assistance from political leaders, especially Governor Rockefeller (Dole's work was conducted, in part, at the Rockefeller Institute), and finally from the press and the public at large.

[21] Gearing, *op. cit.*, Figure 11.

[22] Dole and Nyswander, "Rehabilitation of Heroin Addicts After Blockade with Methadone," p. 2017.

Table 1. Maintenance Therapy of Ex-Addicts With Methadone Hydrochloride, Summary of First 15 Months (February 1964 to May 1965)

Ethnic Group[1]	Age[2] Years		Previous Treatment[3]	Arrests	Education	Best Job[4]	Time on Program, Months	P[5]	HS[6]	Present Activity
	FD	A								
E	16	22	6	6	8th grade	Truck driver	15	1a	Cert	Preparing for college (Sept. 1965)
E	18	31	8	8	1 year high school	Odd jobs (few months each)	15	1a	Cert	Horticulture school
P	21	33	6	14	2 years high school	Office clerk	10	1a	Cert	Employed (rehabilitation work)
E	20	30	7	1	Graduated high school	Store manager	10	1a	..	Employed (usher-cashier in theater)
E	17	22	6	4	2 years high school	Shipping clerk	11	3	..	Employed (parking lot foreman)
E	21	25	12	1	2 years college	Musician	10	3	..	Employed intermittently (musician)
E	18	25	2	6	Graduated high school	Radio operator in military service	3	2	..	Employed (office work)
N	17	32	3	9	2 years high school	Clothes presser	1½	1	NS	Seeking employment
N	22	37	2	3	2 years high school	Truck driver	1½	1	NS	Seeking employment
P	15	23	0	1	2 years high school	Head usher	1½	2	Cert	Working as waiter
N	16	27	5	1	3 years high school	Stock clerk	1½	1	NS	Army
E	18	22	8	4	1 year college	Mason	1	1	..	Seeking employment

Group	Age FD	Age A	Adm.	Adm.	Education	Job (best position ever held)		Phase	HS equiv.	Status
P	25	35	3	3	1 year high school	Paint sprayer	½	1	..	Employed
P	20	32	5	9	2 years high school	Supervisor of shipping department	1	1	NS	Employed
N	18	30	2	6	3 years high school	Shipping clerk	¼	1	NS	Seeking employment
E	18	24	10	0	8th grade	Installing window screens	3	2	NS	Employed
P	14	30	0	2	2 years high school	Office clerk	3	2	NS	Welfare (seeking employment)
P	19	25	16	10	2 years high school	Office clerk	3	2	NS	Employed (hospital record room)
E	17	19	2	0	Graduated high school	None	3	2	..	Vocational school (barber)
P	13	20	1	2	3 years high school	Stock boy	3	2	NS	Employed (hospital laundry)
E	19	26	2	8	2 years high school	Construction laborer	1½	2	NS	Seeking employment
N	14	30	0	2	8th grade	Shipping clerk	1½	2	Cert	Leather goods company interpreter

[1] For comparison with other treatment series, patients classified into three groups: Western European ancestry (E), Puerto Rican and Cuban (P), and Negro (N).

[2] Age first used diacetylmorphine (FD); age at admission (A).

[3] Number of admissions to Federal Hospital—Lexington, Ky. (F), state hospitals—Manhattan State, Central Islip (S), municipal hospitals—Manhattan General, Metropolitan, Riverside (M), private clinics and groups, including Synanon (P).

[4] All but two patients were employed at time of admission. Job indicated is best position ever held.

[5] Phases of treatment: 1a—four patients, residents on metabolic ward of Rockefeller Institute: 1—new patients being stabilized on methadone therapy, they sleep in hospital but may leave during day for school, shopping, or job; 2—patients newly discharged, living at home or rooming house, needing social support; 3—ambulatory patients who are self-supporting.

[6] High school equivalency status: If not a high school graduate, each patient was encouraged to enroll in night school to prepare for high school equivalency certificate. Those who have completed this course, passed examination, and received certificate are indicated by "Cert"; those now in night school indicated by "NS."

Source: From Vincent P. Dole, and Marie Nyswander, "A Medical Treatment for Diacetylmorphine (Heroin) Addiction: A Clinical Trial with Methadone Hydrochloride." *Journal of the American Medical Association*, Vol. 193 (August 23, 1965), p. 647.

heroin addiction; an evaluation of the Dole-Nyswander program conducted by the Columbia University School of Public Health and Administrative Medicine, which we will examine later, and reports from other methadone projects. There are a number of reports based on independent investigations which have used methadone in approximately the same way as the MMTP does. Still, because of the variation in the ways in which the projects have been designed, it is difficult to compare results from any two tests or studies. For instance, in the methadone maintenance projects reviewed below there are critical variations, first in the characteristics of the groups of addicts admitted to the different programs (some groups being primarily criminals, others not), in the methadone dosages administered (most groups receiving the high dosages which are suggested to block the effects of heroin, one group being maintained on much lower dosages), and also in the way "success" was defined and measured (three projects calling for the addict's abstinence from heroin use along with social rehabilitation—two of these projects monitoring heroin use with urine tests—and one project defining success mainly in terms of the patient's behaviors other than drug-taking and measuring these behaviors through an interview). It seems impossible to combine all experimental results and determine any one figure as an index of effectiveness. Of the studies that are reasonably comparable to the Dole-Nyswander project, we will review two with substantial figures (one following a group of 176 patients for periods up to five years, another following a group of 32 patients up to three years) and two with few patients involved (a one-year, nine-patient study, and a twenty-one-month, sixteen-patient study). These independent investigations of methadone maintenance therapy provide general support for the efficacy of the Dole-Nyswander approach, although they vary a good deal in the degree and persuasiveness of that support.

A small study was conducted by Dr. Alfred Freedman to compare the effectiveness of methadone and cyclazocine (a synthetic analgesic used as an antagonist to both the central and systemic effects of opiates).[23] The methadone segment of the program included sixteen volunteers who received methadone orally. After an initial in-patient period, during which patients are maintained on a 60–180 mg. daily dosage, patients were discharged on a maintenance regimen of a single daily dose of methadone, 75–130 mg. daily. Nine patients returned to the hospital three times weekly for twelve to twenty-one months.

---

[23] Alfred M. Freedman, Max Fink, Robert Sharoff, and Arthur Zaks, "Cyclazocine and Methadone in Narcotic Addiction," *Journal of the American Medical Association*, Vol. 202, No. 3 (October 16, 1967), pp. 119–122.

Freedman describes his goals in terms of a hierarchy on four levels:

1. Improved health and prevention of illness;
2. Increased participation in conventional activities such as satisfactory job performance and relationships with family, friends, and community organizations;
3. Decreased participation in criminal activities, leading to their elimination; and
4. Complete cure and maximal social functioning.[24]

The evaluation of the patients' progress in the *Journal of the American Medical Association* reads: "Their social adjustment has been equal to or better than that on admission, as seven have worked steadily and one has maintained his school enrollment."[25] Alcoholism and other mixed addictions interrupted rehabilitation in three cases, and four other patients who "had not had a satisfactory induction" quit the program. Thus nine out of sixteen patients continued in the program for twelve to twenty-one months and "within the limits of their own rehabilitation efforts, they have maintained themselves in the community without extending a life of crime or a deterioration in social status."[26]

Another small project was set up by Dr. Jerome Jaffe and Leon Brill to test the Dole-Nyswander method with several variations.[27] They wished to establish a more flexible and less expensive procedure with fewer possibilities for illicit distribution of methadone.[28] They eliminated the hospital stay (except for one or two weeks in some cases), treated the addicts on an outpatient basis, charged them part of the cost of their maintenance (the cost of the methadone), and avoided inculcating any group spirit among their patients. They had nine volunteer patients and the program continued for one year. For a time, weekday doses were taken under the supervision of Dr. Jaffe, Saturday doses were given by local pharmacists, and only the Sunday dose was self-administered. As the program continued, more of a role was given to the local pharmacists.

---

[24] Alfred M. Freedman, "Drug Addiction: An Eclectic View," *Journal of the American Medical Association*, Vol. 197, No. 11 (September 12, 1966), p. 157.

[25] Freedman, Fink, Sharoff, and Zaks, *op. cit.*, p. 120.

[26] *Ibid.*

[27] Leon Brill, Jerome H. Jaffe, and David Laskowitz, "Pharmacological Approaches to the Treatment of Narcotics Addiction: Patterns of Response," Paper presented at the 29th meeting of the National Academy of Sciences, National Research Council Committee on Problems of Drug Dependence, February 16, 1967.

[28] When injected by a hypodermic needle, methadone is said to produce a "high" comparable to that resulting from the use of heroin. The oral administration of methadone seems to have a much weaker effect. Methadone is sold on the illegal drug market, although currently it is believed to constitute only a small portion of the illegal drug traffic.

Jaffe and Brill evaluate their patients in terms of vocational adjustment —the ability to maintain a steady job as part of the community—and the regulation of anti-social behavior—generally taken as involvement with the law on other than narcotic possession charges, *e.g.*, theft. The researchers rate seven of their nine patients positive in these two areas.

Overall, the small numbers of patients involved suggest that these two studies may, at best, be considered illustrative evidence. The first study reported a lower rate of "successes" and a higher discharge rate than does the MMTP. It should be noted, however, that three of the seven "failures" were attributed to problems associated with mixed addictions (*i.e.*, addictions involving drugs other than heroin). The Dole-Nyswander program generally does not accept individuals who use drugs other than heroin in significant quantities—a limitation which may preclude treating a sizable segment of the addict population.[29] The second study reports a success rate more in line with the MMTP data, which is based upon an atypical sample of addicts—they are reported to have "previous histories of social competence and very little contact with the law enforcement agencies,"[30] unlike the majority of heroin addicts. This factor is of interest because it has been suggested that the comparable success rate of the MMTP in prompting social rehabilitation is related to its selective admission of the most motivated and promising individuals in the addict population.

A larger maintenance program along the lines of the Dole-Nyswander program was conducted in British Columbia by the Narcotic Addiction Foundation under the direction of Dr. Robert Halliday. The use of methadone for maintenance arose from the report of the Rolleston Committee in Great Britain which concluded that patients might be maintained on narcotics where it was clearly demonstrated that the patients had failed all other attempts at cure and yet were capable of leading normal lives with a certain minimum dosage and incapable of doing so without it. Cases where discontinuance would lead to withdrawal symptoms too severe for the patient are also considered. Accordingly methadone maintenance in this context meant a dosage level intended primarily to avoid withdrawal symptoms rather than to attempt to block the effects of heroin.

Dr. Robert Halliday used two modes of treatment.[31] The first is the provision of decreasing doses of methadone—this is a withdrawal treatment. The second is the provision of maintenance doses for an indeterminate

---

[29] "Methadone and Heroin Addiction: Rehabilitation Without a Cure," *Science*, Vol. 168 (May 8, 1970), p. 686.

[30] Brill, Jaffe, and Laskowitz, *op. cit.*, p. 5149.

[31] Robert Halliday, "Management of the Narcotic Addict," *British Columbia Medical Journal*, Vol. 5 (October, 1963), pp. 412–415.

length of time. Dr. Halliday and Dr. Ingeborg Paulus conducted this comparative maintenance and withdrawal program in Vancouver from 1959 to 1964.[32] The withdrawal treatment involved the oral administration of methadone in a hospital setting "over a 12-day period in doses diminishing from 10 mg. four times a day to 5 mg. twice a day, supplemented with tranquilizing medication where necessary." The maintenance procedure was a daily administration of up to 40 mg. of methadone orally continued "until it is desirable or necessary to discontinue treatment."[33] The work was originally done with 176 subjects, all voluntary, of whom 105 were withdrawn from narcotics use entirely, and 71 were maintained on methadone. All were street or criminal addict types according to the researchers. Those who were maintained on methadone had all previously failed withdrawal treatments. One hundred and fifty-three of the original group were contacted and interviewed from one to five years after their first clinic contact. Progress was evaluated on a scale of rehabilitation again, rather than by abstinence. Rehabilitation, defined as the achievement of specific, measurable changes in a patient's life in accordance with the goals of the Foundation, aimed to:

1. Detoxify the addict and teach him to function without the aid of drugs;
2. Enable him to secure or maintain work in an appropriate occupation;
3. Diminish his involvement in criminal activities;
4. Change his companions to non-drug users and non-delinquents; and
5. Guide him to act in a responsible way in his family.[34]

To evaluate the various patients' development, a precoded interview schedule was used which probed, among other areas, the individual's "work (qualitatively and quantitatively); associations with criminal or near-criminal people; relationships with family; responsibility for dependents; development of healthy social and recreational outlets (not necessarily judged on middle-class standards); and development of useful insights into his psychosocial conflicts."[35] The interviewers made judgments as to whether changes in these and other areas, particularly drug usage, had occurred. They reported that "some signs of positive change" were found in 41 percent of those on the withdrawal program and 47 percent of those on the prolonged maintenance program. Improvement was found more often among women than among men in the withdrawal program (more women than men being

---

[32] Ingeborg Paulus and Robert Halliday, "Rehabilitation and the Narcotic Addict: Results of a Comparative Methadone Withdrawal Program," *Canadian Medical Association Journal*, Vol. 96 (March 18, 1967), pp. 655–659.

[33] *Ibid.*

[34] *Ibid.*, p. 656.

[35] *Ibid.*

drug-free after one year, 19 percent being reported as drug-free after two years). In the maintenance program, older patients seemed less involved in criminal activities than the younger ones (while the majority of the patients were over thirty-years old, all who were in jail at the time of the interview were under forty years of age).[36] Paulus and Halliday consider long ambulatory maintenance with many supportive counseling interviews as very beneficial for the group selected for this treatment. They note that "only maintenance medication seems to keep the hard-core addicts from continuing the in-and-out-of-jail pattern until death."[37]

Although the composite nature of the measure of success used by Paulus and Halliday limits its comparability to the MMTP's several indices of rehabilitation (employment, arrests, drug usage), the figure of 47 percent of the patients reported as exhibiting "positive changes" seems roughly one-third below the MMTP's reported success rates (*e.g.,* 74 percent of the patients employed two years after admission). The subjects in the Dole-Nyswander and Paulus-Halliday projects are similar in several major respects: they are older than the general addict population, they are volunteers, have criminal records, and have failed previous withdrawal treatments. A major reported difference in the Paulus and Halliday maintenance regimen was the relatively lower dosage of methadone administered—40 mg. per day or less. This dosage was lower than the MMTP dosage levels which are suggested to block the effects of heroin. Since Paulus and Halliday indicated at several points that their interest was in achieving social rehabilitation rather than complete abstinence from drugs, and since they apparently did not use urine tests to monitor for drug cheating, it seems possible that their patients returned to the use of drugs more frequently than have the MMTP patients, contributing to the lower reported success rate.

Another methadone maintenance study was set up by Drs. William F. Wieland and Carl D. Chambers as part of the Philadelphia Narcotic Addict Rehabilitation Program.[38] The study's purpose was to test a variation of the Dole-Nyswander maintenance program: the ambulatory induction of patients. From August, 1966, to February, 1968, thirty-two "hard-core" heroin addicts were stabilized on methadone and remained in the program through August, 1969. Thirteen patients were inducted as in-patients and nineteen were initiated into the program as out-patients. Most patients received methadone doses of 100–180 mg. daily and urine samples were taken frequently as a check on the use of heroin and other drugs.

---

[36] *Ibid.,* p. 657.

[37] *Ibid.,* p. 658.

[38] William F. Wieland and Carl D. Chambers, "Methadone Maintenance: A Comparison of Two Stabilization Techniques," *International Journal of the Addictions,* No. 3, 1970, mimeographed.

Methadone

All of the patients were examined by a psychiatrist at induction and again after an average period of twenty-four months in the program. "Marked and sustained clinical improvement, as judged by global ratings of mood, attitude and emotional stability, was noted for 25 (78.1%) of these patients."[39] No significant differences in improvement were found between those patients who were admitted as in-patients and those admitted as out-patients. The report provides no further specification of either the nature of the psychological evaluation or of the results. Still, this observation is of interest because psychological characterizations of methadone patients are fairly scarce. The thirty-two reported job histories are also of interest in this regard as they could reveal possible effects of methadone maintenance upon occupational capacity (see Table 2). However, no uniform effect upon functional capacity is evident.

The authors report that the rate of employment among the patients rose from 34.4 percent at the time of induction to 78.1 percent after maintenance with methadone. Seventy-seven percent of the patients who had previously supported themselves illegally were reported to have secured and maintained full-time legitimate employment.

Ninety percent of the patients reported that they had been arrested before entering the program and indicated an average of 8.6 arrests apiece. After methadone maintenance began, 18.8 percent were arrested and these individuals averaged one arrest apiece.

A comparison of the results for patients inducted on an ambulatory basis with the results for those inducted as in-patients showed that in none of the examined personal or social dimensions was rehabilitation significantly related to the admission technique.

Of the two larger projects only the Wieland and Chambers study used measurements of success that were comparable to those of the MMTP, and it reported quite similar rates of success (78 percent of the patients employed, 81 percent arrest-free after two years,[40] as compared with the MMTP's rates of 74 percent employed[41] and 88 percent arrest-free[42] after two years). The other, smaller, program that reported a similarly high success rate (seven patients out of nine rated as successes) was also similar to the Wieland-Chambers project and to the MMTP (and different from the two other reviewed

---

[39] *Ibid.,* p. 6.

[40] Wieland and Chambers, *op. cit.,* pp. 14–15.

[41] Marie Nyswander, "Methadone Treatment of Heroin Addicts," *The Bulletin, American Psychiatric Association* (January, 1967), p. 7.

[42] Vincent P. Dole, Marie E. Nyswander, and Alan Warner, "Successful Treatment of 750 Criminal Addicts," *Journal of the American Medical Association,* Vol. 206 (December 16, 1968), p. 2710.

Table 2. The Primary Means of Support Before and After a Minimum of 20 Months of Methadone Maintenance

Subjects — Race Age & Sex	Primary Means of Support — Before Treatment	Primary Means of Support — After Treatment	Current Earned Monthly Income
In-patients			
1. 38—WM	Musician	Musician	580
2. 26—NM	Illegal	Machine Operator	385
3. 27—WM	Illegal	Clerical	320
4. 30—WM	Mechanic	Mechanic	600
5. 25—WM	Welfare	Welfare	None
6: 26—NF	Illegal	Service	200
7. 22—WM	Illegal	Laborer	440
8. 37—WF	Illegal	Waitress	320
9. 21—WM	Illegal	Laborer	525
10. 39—NM	Illegal	Porter	330
11. 29—NM	Illegal	Welfare	None
12. 35—WM	Waiter	Waiter	500
13. 28—NM	Illegal	Clerical	465
Totals	23.1% Employed (N = 3)	84.6% Employed (N = 11)	X̄ Earned Income $425
Out-patients			
14. 32—WF	N.I.L.F.	N.I.L.F.—Spouse	None
15. 23—WM	Illegal	Laborer	340
16. 41—WM	Proprietor	Proprietor	1,500
17. 23—WM	Illegal	Bartender	100
18. 23—WM	Stevedore	Stevedore	600
19. 21—WM	Illegal	Cook	400
20. 35—WM	Typesetter	Typesetter	480
21. 39—WM	Proprietor	Bartender	430
22. 28—WM	Illegal	Laborer	320
23. 52—WM	Truck Driver	Truck Driver	330
24. 37—WM	Skilled Manual	Foreman	1000
25. 32—WM	Sales	Sales	700
26. 23—WF	N.I.L.F.	N.I.L.F.—Family	None
27. 30—WM	Illegal	Welfare	None
28. 53—WM	Illegal	Truck Driver	576
29. 39—WM	Illegal	Welfare	None
30. 34—WM	Butcher	Butcher	600
31. 37—WM	Illegal	N.I.L.F.—Spouse	None
32. 41—WM	Illegal	Sales	450
Totals	42.1% Employed (N = 8)	73.7% Employed (N = 14)	X̄ Earned Income $600

Source: William F. Wieland, and Carl D. Chambers, "Methadone Maintenance: A Comparison of Two Stabilization Techniques," *International Journal of the Addictions*, Vol. 5, No. 4, Marcel Dekker, Inc., N.Y., 1970, pp. 645–659. Reprinted by courtesy of Marcel Dekker, Inc.

projects) in that it used urine tests to attempt to detect heroin cheating. However, the patients in this project did not have criminal backgrounds, and might be expected to continue their previous record of employment and freedom from involvement with the law while being maintained on methadone. Of the two projects that reported comparatively lower success rates, the larger Paulus-Halliday project (with a 47 percent success rate) differed from the MMTP in that it did not treat abstinence from heroin use as a central goal, and also used lower maintenance doses of methadone. On the other hand, the project conducted by Freedman *et al.* with seven failures out of sixteen admissions resembled the MMTP in that it used high methadone dosages (60–180 mg. daily) and was concerned about heroin cheating. However, they accepted patients who used alcohol, amphetamines, and barbiturates in addition to heroin, a type of patient which the MMTP avoids accepting. The investigators suggest in conclusion that such patterns of drug usage are a contraindicator to the use of methadone maintenance.[43] Overall, although the reviewed studies were not intended to be experimental replications of the Dole-Nyswander project, and although the process of suggesting post-facto explanations of the studies' varying outcomes can easily be misleading, the information provided by the reviewed methadone maintenance projects appears to generally support, and not to be incompatible with, the reports from the Dole-Nyswander project.

The second major source of data directly bearing on the effectiveness of the MMTP, other than the reports of Drs. Dole and Nyswander and other project personnel, are the reports prepared by the Methadone Evaluation Unit of Columbia University School of Public Health and Administrative Medicine. These reports constitute an independent evaluation in the sense that they check at several points the reliability of the MMTP's data-gathering procedures and also present the data in a manner intended to facilitate the examination of its generalizability to the addict population at large.

We will initially review the general outlines of the data provided in the evaluation report and secondly consider several methodological problems hindering the report's attempt to present the data in the manner of an experimental report.

The evaluation report includes summarized data relating to the achievement of the objectives of the Dole-Nyswander project. The stated objectives of the MMTP are:

1. To establish and maintain a level of methadone sufficient to produce a blockade to the effects of heroin;

---

[43] Freedman, *et al., op. cit.,* p. 120.

2. To reduce anti-social behavior;
3. To increase productivity in a "hard-core" addict.[44]

With regard to the first objective the evaluation report notes that "none of the patients who have remained in the program have become readdicted to heroin."[45] The Wieland-Chambers report discussed above indicated that 28.1 percent (nine) of the patients in the Philadelphia methadone project were detected by the urine test as occasional "cheaters" with heroin.[46] However the evaluation of the Dole-Nyswander project includes no discussion of heroin cheating or of possible discharges for continued use of heroin, although it does report a continuing problem with the abuse of other drugs and alcohol and the continuing discharge of individuals for these offenses up to three years after admission.

The reported alcohol- and drug-abuse rates are of special interest because they provide a possible indication of ex-heroin addicts adopting alternate means of handling psychological stress. As of September 15, 1969, there had been 2,205 admissions and an 18 percent discharge rate (by December 1, 1971, there were 17,550 admissions and 82 percent retention rate and 14,400 patients in treatment[47]). Of the 343 men who were discharged 48 percent, or approximately half, were discharged for either drug abuse (30 percent) or alcohol abuse (18 percent). While the number of individuals discharged decreases for each successive year in the program (first year, 263; second year, 97; third year, 36) the proportion of those individuals discharged for drug or alcohol abuse rises during the first year from 33 percent of all those who are discharged to 64 percent in the second year, to 79 percent in the third year. The observation that long-term attrition occurs primarily through abuse of alcohol or of drugs would seem to suggest that for some individuals heroin addiction may serve certain deep psychic needs.

With regard to the second goal, the reduction of anti-social behavior, arrests appear to decrease with number of years in the program, from 20 percent in the year before admission to 6 percent the first year, 3 percent the second year, and 2 percent the third year. These data are open to a variety of interpretations. They could reflect the effect of the suggested heroin blockade, or they may reflect the patient's reduced need for heroin even if it is still used occasionally. Additionally patients who have been arrested and con-

---

[44] Frances R. Gearing, *op. cit.*, pp. 1–2.

[45] *Ibid.*, p. 9.

[46] Wieland and Chambers, *op. cit.*, p. 11.

[47] F. R. Gearing, "Methadone Maintenance Treatment Programs in New York City and Westchester County: Progress Report for 1971—The Year of Expansion." Submitted to New York State Narcotics Addiction Control Commission, April 28, 1972. Mimeographed. See Tables 1-A and 2-A.

victed are dropped from the program so the more crime-prone patients are progressively eliminated.

With regard to the program's third goal, that of increasing productivity, the report indicates that among a group of 990 men the percentage of those employed or in school more than doubled in the first year, from 29 percent on admission to 65 percent at twelve months, increased by approximately one-sixth (from 65 percent to 74 percent) the second year, and increased again by one-fourth to 92 percent by the end of the third year. The percentage of men being supported by welfare or by their families falls 16 percentage points (from 51 percent to 35 percent) in the last six months of the first year (the first reported data), and then takes three times as long to fall a further 15 percentage points (from 35 percent to 20 percent in eighteen months).

An important question concerns the nature of the jobs held by methadone patients before and during methadone maintenance. This sort of information provides an insight into the psychological capacities of individuals being maintained on methadone. Two short comparative job listings are available, a 1965 listing of twenty-two MMTP patients[48] and a 1970 listing of thirty-two patients in the Philadelphia Narcotic Addict Rehabilitation Program.[49] These listings do not reveal any change in the level of work skills displayed by methadone patients. Additionally the New York State Motor Vehicle Bureau has recently begun to permit methadone patients to obtain driver's licenses, altering an earlier attitude of reluctance to do so.

The objectives of the Methadone Evaluation Unit's reports are:

1. To describe the sample of volunteers accepted into the program in order to attempt to delineate what portion of the addict population they represent;

2. To describe those who are dropped from the program with reasons for drop-out in order to determine how these patients may differ from those who remain in treatment;

3. To document reported information on all patients admitted to the program through objective sources with regard to events prior to admission and to document arrests, employment and school records as well as welfare status while under treatment;

4. To maintain surveillance of urine testing in order to determine degree of heroin use, as well as chronic abuse of barbiturates and amphetamines;

5. Selection of an appropriate contrast group to be followed in similar fashion especially with regard to arrests and incarcerations.[50]

These five objectives may be seen to constitute specifications of two basic areas of concern; assuring that the MMTP data provides a specific and ac-

---

[48] Dole, "A Medical Treatment for Diacetylmorphine (Heroin) Addiction," p. 647.
[49] Wieland and Chambers, *op. cit.*, p. 9.
[50] Gearing, *op. cit.*, p. 4.

curate statement about events within the patient population, and estimating to what extent such a statement may be generalized to the addict population at large. The report of the Methadone Evaluation Unit only partially achieved these suggested objectives.

Objectives 3 and 4, which concerned "documenting reported information" and maintaining "surveillance of urine testing" respectively, focus upon verifying the accuracy of data collected by the MMTP. While the evaluation unit's objective verification of the MMTP statistics did utilize independent sources of information (*e.g.*, police records and the Narcotics Register), at several points the verification is based upon the data collected by the project (*e.g.*, employment record interviews and urine test examinations) and actually constitutes a check upon the flow of information within the MMTP. Objectives 1 and 2 may be seen to focus upon clarifying the generality of the MMTP's findings in that they call respectively for the description of the program's admitted patient population relative to the general addict population and within the group of patients for the description of those who are discharged—generally the failures—thus clarifying the relationship of whatever effect the program's data reveal to the general addict population. The evaluation report does clarify the skewed relationship of the admitted patient population to the heroin addict population at large. The patients in the MMTP may be seen to be disproportionately white and older than the general population of heroin addicts as represented by the New York City Narcotics Register. MMTP patients in 1969 had a mean age of thirty-three years and 67 percent of the patients were over the age of thirty, while addicts on the Narcotics Register had a mean age of twenty-eight and 34 percent were over the age of thirty. Similarly the population of MMTP patients was 39 percent white, 41 percent black, and 19 percent Puerto Rican as compared to 25 percent white, 41 percent black, and 27 percent Puerto Rican on the Narcotics Register.[51]

There are some grounds for suggesting that by selecting a disproportionately older group of addicts the MMTP has chosen patients who would respond particularly well to many forms of treatment or perhaps achieve some degree of rehabilitation without any specialized attention at all. It has been observed by many investigators that there is a diminishing drug use with advancing age, a process termed "the maturing-point process" by Winick.[52]

---

[51] Further data on both applicants to the program and those who are accepted, reflecting the selectivity of admissions, is presented in Marvin Perkins and Harriet Bloch, "Survey of a Methadone Maintenance Treatment Program," *The American Journal of Psychiatry,* Vol. 126 (April 1970), pp. 1389–1396.

[52] Charles Winick, "Maturing Out of Narcotic Addiction," *Bulletin on Narcotics,* Vol. 14 (1962), p. 1.

Similarly the observation that blacks display a somewhat lower probability of staying in the MMTP than whites do might initially suggest that the disproportionate number of whites in the patient population constitutes a biasing factor in favor of the program's success.

Inasmuch as the MMTP is an attempt to test the effectiveness of a particular approach to the social rehabilitation of heroin addicts—long-term maintenance on high dosages of methadone supported by a variety of rehabilitative services—it is important that the program be able to demonstrate that any observable change, and particularly apparent success, is due primarily to the therapeutic regimen, and not to other, circumstantial, factors.

Objective 5, the selection of a contrast group, appears to be a response to such considerations. The evaluation unit chose to collect information relating to arrests from a contrast group, "matched by age and ethnic group selected from the Detoxification Unit at Morris Bernstein Institute." When the arrest records of the MMTP patients and those of the contrast group are compared over a six-year period they are roughly comparable up until the third year, when the MMTP patients entered the treatment program, and thereafter the arrest rate for MMTP patients declines sharply while that of the contrast group remains stable.

While this rather limited and specialized approximation of the use of a control group provides some helpful information, its significance may easily be overemphasized as its utilization is limited to this single comparison and there are serious problems with the equivalence of the two groups even here.

While the two groups were matched with regard to race and age, they may be seen to differ significantly in the probable motivations of the men constituting them. While addicts frequently enter a detoxification unit in order to prepare for court or a jail term, or simply to lower the cost of their habit, an addict entering the methadone program usually has undergone an extended waiting period and is apt to expect to remain on methadone for a long time—perhaps a lifetime. The motivations underlying entrance into these two forms of treatment seem likely to be significantly different. For the purpose of evaluating the adequacy of the contrast group as an approximation to a control group it is sufficient to locate the contrast group's limitations. This in turn suggests that the report's data essentially presents information about an uncontrolled experiment and does not clearly distinguish the causal factor (*i.e.,* the MMTP program or its admissions criteria), nor provide a comparative measure of its "effect" (although a comparison may be inferred by reference to the lack of effectiveness of other rehabilitative programs).

It should be noted however that these observations do not suggest any reasons why the utilization of a more adequately matched control group would tend to alter the general impression of effectiveness gained from the MMTP's statistics,[53] although at present they do provide an imprecise picture of the causal sequence that is occurring.

The evaluation report is clearest while demonstrating the MMTP's achievement in promoting employment, and reducing arrests among former heroin addicts. On the other hand, while it does present material that might be used as a basis for speculating about the precise means by which these effects have been achieved (*i.e.,* data on the characteristics of the discharged patients—the failures—and the continuing patients—generally the successes), it does not attempt any interpretation of this data. The nearest the report comes to considering an interpretation or explanation of how the program achieves its results is its use of the contrast group in a partial refutation of the idea that the program's success is due to its selection of a group of patients who are not typical of the general addict population and who might be particularly susceptible to social rehabilitation. Beyond this inferred refutation of one explanation of the MMTP's effectiveness the question is not approached in the report.

Clarifying the precise manner in which the MMTP achieves its results is important because only this process will permit a thorough evaluation of the MMTP's value relative to other therapeutic approaches. For only by specifying which are the critical ingredients in the program can one clarify which of the costs and dangers associated with the program are intrinsic and unavoidable, and which are avoidable. For example, should it appear that the MMTP's effectiveness is due mainly to its selecting promising candidates from the addict population and providing them with social and psychological supportive services, then the problems, or "costs," associated with maintaining a large population indefinitely on a narcotic would appear less essential to the handling of addiction than would the problem of maintaining supportive services. The methadone program might then be adjudged less valuable than a program primarily using psychotherapeutic approaches.

Usually when different investigators are exploring a variety of approaches to a single general problem, it is deemed inappropriate to ques-

---

[53] This seems particularly likely since Dr. Dole and others conducted a study at the New York City Correctional Institute for Men in 1968 which utilized a control group and reported results comparable to those of the MMTP generally. During the fifty weeks after they were released from the Institute all of a randomly selected untreated control group became readdicted to heroin and fifteen out of sixteen were convicted of new crimes, while none of a randomly selected group being maintained on methadone became readdicted to heroin and three of twelve were convicted of new crimes. Dole, Vincent, *et al.,* "Methadone Treatment of Randomly Selected Criminal Addicts," *The New England Journal of Medicine* (June 19, 1969), pp. 1372–1375.

tion one program's selection of its particular exploratory tack, and to suggest that it is neglecting another approach. This professional courtesy may be appropriate to the earlier phases of the exploration of a problem; when a particular remedial approach becomes a candidate for adoption as public policy, however, the consideration of comparative costs becomes necessary.

As the MMTP has grown, it has come to involve an increasing number of patients (14,400 in December, 1971)[54] and to utilize larger amounts of public funds. Thus the interests of the patients and of the public suggest the desirability of clarifying both the overt effectiveness of the program in achieving its chosen goals and the precise means used to achieve any observed effectiveness. We do not mean to examine the comparative efficacy of methadone maintenance and other means of handling addiction, such as psychotherapy, hospitalization with rehabilitative services, or residence in therapeutic communities[55]—that would clearly be beyond the scope of this study. However, since the question of the precise means by which the MMTP achieves its results is important for evaluating the program's overall effectiveness and since there is as yet no answer generally agreed upon, it will be useful to briefly review some of the possible interpretations.

INTERPRETATIONS

Five fairly distinct categories of causal hypotheses related to the observed results of the MMTP will be reviewed. All have either been explicitly proposed as explanations of the methadone project's effectiveness, or may be inferred from published discussions of the project. The various suggested causal mechanisms are compatible—all could be simultaneously involved in the program's effects. However, they are discussed separately here because they have differing implications as to the "costs" of the MMTP's effectiveness relative to other means of handling addiction. Proceeding from interpretations that stress factors more or less extrinsic to the MMTP's most distinctive characteristic—the use of the narcotic methadone—to interpretations of the effect of the drug itself, we will briefly note the implications of the possibilities that the program's effectiveness is *primarily* due to: 1) its admissions criteria; 2) its social and psychological supporting services; 3) methadone's serving to sedate or tranquilize patients' sensitivity to psycho-

---

[54] Gearing, "Methadone Maintenance Treatment Programs in New York City and Westchester County: Progress Report for 1971—The Year of Expansion," Table 2-A.

[55] For a comparative examination of eight rehabilitation programs for heroin addicts, see Judith Calof, *op. cit.*

logical problems; 4) methadone's blocking the pleasurable effects of heroin; 5) methadone's acting to remedy a physiological deficiency.

The possibility that the MMTP's relative success at socially rehabilitating heroin addicts might be due to its having selected addicts who have a higher than average probability of abandoning heroin use spontaneously has already been discussed. It was found that (a) methadone helps a sufficient variety of people to make it unlikely that they all would have "recovered" without any help; (b) the program still works best for those who volunteer to participate. But even if it does not work for others, the proportion of heroin addicts willing to volunteer is high enough to make the program worthwhile. It should be stressed, there is no evidence it would not work for the others.

Secondly, it is possible that the MMTP's effectiveness is due to the program's providing psychologically induced relief for psychologically and sociologically induced problems. Drug addiction has been viewed as a response in part to psychopathology. Studies have suggested that personality disorders are more common and more severe in young drug addicts than among their peers in the same environment.[56] Additionally, research has indicated that juvenile addicts come disproportionately from the poorer sections of large cities.[57] Thus it has been suggested that the nature of an individual's social environment, as well as psychopathology, can predispose him to drug addiction. To the extent that the MMTP patients include individuals who became heroin addicts in response to social and psychological problems, the program's psychiatrists, social workers, counselors, and vocational counselors might centrally contribute to these patients' rehabilitation by helping to resolve some of the problems that initially led to their addiction. If the MMTP's effectiveness is seen to be due primarily to this kind of remedial work, then the program's most distinctive feature, the administration of methadone, would appear unnecessary. But many other programs,[58] which provide the same amount or more isolation from previous social en-

---

[56]John A. Clausen, "Drug Addiction," *Contemporary Social Problems,* Robert K. Merton, Robert A. Nisbet (eds.) (New York: Harcourt, Brace and World, Inc., 1966), p. 221. However the application of standard procedures for identifying personality disorders to a drug addicted group is particularly difficult. For an attempt to deal with some of the problems see Charles A. Haertzen, "Addiction Research Center Inventory (ARCI): Development of a General Drug Estimation Scale," *Journal of Nervous and Mental Disease,* Vol. 141 (1965), pp. 300–307.

[57] Isadore Chein, *et al., The Road to H: Narcotics, Delinquency, and Public Policy* (New York: Basic Books, 1964), p. 273.

[58] Reference is to programs such as individual and group psychotherapy and not to those which provide total involvement such as Synanon. MMTP provides no total involvement, and hence should not be compared to Synanon from this viewpoint.

vironments and psychological services, are much less effective than methadone programs, which would suggest the drug is of significant use.

A third possible interpretation of the effectiveness of the MMTP is that the narcotic methadone acts to sedate, or tranquilize, the patient, thus reducing his distress arising from sociologically or psychologically based problems. To the extent that such tension-reducing sedation is the primary attraction of heroin for addicts, and to the extent that methadone also fulfills this function, methadone maintenance is a procedure quite comparable to legalizing heroin. Methadone may have some features that would make the provision of legalized methadone simpler than the provision of legalized heroin. Methadone is said to be longer acting than heroin (effective for twenty-four hours as compared to less than six hours for heroin) and to permit the use of a stable dosage (one that produces fixed psychological and physiological effects and does not require a continually rising dose in order to maintain the same effects as tolerance develops). Additionally, the fact that methadone is taken orally while heroin is usually taken intravenously may contribute to the apparently milder reaction of the individual to methadone than to heroin. Similarly, the possibility that part of the effect of heroin upon an individual may be due to the quinine which is usually mixed with a dose of heroin, but not with a dose of methadone, may also help account for the evidently milder effects of using methadone. However, it seems likely that some of the problems associated with the idea of legalizing heroin would also apply to the widespread adoption of methadone maintenance. Even if the MMTP's goal of socially rehabilitating its patients is achieved in every case, so they will lead "normal" lives of work and family, the program would still be vulnerable to charges that it inhibits the patients' psychological maturation, and possibly addicts people to methadone who might otherwise have overcome their drug addiction. Admittedly this line of reasoning weighs the effects of methadone treatment against goals other than those of the MMTP: it does not question the effectiveness of methadone for those goals the program seeks to serve.

Another possible physiological explanation of the MMTP's success is that methadone prevents patients from obtaining satisfaction from the use of heroin. Drs. Dole and Nyswander have stated:

> Detailed clinical and psychometric studies, conducted at Rockefeller University and Beth Israel Medical Center, have shown that a constant, daily dose of methadone maintains the patients in a state of narcotic blockade without producing narcotic effects in itself. The patients become refractory to the euphorigenic action of heroin and other narcotic drugs. After the blockade is established, patients may try to use heroin again—in which case they are disappointed by the lack of effect—but in no case has a patient become readdicted to heroin while being treated with methadone. The blockaded patients lose interest in

narcotic drugs and are able to work and live in the city despite the presence of heroin on the streets.[59]

This conception of the effectiveness of the MMTP views methadone as combating heroin addiction in much the same fashion as a non-addictive antagonistic agent, cyclazocine. Leon Brill, Director of the New Jersey State Narcotics Program, has noted:

> When given in appropriate doses, cyclazocine reduces the subjective and physiological effects of any morphine-like drug. When given to subjects already physically dependent on an opiate drug such as morphine, cyclazocine, like nalorphine, can also precipitate a severe withdrawal syndrome. The regular use of cyclazocine reduces or prevents the development of physical dependency on morphine-like drugs. Presumably, once present, cyclazocine prevents morphine from reaching the usual receptor sites in the nervous system. As a result, patients pretreated with cyclazocine in appropriate doses will not feel the effects of ordinary doses of morphine-like drugs and will not become physically dependent even with regular use of such drugs.[60]

Thus although heroin addicts have to be initially withdrawn from their overt dependence on heroin (*i.e.,* detoxified), once in that state and being given regular doses of cyclazocine it is suggested that they would neither experience the effects of heroin, nor become readdicted to that drug.

However, it has not been clearly demonstrated that methadone maintenance does block the euphoric effects of heroin. While the reports from Drs. Dole and Nyswander and the Methadone Evaluation Unit are unclear about the extent and intensity of heroin use among methadone patients, there does seem to be some use.[61]

However, a potentially significant difference is that cyclazocine is not seriously addictive[62] while methadone is. Accordingly when methadone is

---

[59] Vincent P. Dole and Marie E. Nyswander, "Rehabilitation of Heroin Addicts After Blockade with Methadone," p. 2012.

[60] Leon Brill, "Three Approaches to the Casework Treatment of Narcotics Addicts," *Social Work*, Vol. 13, No. 2 (April, 1968), p. 30. For a discussion of current research on narcotic antagonists see Allen L. Hammond, "Narcotic Antagonists: New Methods to Treat Heroin Addiction," *Science*, Vol. 173 (August 6, 1971), pp. 503–506.

[61] Dole and Nyswander, "Successful Treatment of 750 Criminal Addicts," *Journal of the American Medical Association*, Vol. 206 (December, 1968), p. 2711. There are indications of heroin "cheating" among methadone patients. See Perkins and Bloch, *op. cit.* A report of continuing experimentation with a variety of drugs among one group of methadone patients is provided by W. R. Taylor and C. D. Chambers, "Patterns of Cheating Among Methadone Maintenance Patients." Paper delivered at the Eastern Psychiatric Research Association, November 1970 (mimeographed).

[62] W. R. Martin, C. W. Gorodetzky, and T. K. McClane, "An Experimental Study in the Treatment of Narcotic Addicts with Cyclazocine," *Clinical Pharmacology and Therapeutics*, Vol. 7, No. 4 (July–August, 1966), p. 456.

conceived of as being an effective means of handling narcotic addiction due to its capacity to "blockade" the effects of heroin, its use seems to be generally comparable to the use of antagonistic agents such as cyclazocine, with the added problem that it is addictive.

Finally, a metabolic conception of heroin addiction has been advanced by Drs. Dole and Nyswander. They have suggested that opiate abuse leads to a metabolic deficiency that contributes to the high rate of relapse associated with most treatments for heroin addiction. Drs. Dole and Nyswander present their theory of heroin addiction in the form of a flow chart tracing a possible sequence of involvement with, and addiction to, heroin. It is suggested that "curiosity" and the "availability of the drug" lead to "experimental drug use" which, in turn, leads either to "normal no addiction" or through the intermediary condition of a "neurological susceptibility" to an "altered response to narcotics" and to "addiction." An attempt to leave the condition of "addiction" through "detoxification" leads to "recurrent symptoms of abstinence" and subsequently back to addiction.[63]

From this perspective the narcotic methadone is seen as satisfying a biological rather than psychological "drug hunger," thus relieving the addict from a chronic, physiologically based pressure to relapse into the illegal use of opiates. If the effectiveness of the MMTP is due to the capacity of methadone as a narcotic to satisfy a physiological deficiency arising from previous opiate addiction, then methadone maintenance would appear to be the most dependable and widely applicable means of rehabilitating narcotic addicts that is currently available. For if the long-term persistence of heroin addiction is due to a metabolic deficiency, even though some individuals with particularly strong personalities or who are being provided with special social and psychological supports (such as occurs, for instance, in a therapeutic community) can remain drug-free despite the physiological craving, the large majority of addicts could be expected to eventually become readdicted.

The suggestion of the existence of a metabolic cause for long-term addiction has been supported by some investigations. Experimental work with rats has suggested that opiate addiction leads to physiological alterations which last far longer than overt dependence upon the opiate and which will later cause distinctive behavior such as a preference for opiate-tainted water which normal rats will avoid.[64] However little data have been presented sup-

---

[63] Vincent P. Dole and Marie E. Nyswander, "Heroin Addiction: A Metabolic Disease," *Archives of Internal Medicine,* Vol. 120 (July, 1967), pp. 19–24.

[64] Herman Joseph, "Heroin Addiction and Methadone Maintenance," *Probation and Parole,* Vol. 1, No. 1 (Spring, 1969), p. 5.

porting the metabolic interpretation of continued heroin addiction and the theory is not generally accepted.

Despite the many hypotheses about possible causal processes underlying the MMTP's effectiveness at rehabilitating heroin addicts, the problem remains unresolved; Drs. Dole and Nyswander's metabolic theories have not gained wide acceptance, the evaluation unit's report does not offer a clear interpretation of the program's apparent effectiveness, and the suggestions of other observers generally remain speculative and unsubstantiated. As yet, there seems to be no answer to the question, Why does it work?

Accordingly the program's "workability" must be evaluated on the basis of its attainment of its specific goal—the social rehabilitation of its patients. At this level of analysis the general implications of the data seem comparatively clear.

In view of the various roughly replicatory studies and the number of years during which the Dole-Nyswander reports have been available for, and subject to, concerned criticism without the project's rather major claims being subjected to a serious challenge, it seems appropriate to grant that the program has been unusually successful, even though it is not clear precisely how this has been accomplished. The MMTP does appear to achieve its chosen goal, it does "work" in that its patients are largely able to avoid re-addiction to heroin, avoid entanglement with the law, and become self-supporting to a notably greater degree than patients in other forms of addiction therapy. If an individual who was previously repeatedly involved in criminal activities, and who was unable to hold a job and maintain a "normal" life-style *is* able to do these things while being maintained on methadone, it is difficult to see what arguments, other than the possibility of the individual's health being endangered in the long run, outweigh the program's benefits to the addicts themselves (as attested by the long waiting lines for the program), and to the community as a whole (in reduced cost of crime and of preventive/remedial activities). One cannot argue the morality or immorality of methadone maintenance as if the alternative to being maintained on drugs was being free of all drugs. It is not. It is not even the "cold turkey" withdrawal as practiced at Synanon. The alternative to maintenance, or any other one type of treatment, for most addicts is the street.

Drs. Dole and Nyswander repeatedly speak of methadone maintenance as giving time—time for the addicts to participate in extensive psychotherapy without being tied to the search for the next fix; time for the medical doctors, psychologists, and psychoanalysts to look at the addicts, hold them still, and search for the causes of physiological and psychological addiction.

Although the preceding review of the results of the MMTP and related projects fairly directly suggest the utility of methadone maintenance, the development of political support for such a program is a different and more complicated process. This aspect of the growth of the MMTP is examined below.

THE RISE OF CONCERN*

Although programs devoted to medical maintenance of addicts on narcotics operated in this country in the early 1920s, these clinics were basically an anomaly. Since the Harrison Act in 1914, drug addiction has been handled chiefly by the courts and penal system, and medical experimentation with the maintenance of drug addicts on narcotics of any kind, including methadone, has been sharply inhibited.[65] Only recently has the view been widely challenged that narcotic addiction is most effectively inhibited by the legal prosecution of addicts and their suppliers—a view promoted over decades by the Federal Bureau of Narcotics.[66]

In the 1950s a vanguard of concerned physicians, lawyers, social scientists, and other professionals whose work brought them into contact with drug addiction and its associated problems, became increasingly aware of, and began to focus their attention upon what they viewed as a crisis—the extent to which drug addiction policy was detached from the reality of a growing social problem. The "reality" that provoked their activity was the growing post-World War II narcotics traffic and usage which indicated a failure of the punitive approach which had characterized the last thirty years of narcotics policy. Their attention was directed to the assumptions behind the approach—that addiction was a crime and thus belonged in the province of law enforcement agencies and officials. Such reasoning had justified the

---

* Pp. 33–48 were researched and written by Lily Hoffman.

[65] Edwin Schur notes that the establishment of municipal clinics were themselves probably a response to the pressure of the Harrison Act and its judicial interpretation, in that individual M.D.s were fearful of taking on addicts as patients. *Narcotic Addiction in Britain and America* (Bloomington, Indiana: Indiana University Press, 1962), p. 63.

[66] For arguments that addicts are "sick" and not criminal and should be treated accordingly, see: Rufus King, "The Narcotics Bureau and the Harrison Act: Jailing the Healer and the Sick," *Yale Law Journal,* Vol. 62 (April, 1953); Marie Nyswander, *The Drug Addict as a Patient* (New York: Grune and Stratton, Inc., 1965); William Eldridge, *Narcotics and the Law,* 1962; Edwin M. Schur, *Narcotic Addiction in Britain and America* (Bloomington: Indiana University Press, 1962); Lawrence Kolb, *Drug Addiction: A Medical Problem* (Springfield, Illinois: Charles C. Thomas, 1962). For collective recommendations of a medical approach see: The Council of Mental Health of the AMA, *Comprehensive Report on Drug Addiction,* 1956, in *Drug Addiction: Crime or Disease? Interim and Final Reports of the Joint Committee of the American Bar Association and the American Medical Association on Narcotic Drugs* (Bloomington, Indiana, 1961).

maintenance of the *status quo* by the Federal Bureau of Narcotics,[67] the branch of the Treasury Department which had monopolized the control of addiction,[68] as well as by the potentially relevant federal knowledge-producing units such as the Public Health Service.

In contrast, the critical groups sought to question the adequacy of this conception, first in light of what they considered the factual realities of the day, secondly in relation to results of their several investigations into the history of drug control policy and the law in the United States,[69] and finally, in comparison with British and European approaches to narcotics addiction which not only were shown to differ from our own but also were felt to be more effective.[70] Before the 1950s and these critical efforts, Americans were generally unaware of these issues and of the existence of differences in approach, either within this country or in comparison to other countries.[71] Thus, this vanguard served a "critical function," mobilizing for change both their own professions[72] and, to a degree, society at large. This movement for

---

[67] Lindesmith, *The Addict and the Law*, chapter 9. He finds that the Bureau is the main exponent of the theory of drug addiction as a crime; that it is dependent on the *status quo* and, in turn, the biggest obstacle to reform.

[68] In 1968, the Bureau of Narcotics of the Treasury Department was combined with the Bureau of Drug Abuse of the Department of Health, Education, and Welfare, and the composite organization, whose administration was dominated by the staff of the Bureau of Narcotics was called the Bureau of Narcotics and Dangerous Drugs (BNDD) and placed under the jurisdiction of the Department of Justice.

[69] *Joint Committee: AMA–ABA.* The Committee reviewed narcotics laws and recommended legal research; cited the ambiguity of laws regulating narcotics and questioned the soundness of the premises they rest on; commented on the inadequacy of the statistics of the Bureau of Narcotics.

Eldridge discussed the ineffectiveness of the American system and its legal history, and in the *Proceedings: White House Conference* questioned the statistics concerning narcotics.

[70] An important use of knowledge by the critics, to support an examination of the community-of-assumptions underlying our policy, was the so-called "discovery" of the British approach to addiction, and the dissemination of information about this different and possibly more effective approach, in various publications, as well as at commissions and conferences, see, for example, books by King, Schur, Eldridge, Lindesmith cited above. See also, articles, particularly E. M. Schur, "Drug Addiction in America and England," *Commentary*, Vol. 30 (September, 1960), pp. 241–248, and Gertrude Samuels, "Report on the British System of Drugs," *New York Times*, October 18, 1964, p. 37.

For collective expressions, see *The Joint Committee: AMA–ABA*. Rufus King presents a comparative view of British and European experiences. The Federal Bureau responded to this information by issuing counterstatements in its pamphlets during the period, stating that the British system is essentially the same as ours.

[71] *Joint Committee: AMA–ABA.* See introduction to report, by Lindesmith.

[72] The early critics cited the need for the medical and legal professions to assume responsibility in this area. Some went as far as to say that the M.D. had given the addict up

reform within the relevant professions came about in the context of inadequate knowledge production, collection and synthesis, leading to an ineffective policy on the part of the unit controlling public policy towards addiction —the Bureau of Narcotics and Dangerous Drugs. For this failure we can locate both symbolic and structural explanations.

First, the knowledge chosen to inform and implement public policy by the Federal Bureau of Narcotics (the organization which had assumed the control of drug addiction and drug traffic since its formation in 1930) seemed not only out of touch with social reality, as indicated by the growth of the narcotics problem, but had become dysfunctional to one of the Bureau's public goals since it tended to create and maintain a drug problem and a drug culture.[73] Several of the critics speculated upon this lack of alignment of knowledge with reality, questioning the accuracy of the Bureau's statistics and indicating that its continual understatement of the size of the narcotics problem was intended to reflect favorably upon the effectiveness of the legislation and enforcement policies in effect during this period.[74] Lindesmith said essentially the same thing when he commented on the "vested interests" that made the *status quo* desirable.[75]

Looking at the Bureau's position over the thirty-year period 1930–1960, we perceive a lack not only of self-critical feedback, but of new knowledge

---

due to fear. The Joint Committee of the AMA–ABA on Narcotic Drugs suggested that the medical profession should "itself lay down criteria"; and that the AMA reconsider its 1924 statement. The Committee also recommended that the legal profession reexamine the legal history of narcotic addiction. *Drug Addiction: Crime or Disease?* (Bloomington, Indiana, 1961).

In *Proceedings: White House Conference* (1962), the Conference recommends that the medical profession develop a code defining legitimate medical practice.

Dr. Wortis, in *New York Academy Bulletin*, Vol. 40 (April, 1964), p. 318 summarized the symposium saying that there has been a "lack of a responsible attitude on the part of the medical profession" and there is a need to "train M.D.'s in medical school to handle this." See also Edwin M. Schur, *Narcotics Addiction in Great Britain and America*, pp. 202–204.

[73] Many observers have pointed out that by defining the addict in moral terms and treating addiction as a crime, we have helped create a criminal way of life for the addict, who must steal to finance his expensive, because illegal, habit.

Lindesmith, *The Addict and the Law*, chapter 10, also suggests that the spread of the "habit" is linked with the prohibitive system of control and that illicit traffic gives it a kind of symbolic importance.

Schur, in *Narcotics Addiction* explores the impact of policy on patterns of addiction.

[74] For example, William Eldridge, speech before the White House Conference on Drug Abuse, 1962. See *Proceedings: White House Conference on Narcotics and Drug Abuse* (Washington, D.C., 1962).

[75] Lindesmith, chapter 9.

—whether medical, sociological, or psychological—reflected in the lack of change in the information published in the Bureau's pamphlets during these years,[76] and in its policy of recommending increasingly severe penalties for drug possession as well as distribution. Particularly noteworthy is the evidence that the Bureau maintained no creative interaction with any knowledge-producing unit, although there were several to which it had access; evidently the research units were not encouraged to do anything more than to test drugs or try variations of the standard approach to treatment—withdrawal.

The role of the Public Health Service throughout this period is interesting because theoretically it could have been a research-oriented, knowledge-producing adjunct of the Bureau. Lindesmith finds the Public Health Service (PHS) supporting the Bureau, although perhaps uneasily, in maintaining the *status quo*.[77] However, he notes occasional disparities in the implications of their research findings or their statements. For example, when called upon to testify at the Daniel Committee hearings in 1955–1956, in regard to the New York Academy of Medicine proposals to dispense drugs to addicts at clinics, the PHS physicians, to the surprise of the investigating Senator Price Daniel, indicated a favorable attitude and urged viewing the addict as a patient.[78] Later they more or less withdrew this position, indicating to Lindesmith the conflict between their own strong professional values and ties, and the pressure of the federal bureaucracy toward keeping its knowledge "stable" and its men in line. According to one prominent retired Public Health Service official active in the area of addiction, the knowledge produced was "largely ignored."[79]

A similar interpretation of the relation between the Bureau and the Public Health Service, but imputing intent to withhold, was made by Dr. S. Bernard Wortis in a symposium sponsored by the New York Academy of Medicine. Referring to the fact that the proceedings of the U.S. Public Health Service Symposium held in 1958 at Bethesda were not published until 1964, he stated:

> I have always had the suspicion that perhaps somebody was holding back its release in Washington . . . (that) some place or agency in Washington blocks

---

[76] U.S. Bureau of Narcotics, Treasury Department, Pamphlets, *Prevention and Control of Narcotic Addiction* (Washington, D.C., U.S. Treasury Department).

[77] Lindesmith, p. 264.

[78] Lindesmith, p. 266. Also, see White House Conference, 1962, *Proceedings:* where Dr. R. H. Felix (PHS) calls addiction a "chronic disease," a potentially troublesome idea in view of the implications of this view of addiction for policy and control.

[79] Kolb, p. 153.

proper action to bring our management of drug addiction in line with present day medical knowledge.[80]

Whether knowledge was ignored or suppressed, coercive tactics, linked with what has been called a generally anti-intellectual stance on the part of the Bureau, show an organization out of tune with the changing times and, in the 1950s and early 1960s, underline strategic weaknesses which, when compared with the strategic gains of the mobilizing reformist elite, foreshadow the loss of some control.

Another factor supporting the mobilization of the professional elite was a rising concern, starting in the 1950s, with the need for a more effective attack upon crime and its sources. Many early critics noted the relation between drug addiction and crime, and observed ironically that the Bureau itself helped fashion the stereotype of the addict as potential rapist and killer through its pamphlets and statements.[81] It was the critics who then turned this relationship back upon the Bureau, pointing out that the Bureau had failed to control addiction; that if anything the punitive approach had created and sustained criminal behavior; and that in order to reduce crime, a new approach to the problem of addiction was needed. Most of the articles and books about addiction published in this period refer to this relation.

The compatibility of the goal of controlling drug addiction with that of a more widespread social problem, the control of crime, can be seen to provide both an important base for coalition formation and mobilization for change. At the same time it seems potentially "dangerous" to the extent that it politicizes the issue as, for example, in New York politics beginning in the mid-1960s. In addition to legitimating change itself, the location of addiction within the larger context of crime helped generate more attention (presidential committees, congressional action, etc.), and the call for research which, as we have noted, seemed to herald the end of the Bureau's monopoly of control.

The structural impetus for the start of a critical movement such as this may well lie in "imbalances," wherein there has been a gain in some of the assets of a societal actor without an accompanying increase in power or control.[82] For example, although post-war developments brought relative prominence and prestige to most knowledge-producing groups relative to others in society, and although medicine shared in this gain, particularly academic medicine, the M.D. as researcher, as well as the private practitioner, was still coerced by the Federal Bureau with regard to the entire problem

---

[80] Wortis, *Bulletin of the New York Academy of Medicine,* 1964.

[81] Lindesmith, "The Dope Fiend Mythology," *Journal of Criminal Law and Criminology,* Vol. 31 (1940), pp. 199–208. Kolb, *Drug Addiction,* chapter 11.

[82] Etzioni, *The Active Society,* chapter 15.

of addiction.[83] Thus we find an unstable situation; not only was new medical and scientific knowledge more or less ignored, but there was the anomaly of a professional group being under the control of a less knowledgeable and more bureaucratic external elite during a period of otherwise growing professional prestige.

The critics' efforts during this period to review the area of drug addiction theory, policy, and knowledge, and to suggest new approaches, whether individual or organized, seemed, on the whole, to have little immediate impact. For example, the New York Academy of Medicine proposals did not get adopted by the AMA and were essentially ignored by the Presidential Advisory Commission.[84] The recommendations of the prestigious Joint Committee of the ABA–AMA in the Interim Report (1958) and the Final Report (1959) which proposed the establishment of experimental outpatient clinics to see what would happen if drugs were dispensed, aroused the Bureau to a bitter rejoinder and attempts to suppress publication of the Reports, and in general led to delaying tactics with calls for more committees and more study.[85]

However, given the imbalances in power and control, and the evolving level of consciousness of the reformers, the frustration of these early collective efforts seemed to further activate the group. We find evidence that the elite examined the failure of their efforts and directed themselves toward a definition of strategies for possible guided change during the next decade.[86] Consciousness, particularly of the control processes, can enable even a small subunit to contribute toward social transformation by designing new structures and systems, although the problem of "unlocking the old" may still remain.

The frustrations of critical and reformist attempts at a national level spurred state and city activity, particularly in New York where the conjunc-

---

[83] Lindesmith, *The Addict and the Law,* chapter 9, discusses attacks on critics, including physicians, lawyers, commission members and himself.

Kolb refers to the repression, particularly in regard to its coercive effect on physicians and on the public mind.

[84] Javits, *Bulletin, New York Academy of Medicine,* pp. 290–293.

[85] *Ibid.*

[86] Despite growing awareness and interest, many observers did not see any change coming from *within* the concerned groups, but felt that the change from viewing the addict as a criminal to the medical viewpoint could perhaps only be accomplished by the President in such form as an executive order. See for example, N.Y. Senator Jacob Javits in *Bulletin of the New York Academy of Medicine,* April, 1964, p. 195; or the sociologist Lindesmith, *The Addict and the Law,* pp. 274–276.

tion of a growing social problem and a large professional elite, provoked early self-awareness and coalition formation.[87]

But collective efforts thus far seemed to suffer from a lack of actual "bits" of new knowledge, preferably "hard" or scientific data, that could be used as leverage to reinforce the demand for a new context.[88] In part this was evidenced by the reformers' demands that the knowledge-production resources of the medical-scientific community be directed toward addiction problems, so as to produce new knowledge which could be used to legitimate change. They also sought to interest researchers in the area of addiction, an area which has been avoided for many years. At the White House Conference on Narcotic and Drug Abuse, 1962, the chairman, Dr. Raymond Trussel, commented on the need for a specific project or research by "some responsible group without at the same time throwing the door open."[89] Dr. Trussel, then Commissioner of Hospitals, City of New York, was to become an active supporter of Drs. Dole and Nyswander's methadone project.

IMPLEMENTATION

In 1962 and 1963, the health professional elite in New York State, seeking to effect substantive change in the societal management of narcotic addiction, were able to recruit and establish two knowledge-producing units which took the study and treatment of narcotic addiction out of the sole domain of the Public Health Service. For the first time since 1924, addicts were legally maintained on narcotics.[90]

These projects at Manhattan State Hospital and Rockefeller Institute mark a deliberate attempt to redirect resources toward addiction and to extend the boundaries of medical-scientific control in an area previously controlled by the federal bureaucratic elite.[91] The Manhattan State project

---

[87] Dr. Paul Hoch, *Bulletin, New York Academy of Medicine*, p. 299. New Yorkers active in national and local efforts included Drs. Trussel, Brill, Freedman, James, and Judge Pluscowe.

[88] The lack of "hard" data was used against the innovating group to delay action, particularly in regard to the proposals to establish clinics. For example, the Council of Mental Health of the AMA in its comprehensive report (1956) states that "the plans are not good" and cites the need for more "scientific knowledge." See *Drug Addiction: Crime or Disease?* (Bloomington, Indiana, 1961).

[89] *Proceedings: White House Conference.*

[90] The two projects were announced in *The New York Times,* March 9, 1964, as a "new attack on narcotic addiction."

[91] A few comments that indicate the deliberate decision to widen boundaries and extend control:

was set up with the aid and support of medical and scientific professionals in the New York State Department of Mental Hygiene, particularly Dr. Paul Hoch, the State Commissioner of Mental Hygiene, who was also a leading medical academician. The Dole and Nyswander study at the Rockefeller Institute was actively encouraged and funded by the Health Research Council of New York City, an elite advisory group to the New York City Department of Health.[92]

These decisions removed some of the hotly debated questions of the past decade from the moral and bureaucratic realm and placed them within a scientific context, thus going beyond the critical efforts of the 1950s and introducing the potential for the production and use of radically transforming knowledge.[93]

These two early and similar projects can be compared for structural and guidance factors contributing to their success or failure. Such a comparison will illuminate an examination of the strategies that made the Dole and Nyswander experiment a crucial element in the mobilization for change between 1963–1969 in narcotic addiction assumptions, policy, and control.

There seem to be no further newspaper accounts or published information about the Manhattan State experiment with controlled dose, but on the basis of a telephone interview we can make some broad comparisons between the state methadone maintenance program, which was in effect since July, 1962, and the Dole and Nyswander methadone project since 1963.[94]

First, Dole and Nyswander utilized important bits of knowledge which Manhattan State did not have. Manhattan State had hit upon neither the effective use of high-dosage methadone, nor liquid medication (with consequent better control over illicit use of the drug), nor the pre-selection of patients that determined in part the MMTP's better statistical results.[95]

Dr. Henry Brill, in *The New York Times*, March 9, 1964, says that previously it was "not a fashionable field";

Dr. Paul Hoch, *Bulletin, New York Academy of Medicine*, says that previously addiction was in the hands of the PHS and that for "such a big problem" we need wider medical responsibility.

[92] The HRC was created in 1958 to encourage and support both basic research, and research applied to city problems such as pollution, addiction, health, etc. at institutions in the city.

[93] The questions early researchers were asking indicate this potential: *e.g.,* Can addicts be kept at level dosage? What are the effects of steady doses of narcotics on behavior? *New York Times,* March 9, 1964.

[94] Private communication.

[95] In contrast to Dole and Nyswander, Manhattan State gave a low dose (30 mg.) in spansules (not dissolved in liquid) to addicts who came to them under the state's Metcalf-Volker Act. Most of the addicts did not remain beyond three years; two-thirds of those in the program went back to other drugs, and the physician reported problems with people

Secondly, a conservative approach to drug therapy with addicts, biased against high dosage, may have affected the results obtained. Another concern was the lessons of medical history in that lack of sufficient knowledge in the past had had the unanticipated consequences of creating new addict populations. However realistic and sound such concerns may be for the administrator—and we find similar expressions of them today—the point we wish to make here is the possible dampening effect of a conservative context on exploratory drug research.

The decision by the Health Research Council to initiate and encourage research regarding drug addiction was of major importance. Furthermore, the recruitment of someone like Dr. Dole was crucial, in view of his status as a prominent biochemist and member of the Rockefeller Institute, the elite scientific knowledge-producing community in New York City. Such a position is not only a "background factor" but is an asset that may be converted to power in use.[96] This is an example of the manner in which an intellectual can serve a critical function, both in challenging "tabooed assumptions" and providing alternatives, particularly where knowledge itself is a key resource.

To be sure, agencies of the state and city were aware of the need for change, for initiating and seeking research, and making funds available, but they needed the right person and the right project. The catalytic addition of an independent intellectual provided, among other things, a network of scientific connections, the confidence and prestige to undertake a controversial project, and those special options available to such individuals, including in this instance, the possibility of initiating research within the relative sanctity of the Rockefeller Institute's small hospital. In contrast to the Manhattan State project, Drs. Dole and Nyswander were working, not on state patients, but with volunteers, not on a public ward, but in a relatively private and inaccessible place. Other supporting factors for the production of more radically transforming knowledge included the advantages associated with being a member of an independent intellectual establishment, as opposed to a bureaucratic structure such as the PHS with its con-

---

secreting and reselling methadone. Thus the program was not particularly successful. In fact, in 1966, following Dole and Nyswander's work, Manhattan State increased the dosage of methadone. They still had problems, and lowered it again last year. They are now in the process of preparing the results of the eight-year-old program.

[96] Dr. Rosenthal has commented on the importance of getting Dr. Dole to work in the program, *Bulletin, New York Academy of Medicine* (1964), p. 13.

JAMA (April 14, 1969), p. 251. The Bureau tried to hinder Dr. Dole but could not do so because of his position.

Dr. Nyswander says that Dr. Dole's entry was "the best thing in the field." Nat Hentoff, "Profiles—Dr. Nyswander," *New Yorker* (June 26 and July 3, 1965), Part I, p. 23.

flicting role demands, and also the differences in recruitment—Dole and Nyswander seemed to come to the work with radical intent.[97]

The complex of options available probably meant that Drs. Dole and Nyswander could work quite differently than the Manhattan State researchers. From their own accounts of the early stages of their work, it is evident that their start was exploratory, playing out leads and seizing upon fortuitous happenings, quite aware of the sense of sanctuary.[98] It seems entirely possible that such explorations in a more public place might have proven difficult or impossible, and might not have been initiated.

In this context, Drs. Dole and Nyswander's first major effort was to prove that the physician or scientist could work in this "illegal area" outside of the Public Health Service hospitals without being stopped or "punished" by the Bureau of Narcotics. They attacked the "psychological walls"[99] that had kept people from conducting research in this area for decades by showing that it could be done, and in so doing, gave the venture more respectability. This conclusion is supported by later references by others in the field to their "courage" and "pioneering work."[100]

Secondly, they were concerned with gaining acceptance of their controversial program both in terms of the scientific-medical community, the authorities, and the public. This involved Dole and Nyswander's primary strategy and objective—to switch drug maintenance from a moral to a scientific context, and also to anticipate and disarm the moral opposition of the public through the mass media.

Consciousness of latent societal structures aids in transformation by enabling the actor to design new structures and policies so as to reduce resistance. We find implicit in the methods of the methadone project some estimation of the nature and kind of opposition, that in turn reflects the increased political awareness of the preceding years, and the attempt to

---

[97] Dr. Nyswander was an early and leading proponent in attempts to establish the validity of medical approach to addiction: Hentoff, p. 54; also pp. 21–23. Hentoff also describes Dr. Dole's recruitment on HRC as a chance substitution, for a friend on sabbatical. He served on a narcotics subcommittee and, in the course of reviewing the literature, found little research had been done. Unable to find anyone to do what he had in mind, he approached the President of Rockefeller Institute and got permission to begin.

[98] Hentoff, p. 52: Dr. Dole's reputed words to Dr. Nyswander were, "Go ahead, do what you want. No one is holding you back now." This is supported by the comment in the *Journal of the American Medical Association* referred to above.

[99] Elites of a lower collectivity may hesitate to challenge a higher one because of "deprivations" experienced in the past—in our case, coercion and punishment. For a discussion of the role of projects in activating internal mobilization, see Etzioni, chapter 15, p. 403.

[100] There were comments by various speakers to this effect at the New York State Narcotic Addiction Control Commission (NACC) Conference held in New York City in 1969.

make strategic use of such knowledge. For example, the criteria for a subject's admission to the program were such as to negate the potential charge that they were addicting anyone who had not already had a chance to be withdrawn from drugs completely.[101] And it is only years later, after the treatment program is widely accepted, that the criteria are lowered so as to experiment with other subpopulations.[102] Another reflection of this informed caution was the strategic concern with records and evaluation. It is said that Dole and Nyswander's program was "the only program in N.Y. that kept complete records from start to finish."[103] This was important because they were also the "first such program to be subjected to independent third-party evaluation,"[104] after three years of operation (1967)[105] and again after five years (1968).[106] The panels convened by the Narcotics Addiction Control Commission of New York State (NACC) were on both occasions composed of prestigious figures in state and national medicine. Even those on the panels who, on one ground or another, seemed to oppose extending methadone maintenance to a widely used program recommended the Dole-Nyswander project's expansion.[107] The critics added the qualification that while the success of the methadone program seemed indicated for a specific addict subpopulation, more research was needed before it could be endorsed for the wider population of addicts.[108]

Drs. Dole and Nyswander made their work highly visible professionally, announcing their results periodically in medical journals, at scientific meet-

---

[101] Their criteria excluded all but hard core users of one drug, who were also older addicts that had tried rehabilitation before, but had relapsed. *Journal of the American Medical Association,* Vol. 193 (August 23, 1965), pp. 646–650.

[102] NACC Conference, 1969. Dr. Trigg speaking on the current methadone program.

[103] John Langrod, *Interviews* re MMTP for the Columbia University Bureau of Applied Social Research, p. 104.

[104] Langrod, *Interviews.* Dr. Frances Gearing, Director of the Evaluation Project of MMTP, Columbia University School of Public Health, p. 125.

[105] *New York Times,* March 10, 1967.

[106] *New York Times,* December 9, 1968.

JAMA (December 16, 1968), "Progress Report of Evaluation of MMTP as of March 31, 1968."

[107] Drs. Dole and Nyswander were not invited to the New York State NACC Conference, 1969 (personal communication).

At the Conference, for example, Dr. Brill commented to the effect that we all agree it is not a drug to be prescribed by the physician in local practice; in England, where they do, they have three hundred methadone addicts. See Dr. Brill's comments, *New York Times,* March 10, 1967. Dr. S. Louria, a member of the evaluation panel, who helped develop the state commitment program, states that "nobody seriously interested in the problem disputes the use of methadone but many of us are opposed to permanent maintenance and feel the addict should be taken off it." *New York Times,* March 10, 1967.

[108] *New York Times,* March 10, 1967. See footnote 103.

ings, and to the press.[109] In scanning the publications about the early period of the project, 1963–1965, we note the relative absence of criticism of the work, not only in the medical journals but also in the popular press.[110]

We can understand why the Bureau of Narcotics could not effectively attack the MMTP. With little input of new knowledge, the Bureau could only attempt to discredit the program on grounds of inadequate and/or dangerous procedures, as it had done in the past to others, or coerce the program by means of intimidation and threat. We find evidence of attempts in both directions. For example, Dr. Dole reported the Bureau's efforts to put pressure on the associated hospitals to shadow research people, to obtain records, to seize methadone prescriptions, and to threaten the pharmacists who filled the prescriptions.[111] The effect of such tactics, as mentioned earlier, served to unite the methadone project, and give it an aura almost of conspiracy, thus contributing to the creation of a very tight (and perhaps slightly paranoid) group.

The Bureau could not discredit the procedures of the MMTP because the doctors in the project exercised extreme caution both in issuing methadone and in recording results. Thus, typical Bureau predictions of what would happen if drugs were distributed proved fallacious, although its literature on the drug situation continued to ignore the new evidence and reprinted the same dire predictions year after year.[112] Additionally, it attacked the MMTP by questioning the validity of the statistics on the reduced

---

[109]Major publications of Dole and Nyswander's work on methadone:

Dole and Nyswander, "A Medical Treatment for Heroin Addiction," *JAMA* Vol. 193 (1965), p. 646.

Dole, Nyswander and Kreak, "Narcotic Blockade," 118 *Archives of Internal Medicine* (1966), p. 304.

Dole and Nyswander, "Rehabilitation of Heroin Addicts after Blockade with Methadone," *New York State Journal of Medicine* (August 1, 1966).

Dole, Nyswander and Warner, "Successful Treatment of 750 Criminal Addicts," *JAMA* Vol. 206, (December 16, 1968), p. 2708.

[110] Of the few negative responses found in the medical journals one, a letter to the editor of *JAMA* (March 14, 1966) by Dr. Vogel (Chairman of the California Narcotic Addiction Evaluation Authority) states that Dole and Nyswander are arriving at premature conclusions, questions their findings in the light of past pharmacological knowledge of the drug methadone, and attacks their press releases as misleading information. (This is reprinted by the Bureau of Narcotics in a bulletin.) Another article essentially attacking the work on "moral grounds" is written by Dr. Ausubel, 196 *JAMA* (1966), p. 946. It is reprinted by the Bureau and by the NACC of New York State to justify compulsory closed-ward treatment. *NACC Reprints*, Vol. 1:5 (June 1968).

[111] *New York Times*, December 9, 1968.

[112] *Prevention and Control of Narcotic Addiction* (Washington, D.C., U.S. Treasury Department). Pamphlets by the Bureau of Narcotics, published in 1959, 1962, 1964, and 1966.

crime rate among patients, hinting that Dole and Nyswander had made arrangements with the police to protect patients from publicity in case of arrest. The Bureau also cited press releases as attempts to falsify various aspects of the project.

The last mentioned criticism by the Bureau—manipulation of information to the press—concerns us in that it seems to have substance; however, the Bureau was never able to make it into an effective attack on the project.[113] In view of the MMTP's advanced scientific context, probably the only successful attack against the project would have had to have been directed against the research itself, through the work of another knowledge-producing unit. Subsequently, attacks against MMTP have usually been tied to new knowledge even though some still show the same old moral dimensions.

The press reports on the MMTP presented a somewhat hazy and shifting description of the properties of methadone and of the nature and purpose of the project. Many of the references to the drug in the *New York Times* and in the popular magazines of the initial period, 1964–1965, evade calling it a narcotic, and refer to it as a "transitional drug," a "cure," "breaking the habit," a "new hope for drug addicts," and "the drug that cures drug addicts," etc. Many of these phrases and their contexts imply cessation of addiction, and further, that methadone is something other than a narcotic. In part this may reflect journalistic confusion, or the dramatization of a "new discovery," but at least in part this seems to reflect the way in which Drs. Dole and Nyswander themselves conceptualized and presented their work, perhaps to avoid arousing the full range of emotional connotations associated with narcotic maintenance.

In the first major *New York Times* report discussing the project and the results, the headline reads, "Patients in Test Substitute Good Addiction for Bad," and the caption is obviously drawn from Dr. Dole's own words, for he states that "methadone is a good drug pharmacologically, while heroin is bad."[114] In the same article Dole refers to the substitution of "pain-killing methadone" for the "crippling addiction to heroin." Such value-laden statements are certainly departures from the more objective language typical of scientific parlance and seem to be essentially attempts at legitimization. Similar confusion as to what methadone really is, is also found in the comments of city officials[115] and in an editorial in the *New York Times* in praise

---

[113] However, it was picked up by a "friend" of the Bureau, Dr. Ausubel. See note 110.

[114] *New York Times*, December 8, 1964.

[115] Mayor Robert Wagner said that the city was opposed to proposals to supply narcotics to addicts but would pursue a demonstration program "utilizing a substitute for Heroin on an ambulatory basis." The fact that methadone is a narcotic was played down

of the program, which falsely describes the drug as both a "non-addictive" and an "antagonistic drug"[116] (which methadone is not).

Behind this confusion, however intentional or circumstantial, lies the question of the goals of the maintenance program and, in turn, the radical context underlying the project, Dole and Nyswander's theory of addiction. They seem to hold that narcotic addiction creates physiologic dependence which, like any chronic disturbance, may make the goal of abstinence unrealistic, demands a redefinition of the concept of cure, and suggests the need for new objectives in treatment.[117] They defined their goals as socially productive behavior, and the reduction in crime rate among out-patients.[118] This theory would seem to be one of the strong points of the project, for it legitimates narcotic maintenance treatment specifically.[119]

---

by both the administration and the researchers, creating in the public mind, as the Bureau itself charges, a certain amount of functional misinformation. *New York Times,* September 21, 1965.

[116] *New York Times,* July 22, 1965. This point was picked up in a letter to the editor, August 17, 1965, by a physician who, while in favor of the project and of radical reform, wanted to clarify the fact that methadone "is a narcotic . . . neither new nor antagonist . . . and that it causes addiction and tolerance, just as other narcotics do."

[117] Dole and Nyswander, "Methadone Maintenance and Its Implication for Theories of Narcotic Addiction" in *Association for Research in Nervous and Mental Disease, the Addictive States* (1968), pp. 360–361.

New York Times, December 9, 1968. Research led to a new theory of addiction.

New York Times, April 23, 1968. NSA Symposium, with Dr. Dole as chairman; the persistence of narcotics was discussed, and additional evidence of physiological dependence at cell level was presented. Dr. Dole commented that "such reasoning justifies the use of methadone in non-narcotic doses to protect former addicts from their craving."

At the NACC Conference in 1969, Dr. Jerome Jaffe discussed Dr. Dole's theory that a narcotic lesion produced narcotic hunger, and noted that this has not been confirmed, and that there seems to be contrary evidence.

[118] Dole, Nyswander and Warner speak of "social productivity," *JAMA, Journal of the American Medical Association,* Vol. 206 (December 16, 1968).

The "crucial test of any treatment program is that the patients become normal members of society . . . that they resist drugs, and work." *New York State Journal of Medicine,* August 1, 1966.

Gertrude Samuels, in her feature article on the project, quotes Dr. Dole as saying "our first goal is normal functioning citizens" and not abstinence. *New York Times,* October 15, 1967.

[119] We note relatively few attacks relative to goals in the early period, before more knowledge became available and more projects were in competition.

In 1965, at the Mayors Conference on Addiction, Rev. O. Dempsey cried, "Narcotics is death," but his outburst was more than countered by the scientific support of Dr. S. J. Holmes of Toronto, who reported another successful methadone program. *New York Times,* February 6, 1965. The "emotional" attacks seem to reappear in new clothing in the vehemence with which some members of the black community attack methadone within the black militant ideology as another way of "keeping us down."

To some extent, the theoretical underpinnings of MMTP may reflect social objectives of those concerned prior to the research, and thus indicate the intention not only to produce scientific bits but to produce them and to interpret them so as to create, in addition to new knowledge, a transforming context, under the partially valid assumption that new scientific findings can be used in our society to mandate policy change, and that a new community of assumptions will hopefully follow.

To the best of our knowledge, what makes the Dole and Nyswander approach distinctive is their discovery of an effective way to use methadone, not the drug itself, which was around since World War II, and which has many of the properties of other narcotics.[120] This distinction is obscured for readers of magazine articles or press releases. What we find instead is the presentation of some pharmacological truths and a good treatment program in emotionally tagged and highly evocative language that few, but critics, see the need to clarify. It appears that whatever distinctions, linguistic or otherwise, could be made between the radical act of appearing to give narcotics to addicts and giving out methadone were strategically utilized. The authors of the project seemed to be at some pains to dissociate themselves from the criticism raised against the American clinics of the 1920s and against the more recent British system of dispensing drugs—a criticism circulated by the Bureau whose pamphlets were distributed throughout the country.[121] They also prescinded from the ineffective attempts by the state medical societies, and by elites at the national level, to initiate trial clinics in the 1950s. Similar distinctions and refinements are still required by researchers, if one may judge by some recent statements. At the 1969 Conference of the New York State Narcotic Addiction Control Commission, Dr. Jaffe, currently working with methadone and the newer antagonistic drugs such as cyclazocine, carefully emphasized how the Dole and Nyswander project differed from the British technique of giving narcotics by prescription for self-administration, without any accompanying rehabilitation services.[122] He concluded that it is too simplistic to say that "a narcotic is just a

---

[120] Letter to the Editor in response to an editorial. Dr. R. L. Marcus sought to correct the paper and stated that it is an old drug but a new way of using it. *New York Times*, August 17, 1965. Also, from Dr. Dole these words: "Use a familiar drug in a new way." *Journal of the American Medical Association*, Vol. 206 (December 16, 1968), p. 2708.

For a description of the properties of the drug, a basic pharmacologic reference is Jerome H. Jaffe, "Narcotic Analgesics" in *The Pharmacological Basis of Therapeutics*, ed. Goodman and Gilman (New York: The Macmillan Company, 1965), pp. 271–272.

[121] NACC Conference, 1969. Dole and Nyswander commented on this issue that "methadone maintenance is not to be confused with giving a narcotic drug as in Great Britain." *New York State Medical Journal*, August 1, 1966.

[122] NACC Conference, 1969.

narcotic." Thus in 1969, there is still concern about presenting narcotic maintenance, although it is possible to be slightly more open about the whole problem. In 1964–1965, most spokesmen avoided even phrasing the issue that way. Rather the implication was that methadone is a medication and the common analogy used by Drs. Dole, Nyswander, and others was that giving methadone is like giving insulin to a diabetic; a chronic disease requires chronic medication.

This comparison of presentations—1964 and 1969—may indicate a gap between the proliferation of methadone maintenance projects in the intervening period and the relative stability of the prevailing community of assumptions, or to phrase it differently, the relative ease of building new contexts as opposed to the difficulty of unlocking the old, although a complete transformation involves both processes.

Indications of a recent alteration in the attitudes of authorities toward the use of narcotics, which methadone is legally[123] and may be medically,[124] for a maintenance program may be found in the positions taken on the drug by the main candidates for mayor of New York City in the 1965 and 1969 elections, and by the candidates for Governor of New York State in the 1966 elections. More important, a review of the nature of the major programs actually supported by the New York City and New York State administrations suggests a rise in support for methadone maintenance of heroin addicts during and after 1967, a year during which the Dole and Nyswander results began to be corroborated by a variety of independent investigators.

During the first three years of its operation the MMTP was supported largely by New York City municipal funds. While the experimental program initiated at Rockefeller University in New York City with two patients had expanded to three public and private hospitals by 1967, the methadone maintenance approach to addiction was treated warily by most political candidates and officials during these years. The Wagner administration had supported MMTP but opposed any extension of methadone maintenance from an experimental procedure to a means of dealing with heroin addicts.[125] Similarly, the candidates in the 1965 mayoral election were generally opposed to the utilization of methadone as a maintenance program for addicts. Although an encouraging report on the first fifteen months of MMTP's operation had been published, and one mayoral candidate, Abra-

---

[123] Paul D. Gewirtz, "Methadone Maintenance for Heroin Addicts," *The Yale Law Journal,* Vol. 78, No. 7 (June, 1969), p. 1195.

[124] N. B. Eddy, H. Halback, O. J. Braenden, "Synthetic Substances With Morphine-Like Effect: Methadone," *Bulletin of the World Health Organization,* Vol. 17 (1957), p. 569.

[125] *New York Times,* February 15, 1965.

ham Beame, did urge the increased use of methadone in handling the city's addicts,[126] the majority of the candidates, including the eventual winner, John Lindsay, called primarily for the expansion of current approaches to drug addicts and did not favor the utilization of methadone maintenance for addiction. While Lindsay expressed support for the experimental methadone program, he also indicated his opposition to the use of the synthetic drug for drug addicts "unless maintenance proves workable."[127] During the campaign Lindsay called for improved police procedures for halting narcotics sales, for the construction of a new hospital for addicts, and for educational programs dealing with addiction.

Further indications of politicians' attitudes toward the handling of drug addiction by methadone maintenance were provided during the 1966 New York State gubernatorial election. Although Drs. Dole and Nyswander published several more articles commenting favorably on the methadone program in medical journals during the year, and although their reports were widely cited in the popular press, the program for handling addicts that the incumbent Governor proposed to the state legislature, that he saw passed by a twenty-to-one margin, and that he then campaigned successfully for reelection upon, was a program under which addicts could be involuntarily committed to state treatment centers for periods ranging up to three years.

Thus, the positions taken on the handling of narcotic addicts by the major mayoral candidates in 1965 suggested at most cautious support for the research or experimental use of methadone but little support for its acceptance as a means of maintaining or treating addicts. Similarly the 1966 gubernatorial campaign dealt with the question of narcotics addicts primarily in terms of their involuntary confinement and withdrawal from narcotics use.

By 1969, however, the mayoral candidates expressed positions considerably more favorable to the expanded use of methadone as an implicit or potential means of dealing with large numbers of narcotic addicts. Candidates Lindsay, Procaccino, Wagner, and Low all promised support for the expansion of the use of methadone in the city.[128] Among the prominent candidates, only John Marchi did not emphasize his support of an expanded methadone program.

Consideration of the city and state administrations' support for major programs for the control of drug addiction suggests a similar alteration in attitude toward the use of methadone. During the early years in which Drs.

[126] *New York Times,* October 16, 1965.
[127] *New York Times,* October 24, 1965.
[128] *New York Times,* February 22, 1969; May 30, 1969; June 13, 1969.

Dole and Nyswander were issuing favorable reports on the efficacy of methadone as a means of rehabilitating heroin addicts (1964–1966) the major programs supported by the state and city administrations emphasized only the addict's withdrawal and abstention from narcotic use. Under the New York State Metcalf-Volker Act of 1962, which both the state and city helped to administer, an addict faced with certain criminal charges could elect to be civilly committed for withdrawal from drug use and rehabilitation instead of standing trial. In 1966 a narcotics program was proposed by Governor Rockefeller and overwhelmingly approved by the state legislature under which addicts who had committed no crime could be involuntarily committed to a treatment center by the courts for a period of up to three years. The high relapse rate associated with such rehabilitation programs was generally acknowledged and the program was often described as one of incarceration. One state assemblyman observed, "We haven't got the medical answer, so we've got to do the next best thing. We've got to keep these people off the streets."[129] In addition, the city government supported several programs in which addicts voluntarily attempted withdrawal and rehabilitation aided by various forms of individual and group psychotherapy. These projects included the Phoenix House program initiated under Dr. Efrem Ramirez, as well as Daytop Lodge, Daytop Village, and others.

During the first three years (1964–1966) of Drs. Dole and Nyswanders' program the state government provided no support and the city supported it explicitly as "experimental research." However, late in 1967 the state government agreed to support the MMTP with an estimated $2.5 million annually.[130] In December, 1968, the New York State government and the New York City government decided, independently, to establish their own programs to maintain narcotic addicts on methadone. While the programs continued to be referred to as "research," due to the Federal Bureau of Narcotics' opposition to any non-experimental maintenance of addiction, the size of the programs and their more permissive admission standards suggest a fairly explicit transition from a program of experimental research to one of maintenance. A bill has also been passed by the New York City Council requiring methadone to be made available to addicts in the city's prisons.[131] The state government has also established a methadone treatment center in New York City and in January of 1970 the state announced that it would increase its support of the MMTP from $2.5 million to $15 million annually.[132]

---

[129] *New York Times,* April 3, 1966.
[130] *New York Times,* November 15, 1967.
[131] *New York Times,* January 8, 1970.
[132] *Ibid.*

Methadone research projects were subsequently established in a number of cities in the United States and Canada, including New Haven, Baltimore, St. Louis, New Orleans, Vancouver, B.C., and Toronto, Ontario.[133] While these projects usually resemble the Dole-Nyswander program in that they administer daily oral doses of methadone to patients and also take frequent urine samples, they vary considerably in their procedures. While most programs handle patients initially in a hospital and only later as out-patients, some programs initiate and maintain individuals on methadone entirely on an out-patient basis. Admissions criteria also vary considerably: some programs use fairly restrictive criteria, similar to those initially used by the Dole-Nyswander project, while others are relatively permissive about admission to methadone maintenance.

In June, 1970, the Bureau of Narcotics and Dangerous Drugs and the Food and Drug Administration jointly issued a set of regulations designed to establish nationwide control over the procedures of the spreading community methadone maintenance centers.[134]

In summary, the political candidates as well as the city and state authorities did shift their positions from opposition to reliance on methadone to extensive use, as the evidence was published, *after* it was supported by other studies than those of the original advocates, and following independent evaluations. In this way the political decision-makers were protected from relying on one expert. But they did "move" once the evidence became relatively convincing. Thus a medically effective approach to the problem of heroin addiction also became politically effective.

---

[133] "Methadone Clinical Trials Under Study," *Journal of the American Medical Association,* Vol. 208, No. 2 (April 14, 1969), p. 251.

[134] *Washington Post,* June 12, 1970.

2

ANTABUSE

DISCOVERY

The possibility of using antabuse[1] (disulfiram) in the treatment of alcoholism was first detected by Drs. Erik Jacobsen and Jens Hald in Denmark in 1945.[2] As in many such discoveries, accident played a large part. Jacobsen was testing the drug for use in the control of parasitic intestinal worms. In keeping with his policy of never giving a drug to a patient without first testing it on himself, he took a small dose. Some hours later, at a dinner party, he became physically ill with just a few sips of beer.[3]

The first reports on the drug and its possible applications in combating alcoholism appeared in 1948 after Jacobsen and Hald had tested the drug's physiological effects and Dr. Oluf Martensen-Larsen had begun clinical work with it.[4] (The beginning of Martensen-Larsen's association with the research is set as 1947.[5])

EFFECT

The basis for the claim that the drug can be of use as a pharmacological and psychological aid in the treatment of alcoholism is the "alcohol-antabuse reaction," which causes a person consuming alcohol considerable discomfort. (It is hence a so-called antagonistic drug.)

---

[1] Or antabus, a trade name for tetraethylthiuramdisulphide, or disulfiram.

[2] G. L. Usdin, "Antabuse in the Therapy of Chronic Alcoholism," *Cincinnati Journal of Medicine,* Vol. 32 (1951), pp. 288–291.

[3] *Ibid.,* p. 288.

[4] Erling Asmussen, Jens Hald, and Erik Jacobsen, "Studies of the Effect of Tetraethylthiuramdisulphide (Antabuse) and Alcohol on Respiration and Circulation in Normal Human Subjects," *Acta Pharmacologica et Toxicologica,* Vol. 4 (1948), pp. 297–304. And in the same journal, the same issue: Jens Hald, Erik Jacobsen, and Valdemar Larsen, "The Sensitizing Effect of Tetraethylthiuramdisulphide (Antabuse) to Ethylalcohol," pp. 285–296.

[5] Letter from Denmark, "The Antabus Treatment of Alcoholism," *Journal of the American Medical Association,* Vol. 139 (1949), p. 732.

The treatment is started by giving the patient initial doses of antaboic, reading him for the alcohol-antaboic reaction. Although it has not been confirmed exactly how disulfiram works chemically, it apparently works by blocking the enzymatic function of aldehyde oxidases in the liver; this prevents the normal metabolic degradation of alcohol in the body. The result is an increased concentration of acetaldehyde in the blood. Earlier investigations suggested that a substance is formed by the disulfiram-prepared individual under the influence of alcohol which "directly or indirectly increases the irritability of the respiratory centre."[6] By inhibiting the oxidation of the acetaldehyde, disulfiram may allow an accumulation of that substance in the body large enough to cause the observed irritation.[7] The early investigators noted certain effects of disulfiram itself on the non-alcoholic-prepared body. They have noted transient symptoms of fatigue and impaired sexual potency;[8] in some cases, headaches, dizziness, gastrointestinal disorders, bad taste, and halitosis have been recorded.[9] In few cases symptoms, such as allergic reaction, have been such that treatment had to be discontinued.[10]

Hypersensitivity to alcohol begins three to four hours after the ingestion of antabuse.[11] The reaction varies from thirty to sixty minutes to several hours in the more severe cases, or as long as there is alcohol in the blood. Mild reactions may occur in the sensitive individual when blood alcohol concentration is increased to as little as 5 to 10 mg. per 100 cc. Symptoms are fully developed when the concentration reaches 50 mg. per 100 cc. Since the disulfiram is only slowly eliminated from the body, unpleasant symptoms following ingestion of alcohol have been observed seven to eight days after a single dose of 1.5 gm.[12] Furthermore, prolonged administration of antabuse does not lead to tolerance for alcohol.

A few minutes after the ingestion of alcohol, there is flushing of the

---

[6] E. Asmussen, *et al.*, p. 301.

It has also been suggested that disulfiram (Antabuse) affects not only the quantity of acetaldehyde but also the vascular reaction to it. See: J. K. W. Ferguson, "A New Drug for Alcoholism Treatment," *Canadian Medical Association Journal*, Vol. 74 (1956), p. 794.

[7] Max Hayman, *Alcoholism: Mechanism and Management* (Springfield: Thomas, 1966), pp. 148–149.

[8] E. Jacobsen and O. Martensen-Larsen, "Treatment of Alcoholism with Tetraethylthiuram Disulfide (Antabus)," *Journal of the American Medical Association*, Vol. 139 (1949), pp. 918–922, specifically p. 919.

[9] Hayman, p. 149. Also E. Glud, "The Treatment of Alcoholic Patients in Denmark with Antabuse," *Quarterly Journal of Studies on Alcohol*, Vol. 10 (1949), pp. 185–197, specifically pp. 193–194.

[10] Jacobsen and Martensen-Larsen, p. 919.

[11] *Ibid.*

[12] See Ruth Fox, ed., *Alcoholism: Behavioral Research, Therapeutic Approaches* (New York: Springer Publishing Company, Inc., 1967), especially pp. 242–246.

addiction: asthma, pregnancy, kidney disease, psychosis, and epilepsy.[23] However, Fox has recently reaffirmed the view that there are few valid contraindications to disulfiram therapy. She feels that the drug should not be given to a full-blown psychotic or to someone who is seriously ill.[24] In fact, a recent study of the use of antabuse with skid-row alcoholics, a group whose level of physical fitness was much below average, found very few serious side effects.[25]

The second danger, and obviously the more considerable, is that from the reaction to consumption of alcohol. Jacobsen and Martensen-Larsen state that this reaction may be "either too severe or too light."[26] If too light, this just means that the effects disappear too quickly and the patient is probably not susceptible to treatment with disulfiram. Severe reactions may result in convulsions and require hospital attention.[27] Another danger associated with the alcohol-antabuse reaction is the possibility of consuming the alcohol in such quantity and so quickly that the alcohol level in the blood surpasses the lethal level, but, to a degree, this is a danger in any heavy drinking.

One disturbing matter in disulfiram therapy arose with the reporting of deaths which occasionally occurred during the treatment. Because of these reports, Jacobsen and others began to investigate the cases of death cited in the literature. It became clear that the deaths had occurred during the disulfiram and alcohol reaction, and that disulfiram by itself had not caused them. As E. Jacobsen noted:

> Neither in the literature nor in the present investigation have any cases of death been seen which can with certainty be attributed to the effect of disulfiram alone. All the unexplained deaths occurred among patients who, while under the influence of disulfiram, drank some alcohol. Thus, the hazard of the treatment exists only in the combination of alcohol and disulfiram.[28]

He further notes that during the three and a half years that disulfiram had been used in Denmark, about 11,000 patients had been treated with the drug; of this total, only three or four had died unexpectedly because of the antabuse-alcohol reaction.[29] In a recent review study, Amador and Gazdas

---

[23] Block, p. 457, and Hayman, pp. 149–150.

[24] Fox, *Alcoholism, ibid.,* p. 246.

[25] P. G. Bourne, J. A. Alford, and J. Z. Bowcock, *op. cit.*

[26] Jacobsen and Martensen-Larsen, p. 919.

[27] *Ibid.*

[28] See E. Jacobsen, "Deaths of alcoholic patients treated with disulfiram (tetraethylthiuram disulfide) in Denmark," *Quarterly Journal of Studies on Alcohol,* Vol. 13 (1952), p. 22.

[29] *Ibid.,* p. 25.

showed that the reported fatalities occurred only during the disulfiram-alcohol reaction, and were not the result of administration of the drug itself. The investigators further suggest that the present dosage of .25 gm. daily would further reduce the reaction:

> . . . the smaller dosage of disulfiram (0.25 g. daily) currently employed, together with the elimination of the therapeutic production of the disulfiram-alcohol reaction, might serve to reduce the incidence of complications.[30]

Another danger referred to in the literature about antabuse is the possibility of precipitating or inducing a psychosis. It has been suggested that for some individuals the alcohol-antabuse reaction may induce the disturbance; however, this is related to a specific and older mode of treatment, and will be dealt with below. It also is maintained that to deprive the alcoholic of his alcohol is to block his primary avenue of escape from his problems. "The therapist should bear in mind that, by blockading the patient's way to drink, he is depriving him of something which is of vital importance, namely his only way of escape. . . . The alcoholist drinks to escape inner tensions and conflicts which will increase and cause different reactions if his way of escape, alcohol, is blockaded by disulfiram."[31] Another writer adds: "It was thought that psychoses occurring while this drug was being used were due to the toxicity of the drug itself. However, now it is believed that it is not the drug but the inability of the patient to escape into his alcoholic oblivion as an outlet for his emotional inability, that precipitates the psychotic episode."[32] The answer to this problem, to many minds, is psychotherapy as a part of treatment for alcoholism, an aspect that will be discussed below.

METHODS OF TREATMENT

The initial step of almost any disulfiram treatment for alcoholism is to withdraw the patient from alcohol for approximately twenty-four hours. Then, the first dose of disulfiram is administered (usually 0.5 gm.) and repeated once a day for approximately one or two weeks. The patient is then maintained on a smaller dosage (0.25 gm.) for a variable length of time—"until the patient seems to be adjusted to his no-alcohol regimen."[33]

---

[30] See E. Amador and A. Gazdas, "Sudden Death During the Disulfiram-Alcohol Reaction," *Quarterly Journal of Studies on Alcohol,* Vol. 28 (1967), p. 652.

[31] J. Smilde, "Risks and Unexpected Reactions in Disulfiram Therapy of Alcoholism," *Quarterly Journal of Studies on Alcohol,* Vol. 24 (1963), pp. 489–494, specifically pp. 493–494.

[32] Block, p. 458.

[33] *Ibid.,* p. 457.

When antabuse was first introduced it was thought that the hospital setting was a necessary adjunct to treatment, particularly for the first alcohol-antabuse test (an intentional induction of the alcohol-antabuse reaction), which was administered shortly after the patient was put on antabuse. It was also initially considered a useful part of the treatment to subject the patient to intermittent alcohol challenges as a reminder of the consequences of departure from the alcohol-less life. This is no longer generally accepted as necessary either as an admonition or as an attempt to establish a conditioned aversion.[34] It is now considered sufficient to describe the extreme discomfort of the reaction to the patient, stressing the risk he incurs by taking any alcohol while under disulfiram treatment.[35]

From the beginning of the use of disulfiram as treatment for alcoholism there has been an assumption of the necessity of concurrent psychotherapy. Jacobsen and Martensen-Larsen stated, without support: "The medication must be combined with intensive psychotherapy in order to obtain permanent results."[36] This dictum was incorporated in what is now called the "Danish Method" of treating alcoholism:

1. The administration of antabuse which induces the patient to shun drinking;

2. Psychotherapeutic care, which supports the patient in his desire to continue medication, to readjust himself socially, and finally to make the necessary changes in his habits.[37]

With reference to the fears mentioned earlier of the possible harmful effects of eliminating the alcoholic's primary escape mechanism, one investigator states: "Psychotherapy, or at least close and frequent contact between patient and physician, are essential particularly during the period of the patient's transition from addiction through the void of initial sobriety, when he is at a loss for another outlet to replace his emotional depressant."[38]

EVALUATIVE TESTS

Among the first evaluations of the effectiveness of disulfiram was that of Dr. Martensen-Larsen who did the first clinical work with the drug after

---

[34] Hayman, p. 150.

[35] Block, p. 457.

[36] Jacobsen and Martensen-Larsen, p. 920.

[37] Glud, p. 186.

[38] Marcus Crahan, "The Treatment of Alcoholism with Tetraethylthiuram Disulfide with Observations on the Effects of Group Reaction Tests and of Test Witnessing," *Quarterly Journal of Studies on Alcohol,* Vol. 11 (1950), pp. 538–546, specifically, p. 539.

Jacobsen and Hald had done their experiments. Dr. Martensen-Larsen's four evaluative categories were:

1. Socially recovered (SR)—"could competently perform in his work and live in harmony with his family";
2. Much better (MB)—"can perform his work with integrity and who has had a few relapses that have not disturbed his social status";
3. Somewhat better (SB)—"somewhat improved but is subject to attacks which influence his work and/or his family life";
4. Unchanged (U).[39]

A longer run evaluation of results from disulfiram treatment in Denmark by Drs. Johannes Nørvig and Borge Nielsen shows that two to five years after the discharge of 114 patients originally treated with antabuse, 43 were rated "good," 45 "fair," and 26 "poor," on a scale of recovery much like that of Martensen-Larsen reviewed in Table 2. Considering good and fair results as positive and poor and unavailable patients as negative, the figures suggest 66 percent positive results.[40]

Another follow-up study two to five years after discharge of 500 alcoholic patients treated with disulfiram in a psychiatric clinic in Basel (Switzerland) since 1949[41] maintained contact with 224 patients (fifty-two women). Of the original five hundred, 43 percent had been committed to the treatment by the courts; the remainder had sought out treatment voluntarily, although a majority of these came because of pressure from employers, physicians, or family. The figures are assumed to be approximately the same for the group actually contacted.

Treatment in the clinic had included psychotherapeutic and social therapy counseling as well as antabuse treatment. Psychoanalysis was employed only where neurosis was definitely present. Disulfiram treatment was continued after discharge under the supervision of counseling centers. One-third continued treatment for up to six months, one-third up to seven years, and one-third continued, with lapses, for several years.

Twelve percent of the men and 20 percent of the women were abstinent during the observation period, two to five years after discharge. It was not

---

[39] The criteria and the following figures are from Jacobsen and Martensen-Larsen, pp. 920–921.

[40] Johannes Nørvig and Borge Nielsen, "A Follow-Up Study of 221 Alcohol Addicts in Denmark," *Quarterly Journal of Studies on Alcohol*, Vol. 17 (1956), pp. 633–642.

[41] H. Zuber, "*Entstehungsbeding ungen des chronischen Alkoholismus und Behanlungsresultate der Disulfiram-Kur* (Antabus)," ("Conditions giving rise to Chronic Alcoholism and Results of Treatment with Disulfiram"), No. 34 (1960), p. 58 f. Abstracted in *Quarterly Journal of Studies on Alcohol*, Vol. 24 (1963), pp. 161–162.

Table 2. Status of Persons with Alcoholism Six Months After Institution of Treatment with Antabuse Compared with Status After Three and After Nine Months

		SR	*MB*	*SB*	*U*	*Total*
Status after 6 months:		52	19	12	16	99
Status after 3 months:	SR	43	2	2	2	49
	MB	5	14	0	3	22
	SB	4	2	10	0	16
	U	0	1	0	11	12
						99
Status after 9 months:	SR	18	2	0	2	22
	MB	1	5	0	0	6
	SB	0	0	3	0	3
	U	1	0	1	9	11
Not observed		32	12	8	5	57
						99

Source: E. Jacobsen and O. Martensen-Larsen, "Treatment of Alcoholism with Tetraethylthiuram Disulfide (Antabus)," *Journal of the American Medical Association,* Vol. 139 (1949), pp. 918–922. The study included a total of ninety-nine patients.

specified what proportion of the abstinent patients were using disulfiram. In the researchers' terms, 30 percent were to be considered recovered, 33 percent improved, and 37 percent unimproved. An explanation of these terms is not given.

The rate of recovery was not found to vary with the patients' status as compulsory or voluntary. Patients over forty responded better to the treatment. The best response was found with the pleasure and habit drinkers rather than with those with severe psychological problems.

Robert Wallerstein records a comparative evaluation[42] of antabuse treatment and three other methods in what he terms a "time-limited mental hospital setting." Of 178 voluntary patients, 47 were treated with disulfiram, 50 were given conditioned reflex treatment, 39 had hypno-therapy and the remaining 42 constituted a control group, who lived side by side with the other patients in what Wallerstein calls a "milieu therapy."

[42] Robert S. Wallerstein, "Comparative Study of Treatment Methods for Chronic Alcoholism: The Alcoholism Research Project at Winter VA Hospital," *American Journal of Psychiatry,* Vol. 113 (September, 1956), pp. 228–233.

The study establishes a so-called "multidimensional measure of improvement." There are four sets of criteria:

1. Degree of abstinence—abstinence is here not considered an absolute but subject to evaluation as to intensity and duration;

2. Overall levels of social adjustment—this is similar to Martensen-Larsen's degrees of social recovery. The variable of central interest here is reintegration into society;

3. Subjective feelings of difference—these are the patient's self-assessments;

4. Structural changes in personality—determined by psychiatric observation and psychological testing.

The results are presented in Table 3.

Table 3. Overall Improvement in the Various Modalities

	Treatment		Results		No Follow Up
	Completed	*Incomplete*	*Improved*	*Unimproved*	*Up*
Antabuse (47)	83%	17%	53%	32%	15%
Conditioned-Reflex (50)	80%	20%	24%	34%	42%
Group Hypno-therapy (39)	64%	36%	24%	34%	42%
Milieu (42)	62%	38%	26%	36%	38%

Source: From Robert Wallerstein, "Comparative Study of Treatment Methods for Chronic Alcoholism: The Alcohol Research Project at Winter VA Hospital," *American Journal of Psychiatry*, Vol. 113 (September, 1956), p. 229.

More patients improved with antabuse than with any other treatment. The researchers assume this to be due to the "externalization" of controls with antabuse. Antabuse provides an external source of motivation, the researchers say; no longer must the alcoholic rely solely on his internal psychological motivation to control his drinking. The tablet has become a strong external (*i.e.*, physiological) deterrent to his drinking.

Drs. Ebbe Hoff and Charles McKeown provide evaluative figures for 560 patients who volunteered to take disulfiram treatment (TETD) at the Division of Alcohol Studies and Rehabilitation Service at the Medical College of Virginia Hospital in Richmond and 232 control patients over a period of three years.[43] The treatment consisted of the administration of decreasing doses of disulfiram (1.5 gm. to 0.5 gm.) over four days with 30 cc. of whiskey administered on the fourth day in order to create the disulfiram reaction. The patients were kept on disulfiram for approximately a year.

The results are evaluated in five categories:

Class I: Totally abstinent;

Class II: Abstinent with a single relapse;

Class III: Not abstinent but showing improvement—wider spacing of drinking sprees, better work record, happier adjustment at home and in the community;

Class IV: No improvement;

Class V: May have earlier been considered Class IV, but then were able to remain abstinent for 6 months;

NT: Discontinued treatment (generally means self-discharge);

NC: Lost contact.[44]

The last two categories are included with therapeutic failures. (See Table 4.)

The researchers combine classes I, II, and III as those benefiting from the treatment (78 percent) while 47.8 percent of the control group benefited from treatment other than antabuse.

Another set of results is recorded by Dr. Ebbe Hoff. His patients had to choose each day to take disulfiram. Each "reexperienced his acceptance of the fact that he could not drink and had chosen to accept another day of abstinence."[45] One thousand and twenty patients who took disulfiram and 484 "controls" who chose not to use disulfiram participated in a therapeutic program. Hoff found that the group that took the disulfiram was a younger group, 35–39 age group, while the control group was 40–44. He thought this indicated that the disulfiram was chosen by a younger, healthier, more highly motivated group.[46] Of the control group, 55 percent benefited from psychotherapeutic treatment, while 76 percent of the disulfiram-

---

[43] Ebbe C. Hoff and Charles E. McKeown, "An Evaluation of the Use of Tetraethylthiuram Disulfide in the Treatment of 560 Cases of Alcohol Addiction, *American Journal of Psychiatry,* Vol. 109 (March, 1953), pp. 670–673.

[44] *Ibid.,* pp. 671–672.

[45] Ebbe C. Hoff, "The Use of Pharmacological Adjuncts in the Psychotherapy of Alcoholics," *Quarterly Journal of Studies on Alcohol,* Supplement Number 1 (1961), pp. 138–150, specifically p. 140.

[46] *Ibid.*

Table 4.   Comparisons of Treatment Results Between 232 Control and 560 TETD Cases

Class	Control Group %	TETD %
I	24.1	37.3
II	9.5	20.0
III	14.2	20.7
IV	18.1	13.7
V	2.2	1.8
NT	20.3	1.1
NC	11.6	5.4
	100.0	100.0

	Male and Female			
	Control		TETD	
	192 Male %	40 Female %	500 Male %	60 Female %
I	27.1	10.0	38.4	28.3
II	9.9	7.5	21.2	8.3
III	13.5	17.5	19.6	30.1
IV	16.6	25.0	13.2	18.3
V	1.6	5.0	1.8	1.7
NT	18.8	27.5	1.0	3.3
NC	12.5	7.5	4.8	10.0
	100.0	100.0	100.0	100.0

Source: Ebbe C. Hoff and Charles E. McKeown, "An Evaluation of the Use of Tetraethylthiuram Disulfide in the Treatment of 560 Cases of Alcohol Addiction," *American Journal of Psychiatry,* Vol. 109 (1953), p. 672.

treated group benefited from the program; the disulfiram group also stayed in treatment longer.[47]

A study of 120 cases of antabuse maintenance and psychotherapy in three hospitals—in Albany, Buffalo, and Trenton—shows a 62 percent record of improvement after nine months (the scale is not specified).[48] Although

---

[47] *Ibid.*

[48] George P. Child, Walter Osinski, Robert E. Bennett, and Eugene Davidoff, "Therapeutic Results and Clinical Manifestations Following the Use of Tetraethylthiuram Disulfide (Antabuse)," *American Journal of Psychiatry,* Vol. 107 (1951), pp. 774–780.

some of the patients were kept on disulfiram throughout the study and some others stopped using the drug, the recovery rates are not reported according to these categories. Combined results were available for twenty-five patients after fifteen months:

Table 5

	3 months	15 months
Abstinence	17	9
Moderate Drinker	1	3
Unimproved	7	13
	25	25

Source: George P. Child, Walter Osinski, Robert E. Bennett, and Eugene Davidoff, "Therapeutic Results and Clinical Manifestations Following the Use of Tetraethylthiuram Disulfide (Antabuse)," *American Journal of Psychiatry*, Vol. 107 (April, 1951), p. 779.

Epstein and Guild give results for 125 patients in an antabuse program using Martensen-Larsen's method and categories.[49] The patients were given initial sensitizing doses of disulfiram followed by a test dose of whiskey and then were provided with tablets of disulfiram to take on a regular schedule. Noting that the "unchanged" and "unknown" categories total 49 percent at 15 months of treatment, Epstein and Guild comment "thus half the patients are improved to some extent since the beginning of treatment, although not all are still taking TETD [disulfiram]."[50]

Another example of results from a study using the Martensen-Larsen method, but this time with a different system of rating, is given by J. N. P. Moore and M. O. Drury.[51]

This is a follow-up study conducted after two years on an original testing group of 118. Seventy-one cases were contacted, forty-three in person and twenty-eight by letter. The obtained results are shown in Table 7.

Kirsten Rudfeld divides his results in 334 cases into three categories of varying degrees of alcohol abuse:[52]

---

[49] Nathan B. Epstein and Julius Guild, "Further Clinical Experience with Tetraethylthiuram Disulfide in the Treatment of Alcoholism," *Quarterly Journal of Studies on Alcohol*, Vol. 12 (1951), pp. 366–380.

[50] *Ibid.*, p. 371.

[51] J. N. P. Moore and M. O. Drury, "Antabus in the Management of Chronic Alcoholism," *Lancet*, Vol. 261 (December, 1951), pp. 1059–1061.

[52] Kirsten Rudfeld, "Recovery from Alcoholism by Treatment with Antabuse Combined with Social and Personal Counseling; a Statistical Calculation of the Prognosis in Different Social Groups," *Danish Medical Bulletin*, Vol. 5 (1958), pp. 212–216.

Table 6

Length of treat-ment (mos.)	Results											Total
	Socially Recov-ered		Much Better		Some-what Better		Un-changed		Un-known			
	#	%	#	%	#	%	#	%	#	%		#
3	16	53	2	6	2	6	2	6	8	27		32
6	10	45	1	5	2	9	7	32	2	9		22
9	5	29	2	12	1	6	5	29	4	24		17
12	5	38	0	0	1	8	3	23	4	31		13
15	11	25	6	14	5	12	10	24	11	25		43
Total	47	37	11	9	11	9	27	22	29	23		125

Source: Nathan B. Epstein and Julius Guild, "Further Clinical Experience with Tetraethylthiuram Disulfide in the Treat-ment of Alcoholism," *Quarterly Journal of Studies on Alcohol*, Vol. 12 (September, 1951), p. 311.

Table 7

Condition	Number of cases		Still taking Antabuse	No longer taking Antabuse
No relapse	36	51%	17	19
One or more relapses	23	32%	21	2
Failure	12	17%	0	12
	71		38	33

Of the whole series of 118 cases:

Success	36	(31%)	}	known improvement
Partial success	23	(19%)	}	59 (50%)
Failure	12	(10%)	}	no known improvement
Unknown	47	(40%)	}	59 (50%)

Source: J. N. P. Moore and M. O. Drury, "Antabus in the Management of Chronic Alcoholism," *Lancet,* Vol. 261 (December, 1951), p. 1060.

1. Good results—complete resocialization with no or normal intake of alcohol in 168 cases (50 percent);

2. Doubtful results—definite improvement or considerable resocialization but with relapses in 58 patients (17 percent);

3. Poor results—unstable resocialization in 108 patients (32 percent).

Another specialized example is from an experiment carried out under the auspices of the Atlanta municipal court. The experiment involved using disulfiram in the treatment of "skid-row alcoholics." The individuals involved in the Atlanta experiment were in two groups—voluntary, and compulsory. Of the volunteer group, who were regularly given disulfiram tablets at home, out of sixty-four, thirty-two were abstaining at the end of nine months. The compulsory group was given a choice of going to jail or being treated with disulfiram at the court by the probation officer every morning. Out of 132, 61 of these individuals were abstaining at the end of nine months. Out of the seventy-one who were not, seventeen had abstained through their entire suspended sentence and then stopped treatment.[53] This type of treatment is considered effective in breaking down the "revolving

[53] Peter G. Bourne, James A. Alford, and James Z. Bowcock, "Treatment of Skid-Row Alcoholics with Disulfiram," *Quarterly Journal of Studies on Alcohol,* Vol. 27 (1966), pp. 42–48.

door pattern" of drunkenness and jail sentences that characterize the life of the typical skid-row drunk.

Stimulation of motivation through court referral (a far less rigid and time-consuming procedure than that used in the Atlanta experiment) has been studied. A comparative evaluation is provided by Frederick M. Davis and Keith S. Ditman in their study of Los Angeles court referrals to the U.C.L.A. Alcoholism Research Clinic.[54] Over a fifteen-week period, twenty-six court-referred patients and thirty-six self-referred patients of similar age, sex, and socio-economic status distribution were treated. Of the court-referred cases, six were given group psychotherapy and twenty were given medication (of these eight were given disulfiram). Of the self-referred patients, six were given group psychotherapy; thirty were given medication of which nine were given disulfiram.

After six weeks it was noted that 10 percent had left both the court-referred group and the self-referred group. This is taken by the authors as an indication of the substitutability of court referral for voluntary participation. There is also a trend toward better attendance over a fifteen week period of patients treated with disulfiram, although the authors call it "nonsignificant."

A CLOSE LOOK AT A DIVERGENT STUDY[55]

Dr. Frederick Baekeland and Thomas Shanahan recently completed a study of forty-two alcoholics treated with disulfiram (antabuse). Under study were a variety of admission variables, along with corresponding outcome variables. The *admission variables* included: (1) age; (2) years of education; (3) income; (4) duration of heavy drinking; (5) current state of abstinence; (6) drinking pattern; (7) presence or absence of blackouts; (8) presence or absence of delirium tremens; (9) previous hospitalization for alcoholism; (10) alcohol-related arrests; (11) assaultive behavior; (12) suicide attempts; (13) past or present contact with Alcoholics Anonymous; (14) life situation

---

[54] Davis and Ditman, "The Effect of Court Referral and Disulfiram on Motivation of Alcoholics," *Quarterly Journal of Studies on Alcohol*, Vol. 24 (1963), pp. 276–279.

[55] The study examined here was subsequently extended and reported by Frederick Baekeland, M.D., D.M.Sc., Lawrence Lundwall, M.A., Benjamin Kissin, M.D., and Thomas Shanahan, M.S.W. in "Correlates of Outcome in Disulfiram Treatment of Alcoholism," *Journal of Nervous and Mental Disease*, Vol. 1 (July, 1971), pp. 1–9. The number of participants using antabuse was increased slightly (14 were added) and the number of patients not using antabuse was increased (78 were added). The experimental design was somewhat altered. Findings of the second study were comparable to those previously reported but added that antabuse is effective in *certain* kinds of patients. Older, more motivated, and less depressed patients are particularly likely to be helped by antabuse. The report should be consulted in its entirety by the reader for a more detailed treatment of the subject.

(lives with someone or alone); and (15) whether or not the patient was initially given a tranquilizer or an antidepressant.[56]

The following *outcome variables* were studied: (1) "patient on antidepressant at time of institution of disulfiram (yes or no); (2) patient on tranquilizer at start of disulfiram treatment (yes or no); (3) patient on antidepressant after 6 months on disulfiram or at termination of disulfiram treatment (yes or no); (4) patient on tranquilizer after 6 months on disulfiram or at termination of disulfiram treatment (yes or no); (5) patient on antidepressant at time of last Clinic visit (yes or no); (6) patient on tranquilizer at time of last Clinic visit (yes or no); (7) proportion of missed appointments from intake to start of disulfiram; (8) proportion of missed appointments while on disulfiram; (9) proportion of appointments kept during entire Clinic stay; (10) length of Clinic stay; (11) patient currently dry at end of Clinic stay (yes or no); and (12) proportion of Clinic visits during the last 6 months of treatment on which the patient was rated as currently dry."[57]

The group on disulfiram more than six months (Group I) was of a higher socio-economic status, was better educated, and had been employed a longer time. However, the other group, Group II, which had been on disulfiram less than six months, had a shorter history of heavy drinking and fewer contacts with Alcoholics Anonymous.

In comparing the Group I patients with those not taking disulfiram, they found that the former group was "younger (39.4 vs. 46.0 years, $p<.01$), better educated (11.9 vs. 10.5 years of school, $p<.05$) and had higher incomes ($4,755 vs. $3,520, $p<.01$)." When Group II was compared to those not using disulfiram, they found that again this group contained patients who were younger (38.1 vs. 46.0 years, $p<.01$). However, patients in this second group had been drinking heavily for a shorter time than the patients not using disulfiram (9.8 vs. 15.5 years, $p<.05$) and were less likely to be currently abstinent at intake (5/20 vs. 53/98, $p<.05$). There were no significant differences on the remaining eleven admission variables.

A comparison of Group I with Group II revealed that the two groups of disulfiram patients differed significantly on a number of the outcome variables. Group I patients did well in remaining off antidepressants throughout the course of the treatment; also, they missed fewer appointments and had been rated as currently dry during a higher proportion of visits over their last six months of treatment.[58]

---

[56] Frederick Baekeland, M.D., D.M.Sc., and Thomas Shanahan, M.S.W., "Disulfiram Treatment of Alcoholism: Another Look," unpublished report, March, 1970, p. 2. This article was subsequently published in *Journal of Nervous and Mental Diseases*. See footnote 55.

[57] *Ibid.*

[58] *Ibid.*, p. 4.

Table 8. Two Disulfiram Groups: Admission Variables

	Group 1 (n = 22) On Disulfiram ≥ 6 months	Group 2 (n = 20) On Disulfiram ≤ 6 months	P
Completed high school	15/22	5/20	<.025
Education (yrs.)	11.9 ± 2.1	10.2 ± 2.1	.05 <p <.10
Age (yrs.)	39.4 ± 8.1	39.0 ± 9.7	n.s.
Income ($)	4755 ± 3971	3584 ± 3645	n.s.
Duration of heavy drinking (yrs.)	14.5 ± 8.8	10.8 ± 8.2	n.s.
Employed	16/22	11/20	n.s.
Lives with someone	14/22	16/20	n.s.
Contact with Alcoholics Anonymous	17/22	11/20	n.s.
Hospitalizations	12/22	8/20	n.s.
Subject to delirium tremens	9/22	4/20	n.s.
Blackouts	16/22	16/20	n.s.
Suicide attempts	4/18	3/20	n.s.
Assaultive behavior	3/18	6/20	n.s.
Dry on admission	11/22	5/20	n.s.
Patient on antidepressant	11/22	13/20	n.s.
Patient on tranquilizer	20/22	19/20	n.s.

Source: Baekeland and Shanahan, "Disulfiram Treatment of Alcoholism: Another Look," p. 8. An extension of this study was reported by Frederick Baekeland, Lawrence Lundwall, Benjamin Kissin, and Thomas Shanahan in "Correlates of Outcome in Disulfiram Treatment of Alcoholism," *Journal of Nervous and Mental Diseases,* Vol. 1 (July, 1971), pp. 1–9. © 1971 The Williams & Wilkins Co., Baltimore, Maryland.

The experimenters selected a group of individuals from those treated without disulfiram and used their records to provide an approximation to a control group. "Controls were matched to patients in the two disulfiram groups on the basis of all admission variables with respect to which significant differences were found between patients receiving disulfiram in either group and those not taking the drug."[59] However this was not an experimental control procedure in which comparable patients are assigned to differential treatments, but rather the selection from among patients who had differentiated treatment histories (*i.e.,* the decision not to use disulfiram had

[59] *Ibid.,* p. 3.

Table 9. Two Disulfiram Groups vs. Non-disulfiram Patients: Admission Variables

	P	Group I (n = 22) On Disulfiram ≧ 6 months	(n = 98) Non-disulfiram Patients	(n = 20) On Disulfiram ≦ 6 months	Group II P
Age (yrs.)	<.01	39.4 ± 8.1	46.0 ± 10.0	38.1 ± 9.0	<.01
Education (yrs.)	<.05	11.9 ± 3.5	10.5 ± 2.5	10.3 ± 2.1	n.s.
Income ($)	<.001	4755 ± 2971	3520 ± 740	3584 ± 3645	n.s.
Duration of heavy drinking (yrs.)	n.s.	14.5 ± 8.8	15.5 ± 10.4	9.8 ± 7.0	<.05
Dry at intake	n.s.	11/22	53/98	5/20	<.05
Daily drinking	n.s.	13/22	61/98	14/20	n.s.
Delirium tremens	n.s.	9/22	29/98	4/20	n.s.
Hospitalizations	n.s.	12/22	43/98	8/20	n.s.
Blackouts	n.s.	16/22	66/98	16/20	n.s.
Suicide	n.s.	4/18	13/98	3/20	n.s.
Assault	n.s.	3/18	17/98	6/20	n.s.
Arrests	n.s.	7/22	30–98	9/20	n.s.
Alcoholics Anonymous	n.s.	17/22	58/98	11/20	n.s.
Lives with someone	n.s.	14/22	64/98	16/20	n.s.
On antidepressant	n.s.	12/22	58–98	13/20	n.s.
On tranquilizer	n.s.	20/22	92–98	19/20	n.s.

Source: Baekeland and Shanahan, p. 9.

71

Table 10. Two Disulfiram Groups: Outcome Variables

	Group I On Disulfiram ≥ 6 months	Group II On Disulfiram 6 months	P
Proportion of missed appointments			
Admission to Disulfiram	0.22 ± 0.66	0.35 ± 0.18	$<.02$
While on Disulfiram	0.20 ± 0.21	0.51 ± 0.28	$<.001$
Length of clinic stay (mos.)	44.9 ± 25.2	23.9 ± 19.0	$<.02$
Proportion dry appts. during last 6 months	0.64 ± 0.35	0.38 ± 0.34	$<.02$
Dry on last visit	16/22	6/20	$<.025$
On antidepressant at start of Disulfiram	6/22	14/20	$<.025$
On tranquilizer at start of Disulfiram	13/22	19/20	$<.025$
On antidepressant after 6 mos. on or at termination of Disulfiram	6/22	13/20	$<.05$
On tranquilizer after 6 mos. on or at termination of Disulfiram	16/22	19/20	n.s.
Antidepressant discontinued during clinic stay	11/12	4/13	$<.01$
Tranquilizer discontinued during clinic stay	3/20	2/20	n.s.
On antidepressant at last visit	6/22	12/20	$.05 < p < .10$
On tranquilizer at last visit	17/22	18/20	n.s.

Source: Baekeland and Shanahan, p. 10.

been made—indicating a probable dissimilarity to those patients who were given disulfiram) of patients who had some characteristics comparable to those in the experimental groups. Investigators have noted that the use of disulfiram provides a physiological support for patients who seem psychologically unable to avoid excessive drinking. To the extent that this consideration figured in the decision to give a patient disulfiram or not those patients not using disulfiram might generally be more motivated or psychologically capable of avoiding excessive drinking than those using disulfiram. It is not clear that comparability on other background factors would assure comparability in this respect.

Baekeland and Shanahan reported that if the two groups (Groups I and II) were compared with "controls," much of the beneficial difference between the two groups disappeared. They found that patients in Group I

Table 11. Two Disulfiram Groups vs. Matched Controls: Outcome Measures

	Group I (n = 21)			Group II (n = 19)		
	On Disulfiram $\geq$ 6 months	Controls (n = 21)	P	On Disulfiram $\leq$ 6 months	Controls (n = 19)	P
Length of clinic stay (mos.)	45.7 ± 25.5	26.6 ± 19.6	<.02	23.5 ± 19.4	27.1 ± 21.2	n.s.
Prop. of kept appts.	0.77 ± 0.16	0.64 ± 0.17	<.05	0.02 ± 0.21	0.61 ± 0.16	n.s.
Dry at last visit	15/21	14/21	n.s.	7/19	13/19	.05 < p < .10
Prop. dry appts. last 6 mos.	0.64 ± 0.35	0.68 ± 0.36	n.s.	0.38 ± 0.34	0.56 ± 0.48	n.s.
Antidepressant discontinued	11/12	4/17	<.005	4/13	4/12	n.s.
Tranquilizer discontinued	3/20	1/19	n.s.	3/20	2/18	n.s.
On antidepressant at last visit	10/21	13/21	n.s.	12/19	11/19	n.s.
On tranquilizer at last visit	16/21	20/21	n.s	17/19	17/19	n.s.

Source: Baekeland and Shanahan, p. 11.

73

were *not* more likely to be abstinent on their last visit (15/21 vs. 14/21 for the control, no significant difference); furthermore, they were not rated as being drier than their controls.

The authors concluded that patients who stayed on disulfiram at least six months did better than those who were using it less than six months. (A 1971 extension of this study—see page 68, note 55—found that older, better motivated and less depressed patients did *better* than controls.) However, caution about resting upon these findings is suggested by the problems hampering alcoholism treatment follow-up studies generally (including those reviewed above) as well as by the nature of the control group and a lack of knowledge about the nature and influence of the program's therapeutic milieu.

Thus, overall we have reviewed a study that suggests that disulfiram contributes little to the treatment of alcoholism, and also briefly examined a number of other studies indicating that the use of disulfiram does help in combatting alcoholism. While the reviewed studies are open to a variety of methodological criticisms,[60] one problem particularly limits the clarity of most of the reported results and may help to account for the varied results noted above. While most of the studies measure roughly the same kind of outcome variable (some combination of social rehabilitation and abstinence from alcohol) often they do not sufficiently specify the input, or independent variable (the disulfiram treatment). In most cases the question of how long the patients who were initially started on disulfiram continued to use it, and what proportion of the sample were using disulfiram at the termination of the study is not specified. (While the Baekeland and Shanahan study does distinguish between those patients who used disulfiram more than, and less than, six months, it does not specify the amounts of time the patients were followed while off disulfiram.) The recovery figures presented in many of the reviewed studies reflect the alcohol-abstinence and general behavior both of patients who have stopped using disulfiram and of patients who are continuing to take the antagonistic drug. Since persons who are continuing to use disulfiram are largely prevented from using alcohol due to fear of the alcohol-disulfiram reaction and persons who are not using disulfiram must rely primarily upon their emotional and psychological defenses to prevent a return to drinking, the proportions of these two conditions that go into any study's reported "recovery" rate, or abstinence rate, is a critical interpretative variable. A recovery rate based upon a situation in which most of the patients used disulfiram most of the time, including the time when

---

[60] For a critical survey of the methodology of alcoholism follow-up studies see Duff G. Gillespie, "The Fate of Alcoholics: An Evaluation of Alcoholism Follow-Up Studies," *Alcoholism,* ed. David J. Pittman (New York: Harper and Row, 1967), pp. 159–173.

"recovery" is evaluated, is a very different thing from the same recovery rate occurring in a situation where most of the patients used disulfiram only a small proportion of the reviewed time.

In part this situation seems to reflect varying conceptions of the therapeutic role intended for antabuse. If the proposed therapy involves the administration of disulfiram to block the patient's use of alcohol for a limited period during which he is supposed to make psychological adjustments permitting him to get along without alcohol (and this seems the most widely held interpretation) then the studies should report the characteristics of only those patients who have stopped using disulfiram. Similarly if disulfiram is used to keep the patients from drinking while their bodies recover from the various forms of physical deterioration due to both the extended use of alcohol and the frequently associated malnutrition (*e.g.*, gastritis, inflammatory changes of the stomach, liver changes leading to cirrhosis, and neuritis leading to memory blackouts and delirium tremens),[61] then the follow-up studies should again focus on the behavior of patients who have used disulfiram for the appropriate period and then stopped. On the other hand, if the proposed therapy is to use disulfiram to permit individuals to stay off alcohol independently of their psychological or physical condition, then the studies should report on the behavior of only those patients who are continuing to take disulfiram. Since most of the reviewed studies include some individuals who are still taking disulfiram at the time "recovery" was evaluated, the reported recovery rates rest, in part, upon the use of disulfiram in the last manner suggested above; as a continuing physiological deterrent to drinking. Thus some of the variation between the results of the Baekeland and Shanahan study and those of the other studies might be explicable if fewer of the Baekeland and Shanahan patients were on disulfiram at the point at which the "outcome" measures relating to alcohol abstinence were taken than was the case in most of the other studies.

Thus although there are a variety of other grounds on which limitations of the validity of the reviewed studies may be suggested (*e.g.*, imprecise measurements and the absence of adequate control groups or other means of comparatively evaluating the obtained measurements of recovery), on the whole, the studies do seem to indicate that disulfiram has a distinct effect in the treatment of alcoholism; even though the question of to what extent this effect persists when disulfiram is evaluated solely in the first two suggested therapeutic modes, those of keeping the patients off alcohol for a limited period while they develop their psychological and physical capacities to handle their problems without alcohol, is not yet clear.

---

[61] Joseph B. Kendis, "The Human Body and Alcohol," *Alcoholism*, ed. David J. Pittman (New York: Harper and Row, 1967), pp. 28–29.

ALTERNATIVES

There are other drugs that are used in much the same way disulfiram is used in treating alcoholism. It has long been noted that alcohol induces a "mal rouge" among cyanamide workers—a reaction much like the alcohol-antabuse reaction.[62] This circumstance has recently led to the development of a treatment for alcoholism using citrated calcium carbimide (Temposil). The effects of this drug are apparently similar to those of antabuse, and so are the problems.[63] Clinical investigations of this drug in the United States have been discontinued.[64]

There have also been attempts to use emetine in the aversion treatment of alcoholism. Here the patient is first given a drink and then the drug, which induces a violent reaction. The patient is intended to associate the reaction with the alcohol and thus develop an "aversion to the sight, taste, smell and thought of alcoholic beverages."[65] It should be noted, however (as it is by the United States Department of Health, Education, and Welfare), that "because of the risk of severe physical reactions, this method of treatment requires close medical supervision."[66]

The dispute over treatment in the United States is not really among proponents of the different drugs but is rather between those who see alcoholism as a character weakness and those who see it as an illness. Alcoholics Anonymous has upheld the prior view by relying primarily upon psychological and socio-psychological means of treatment of alcoholism and avoiding the use of drugs.

When antabuse was introduced to facilitate alcoholic treatment, Alcoholics Anonymous reacted to it negatively. AA does not generally use antabuse and permits its use for its members only by special permission in its rest homes.[67] In short, one of the most powerful groups in the treatment of alcoholism has exhibited a continuing resistance to the introduction of antabuse. This resistance derives from that group's conception of the problem, the view that the alcoholic can help himself if he wants to do so, without the aid of a drug.

---

[62] Usdin, p. 285.

[63] See Ferguson, pp. 793–795, and Hayman, pp. 151–152.

[64] According to private communications with Lederle Laboratories such investigations have been discontinued "due to the difficulties with the governmental agencies" (January 3, 1968).

[65] Frederick Lemere and Walter L. Voegtlin, "An Evaluation of the Aversion Treatment of Alcoholism," *Quarterly Journal of Studies on Alcohol*, Vol. 11 (1950), pp. 199–204, specifically p. 200.

[66] National Institute of Mental Health, "Alcohol and Alcoholism," Public Health Service Publication No. 1640, p. 33.

[67] Interview with Dr. Ruth Fox, New York City.

Similar resistance comes from psychotherapists, who perceive the use of antabuse as a minor, or tangential, rather than a major aid in treating the alcoholic. An example is the continued resistance of Dr. Benjamin Kissen, Director of the Sunset Park Alcoholic Clinic, who administers the largest alcoholism control program in New York City.

These sources of opposition have done much to limit the use of antabuse. Dr. Fox, former director of the National Council on Alcoholism and former chairman of the American Medical Association's committee on alcoholism, has said that the number of physicians using antabuse was relatively small. Dr. Fox, among others, feels that antabuse can be an effective *part* of the total treatment leading to the recovery of the alcoholic. She used it in treatment combinations for alcoholics involving hospital stays, AA rest home abstinence intervals, and group therapy (didactic and psychodramatic). Thus, she uses antabuse as a part of a treatment program, and not by itself.

The two positions are not irreconcilable though. An organization much like Alcoholics Anonymous, called "Ring in Ring," was started in Denmark by Dr. Martensen-Larsen to generate mutual support and building of strength among patients taking antabuse.[68]

CONCLUSIONS

Much of the data available suggest that antabuse is a relatively nontoxic drug which can be quite helpful in the treatment of alcoholism. Of course, as all the studies show, antabuse cannot be administered indiscriminately. Patients are reported to require support and encouragement to continue taking the drug. There is also the danger of a severe reaction if the patient does take alcohol while under treatment but not under supervision. Many critiques of the drug indicate that it can serve most usefully as a sort of "pharmacological fence." As one study put it, the drug "forces his [the patient's] cooperation at the time of his greatest impulsive craving for drink."[69] Authorities in this country maintain that the drug treatment is "best used in conjunction with social and psychological efforts to modify the patient's behavior patterns."[70] The fatality rate from the use of antabuse has been low, even in the period in which patients were being given excessive overdoses by present standards. The question arises as to how many more fatalities might have resulted if the alcoholics had been permitted to go untreated.

---

[68] Glud, p. 188.

[69] Crahan, p. 540.

[70] Private communication from Thomas F. A. Plaut, former Assistant Chief, National Center for Prevention and Control of Alcoholism, December 18, 1967.

3

ALCOHOL AND TRAFFIC SAFETY: SCREENING OUT THE DRUNKEN DRIVER

LILY HOFFMAN

INTRODUCTION

In both human and economic terms traffic accidents are a major social problem. In 1969, there were 56,400 deaths, two million disabling injuries, and costs (medical expenses, insurance, property damage, wage loss) of almost 12 billion dollars.[1] Alcohol is conceded to be one of the major if not the most important causal factors in fatal and severe traffic accidents.[2] Several well-controlled studies have shown that 44–60 percent of drivers involved in fatal crashes have blood alcohol levels (BALs) greater than .10 percent (a level that is generally agreed will cause significant impairment), and there is similar though less spectacular implication of alcohol in other vehicular accidents. In general, with increasing levels of blood alcohol, there is increasing likelihood of a driver becoming involved in an accident, that he will be responsible for the accident, and that the accident will be severe or fatal.

This correlation between alcohol and auto fatalities is not new knowledge. For example, at least one of the major controlled studies still cited dates back to the 1930s.[3] But even though many countries have had laws

---

[1] National Safety Council, *Accident Facts: 1970* (Chicago), February, 1970.

[2] Among many references, see publications of the National Safety Council, U.S. Department of Transportation reports, and in the popular press, Howard A. Rusk, M.D., "Death on the Highway," *New York Times,* July 5, 1970.

[3] R. L. Holcomb, "Alcohol in Relation to Traffic Accidents," *Journal of the American Medical Association* (*JAMA*) 111 (September 17, 1938), pp. 1076–1085. (This journal will be cited as *JAMA*.)

Table 1.   Summary of Findings on the Association of Alcohol in Traffic Accidents of Increasing Severity

	Percentage of drivers with BAL in the high concentration range of .10% and over
Drivers using road but not in crash	1–4%
Drivers in run-of-the-mill crashes	6%
Drivers seriously injured in non-pedestrian crashes	25%
Drivers fatally injured in multi-vehicle crashes where another vehicle believed responsible	12%
Drivers fatally injured in multi-vehicle crashes where no other vehicle believed responsible	44%
Drivers fatally injured in single vehicle crashes	48–57%

Source: U.S. Department of Transportation Report: Alcohol and Highway Safety (Washington, D.C.: U.S. Government Printing Office, August, 1968), Chapter 2.

against driving while intoxicated, it is only a few that have actively enforced such programs.[4] In addition to the lack of societal will, a less obvious impediment to increased legislation and active enforcement has been the state of the technology involved.

With the recent adoption of legislation utilizing a new technology, the breath screen test, which has made it considerably easier to identify the drinking driver, Great Britain has claimed an immediate drop in fatalities and serious injuries.[5] The United States is now beginning to embark upon similar programs and thus it might seem that a "solution" is close at hand. However, an examination of the problem as well as the proposed technological solution shows that, although technology has in fact extended our options for legislation and enforcement, it is not a blank check and its usefulness is constrained along many dimensions.

THE TECHNOLOGY

Before the technical tests for measuring human alcohol levels were developed, intoxication could only be determined by simple observation and

---

[4] Scandinavian countries in particular. For example, Sweden began an active enforcement program in 1920, continuing to up-date her efforts as new data on the problem were generated. *Vide* infra, "Sweden—The Total Package," p. 90.

[5] The Ministry of Transport press notice of December 22, 1969, entitled, "Two Years of 'Breath Tests.'" These data are presented in Table 3, p. 97.

performance—the odor of alcohol, walking a straight line, touching the nose —all subjective procedures, neither scientifically accurate nor legally viable.

In contrast, the standard tests for quantifying alcohol levels replaced this relatively "soft data" with a number—the blood alcohol level reported in percentage weight by volume. These tests, in use in modified form for about forty years, take blood or urine samples, preferably blood because of greater accuracy.[6] The procedure is a complex one: for the blood test, a sample must be taken under sterile conditions by a doctor, nurse, or medical technician and sent to a well-equipped laboratory to be analyzed by other highly-trained personnel. In all, this takes a team of skilled personnel, considerable equipment and time, as well as careful supervision and record keeping, because the medical-legal implications of the test, as evidence in court, make it vulnerable to the many hands the sample has passed through and the general complexity of the process.[7]

The first controlled study utilizing these tests to determine the incidence of alcohol impairment in accidents leading to death or hospitalization yielded a figure ten to forty times higher than what was usually found in police statistics, which, for reasons we shall clarify, utilize the behavioral signs of drunkenness as the index of suspicion.[8] Thus as a research tool, the technology has allowed us to grasp the magnitude of the problem. It would seem that this ability to quantify alcohol impairment would have given us greater leverage with the problem, as it has, for example, in Sweden.[9] However, the primary use of the technology in this country has been to obtain corroborative evidence for the conviction of the drunken driver, that is, to confirm the gross physical signs of drunkenness.[10] The time, cost, and general complexity of the process did not particularly facilitate its preventive use, but this can be only a partial explanation.

In comparison to the highly elaborate collection and analytic procedures

---

[6] The first description of quantitative tests for alcohol with application to drivers appeared in 1914, by Widmark. The first application of quantitative tests in the U.S. is described by E. Bogen, "Drunkenness," *JAMA* 89 (October, 1927), p. 1508. The tests were endorsed by the American Medical Association (AMA) in 1937—see *JAMA* 108 (1937), p. 2137, and the National Safety Council in 1937.

[7] Committee on Medico-Legal Problems of the American Medical Association, *Alcohol and the Impaired Driver* (Chicago: American Medical Association, 1968). Chapter 6 describes and evaluates the chemical tests. This basic text will be referred to as the AMA *Manual*.

[8] Holcomb, "Alcohol in Relation to Traffic Accidents."

[9] See pp. 90–94.

[10] For example, the *Department of Transportation Report* (Washington, D.C.: U.S. Government Printing Office, August, 1968), p. 118, states that the use of the chemical test has helped to convict because "it is harder to contradict objective laboratory evidence than oral testimony that the defendant drove 'erratically.' "

for blood or urine tests, the recent development of the alcohol breath test provides a simplified alternative,[11] which has the further advantage of being less physically onerous. Breath sampling involves less bodily intrusion than taking a sample of blood, thus making it a more acceptable test in a culture like ours where the needle puncture is somewhat equivalent to rape. The subject just blows into a balloon or tube; there is no discomfort and medical personnel are unnecessary.[12] The analysis itself is semi-automated, fast, does not require ancillary laboratory facilities, and is inexpensive. Most of the commercially available units are self-contained and several are in fact fairly portable units, which after a brief warm-up period, will give a BAL reading in five to ten minutes.[13] This means that the testing process can be decentralized to local police stations rather than a few central laboratories, and the automation in turn decreases the requirements for time, manpower, and individual competence.[14] Although there are still problems in relation to reliability and ease of use, this represents a considerable technical refinement.[15] But even this has not greatly changed the use of the quantitative alcohol tests in the United States from that of obtaining corroborative evidence to something closer to general deterrence. We cannot be quite certain why the options presented by these tests have not been better utilized; but some of the evident factors are that, until recently, the tests were cumbersome and physically obtrusive; that legal questions were difficult, as the tests couldn't be administered prior to making an arrest and, given the present convoluted legal processes, police were loath to touch anyone but the grossly drunk driver; and that society at large did not demand the evidence produced by the tests—for in spite of exhortation, the United States has been relatively tolerant of the traffic costs and has not at any point fully utilized available options to reduce them.[16]

BREATH TESTS AND BREATH SCREEN TESTS

Although press releases and magazine articles tend to refer to both kinds of tests as "breath tests," the breath test reported responsible for the dra-

---

[11] The most recent AMA *Manual* (pp. 102, 136) says that it is interchangeable with direct blood analysis.

[12] AMA *Manual,* chapter 6.

[13] For example, the Breathalyzer, Drunkometer, Portable Intoximeter. See AMA *Manual,* chapter 6.

[14] A police officer can be taught breath test operation and procedures in forty-four hours (the time recommended by the National Safety Council). See AMA *Manual,* p. 137.

[15] H. Herbert Spector, "Alcohol Breath Tests: Gross Errors in Current Methods of Measuring Alveolar Gas Concentrations," *Science* (April 2, 1917), pp. 57–59.

[16] The only notable spurt of mobilization, with attendant public focus, was during the Nader period, was directed at the vehicle, and has since died down.

matic drop in highway fatalities in Great Britain, and recently legislatively introduced in New York State, is not the quantitative instrument described above, but a version of it, appropriately named the "screening test." In contrast to the quantitative breath test, this breath screen test is not developmentally a refinement, but rather a quickie version—a device with a different function and utility for our problem.

The test is simple—the subject breathes into a tube or balloon—and the results are instantaneous. The color change of chemical reactants in the tube or balloon gives a rough indication of his breath alcohol concentration.[17] However this is not precise information and, unlike the quantitative tests, cannot be used as evidence in court. When positive, the suspect must be given further blood or breath tests to quantify the amount. The advantages of this test relate not to its precision, but rather to portability, cost, and ease of use. For example, the screening test can be kept in the police car (or in a pocket), in contrast to the larger and more expensive quantitative breath test units, and requires only the most minimal instruction as compared to the forty-four hours recommended for the quantitative breath tests.[18]

This means that for the first time we have an epidemiological tool—a way to cover ground quickly and pick up abnormalities. The policeman, or any other agent, with a compact kit can determine who is probably under the influence of alcohol. This is simple detection, introducing the possibility of screening procedures and creating new options for deterrence.

ALCOHOL AS SYMPTOMATIC

Continuing research into the relation of alcohol to traffic safety has both complicated and revealed a depth to the problem that may limit the effectiveness of current efforts. For example, examination of the biographies, previous records, and alcohol levels of drivers involved in fatal and serious accidents has shown the diversity of the drinking-driving population and defined a lethal subset of chronic drinkers, the alcoholic in contradistinction to the social drinker.[19] Perhaps two-thirds of drinking drivers involved in fatal accidents are alcoholics; they are implicated in 40–50 percent of all

---

[17] AMA *Manual,* chapter 6.

[18] The quantitative breath tests would still need a van and are too costly to put in patrol cars—*e.g.,* the Breathalyzer unit costs approximately $650.

[19] The evidence is summarized in the *Department of Transportation Report,* chapters 2, 4. Also in the AMA *Manual,* chapter 5, and has by now achieved some degree of general acceptance. For example, the presidents of the National Safety Council and the American Medical Association recently stated that "the chronic drinker, not the social drinker, is responsible for most accidents," *New York Times,* December 21, 1969.

the traffic accidents in which a driver has been drinking. Since alcoholism is an addiction—a compelling need to drink to the detriment of the alcoholic's physical, social, and economic functioning—and the prognosis for its treatment, particularly if treatment is not voluntary (unlike that provided by Alcoholics Anonymous), is poor, this subgroup of drinking drivers cannot be expected to readily respond to exhortation or the deterrence of *post-facto* penalties.[20]

Not only do we seem to have a diverse population; when the problem is looked at from a somewhat different perspective, we find that among the drivers involved in fatal accidents there is a high incidence of mental illness, social deviancy, violent and suicidal behavior,[21] as well as lower socio-economic class origin which cuts across the spectrum of social drinker and chronic alcoholic and raises the possibility that alcoholism (at least in part) may be an epiphenomenon—that the drinking driver "drives as he lives,"[22] and that the use of alcohol may be symptomatic. Similarly the high accident rate associated with males under twenty-five, who as a group have relatively low alcohol levels[23] and which is often interpreted in terms of inexperience both with alcohol and driving, can also be viewed within the broader context of social deviance and alienation which are high during this life stage.

Similar conclusions are suggested when the problem is viewed in the wider societal context. We find the problem of traffic safety is not just endemic to capitalist countries with unchecked industry, but a rising concern wherever one finds a high ratio of cars to people—any industrialized, motorized nation.[24] This points out the oversimplification of periodically popular "devil theories" and suggests instead at least two underlying themes—on the one hand, that technology is out of control in diverse modern societies (rather than "runaway capitalism"), and on the other, that deep human needs exist unmet (in some cases variably manifested as alcoholism or sociopathic behavior) for which the current technology then becomes an instrument and the resultant problem a symptom.[25]

---

[20] For a discussion of alcoholism, see National Institute of Mental Health, *Alcohol and Alcoholism*, Public Health Service Publication No. 1640 (Washington, D.C., 1960).

[21] The evidence is summarized in the *Department of Transportation Report,* chapter 4. Note particularly the work of M. Selzer, *e.g.*, M. Selzer and S. Weiss, "Alcoholism and Traffic Fatalities—Study in Futility," *American Journal of Psychiatry*, Vol. 122 (1966), pp. 762–767.

[22] The phrase was used in a paper by W. A. Tillman and G. E. Hobbs, "The Accident-Prone Automobile Driver," *American Journal of Psychiatry*, Vol. 106 (1949), p. 321–332.

[23] *Department of Transportation Report,* chapter 4.

[24] For example, a recent Communist Party weekly newspaper was reported to have condemned the "dreadful level of USSR traffic deaths." In the past decade control programs have been initiated in communist countries.

[25] See Amitai Etzioni, *The Active Society* (New York: The Free Press, 1968), pp. 208–

A relation of drinking-driving to deep underlying needs does not mean that pragmatic solutions cannot be devised, but, short of total societal change, it may be possible to treat symptoms only if we can overcome our medical, scientific, and moral biases against such relief. Our bias surfaces, for example, as the tendency to suggest "cures," such as a major attack on alcoholism or rehabilitation programs for problem drinkers (now beginning to proliferate)[26] rather than to attempt shortcuts that either offer effective deterrence or make it hard, harder, or impossible for alcoholics to drive, *e.g.*, revoking registration, taking license plates, or initiating insurance penalties.

LEGAL-MORAL ISSUES

In addition to constraints introduced by the "depth" of the problem, we seem to have difficulty in providing a favorable legal context for the effective use of the quantitative breath tests. To begin with, in this country, to approach the problem at all, we have tread gently, side-stepping problems of self-incrimination, due process, unreasonable search and seizure, by the legal fiction of implied consent legislation[27] which as defined in the Uniform Vehicle Code states that:

> Any person placed under arrest for operating a motor vehicle while intoxicated or under the influence of alcohol is deemed to have given his consent to a chemical test of his blood, breath or urine, for the purpose of determining the alcohol content of his blood.[28]

Even as it stands, the implied consent legislation has been diluted. As of

---

211 for a discussion of the "low capacity" for controlled use of knowledge and the passivity before technology of various countries and, conversely, the asocial effect of technology on diverse societies.

[26] See for example, the *Report of the Secretary's Advisory Committee on Traffic Safety*, U.S. Department of Health, Education and Welfare (February 29, 1968), which recommends: "Traditional punitive measures can be expected to have little effect on behavior that arises from illness. The problem requires a massive Federal program concentrating on alcoholism." And it also recommends the establishment of a center for the study of violent behavior.

The New York State Experimental Driver Rehabilitation Program is an example of current attempts to change the behavior of drinking drivers. The drivers will be divided into tracks on the basis of whether they have driving problems, attitude problems, or alcohol problems and given 10–30 hours training. See *New York Times*, May 16, 1970.

[27] The legal aspects of the chemical tests are discussed by Robert L. Donigan, *Chemical Tests and the Law* (Illinois: The Traffic Institute, Northwestern University, 1966).

[28] See the *Department of Transportation Report*, Appendix 5, for the National Uniform Standards for State Highway Safety Program, Standard 8:II—"Alcohol in Relation to Highway Safety."

April, 1970, forty-six states have some type of implied consent law,[29] but there are many variations which "hamper rather than aid enforcement," weakening the law by restricting the use of the chemical test, complicating the grounds for license revocation, and allowing the test only as corroborative evidence.[30]

Furthermore, most states have set legal alcohol limits too high. Laboratory research indicates that the threshold of driving impairment is about .04 percent and at levels of .10 percent there is a "severe, significant and dangerous deterioration."[31] In line with these findings, many concerned countries have defined lower limits. For example, Norway and Sweden have set .05 percent; Denmark, Great Britain, and Canada, .08 percent.[32] In contrast, in the United States, a limit of .15 percent which corresponds to severe intoxication is still in effect in twenty-four states and three states have no presumptive level of intoxication at all although the Uniform Motor Vehicle Code, the National Safety Council, and the A.M.A. have all recommended adoption of a level of .10 percent since 1962.[33]

The major weakness of the implied consent law is probably the requirement that the driver can be tested only after arrest. In effect, this means that it is those drivers who appear grossly intoxicated enough to be arrested in the first place who will be tested. Thus paradoxically, we are in the same position as we were thirty years ago, relying on gross subjective evidence of drunkenness to detect the drinking driver. The only difference is that now it is easier to obtain corroborative evidence—to "get the goods" on the offender.

In the United States, where there has not really been a sense of urgency,[34] efforts to widen the sieve and increase the proportion of drinking drivers detected (or apprehended as the case may be) seem to have awaited the development of the breath screen devices which make simple, on-the-spot testing practicable. When used in the pre-arrest situation, it becomes a viable approach to the problem of deterrence. The legislative interest in this approach since the appearance of the breath screen test illustrates the subtle

---

[29] "State Legislation *re* Alcohol," *Traffic Safety* (April, 1970), p. 20.

[30] Donigan, p. 180.

[31] AMA *Manual*, p. 59.

[32] *U.S. News and World Report* (October 16, 1967).

[33] The National Safety Council's Alcohol Statistics Fact Sheet (A1–185) states that drivers with a BAL of .15 percent have twenty-five times greater chance of causing an accident than if they were not drinking.

[34] K. J. B. Teasdale notes the importance of this in his review, "Vehicle Accident Studies," in *1970 International Automotive Safety Conference Compendium*, P–30, May 13–15, 1970, Detroit, Michigan, June 8–11, 1970, Brussels (Society of Automotive Engineers), pp. 1266–1279.

relationship between the ease and cost-effectiveness of a technology and its legal and social acceptance—there seems to be a continuum along which trade-offs are possible.

It is in this context that Great Britain adopted the use of the breath screen test. In the United States, New York State and Baton Rouge, Louisiana have recently adopted versions of the British Road Safety Act, and similar legislation is pending elsewhere. The New York State Law, adopted May, 1969, broadened its previous implied consent statute to include pre-arrest testing with a breath screen test.[35] Interestingly, New York, a state generally innovative in traffic safety measures (*e.g.*, the first implied consent law and a prototype safety car project) weakened the British type law by placing restrictions on the test and most crucially failed to provide penalties for refusal. So far the new law has not been well publicized nor fully implemented. The Baton Rouge statute, in effect since November, 1969, is closer to the British model, providing penalties for refusing the pre-arrest test ($200 and/or up to sixty days in jail).[36]

Although the Baton Rouge statute is a better model for the effective use of the breath screen test, the pre-arrest test is itself only a first step on a continuum of increasing pressure which might include, for example, graded randomized testing of all accidents, all moving violations and, ultimately, random roadblocks or spot checks. However such policies have obvious social as well as economic costs that may make them prohibitive for the United States. In addition to the bias against dragnet procedures here, there is the impracticality of stopping every car and screening every driver to get the random 1–4 percentage of drivers that are intoxicated.[37]

No results are available yet on the potential American experience, but legislative advances may not necessarily make any impact because of the way in which implementation is in turn dependent upon attitudes which don't necessarily change with the law. This is illustrated by the experience of two Missouri cities, Kansas City and St. Louis—one with a history of strong enforcement, and the other with relatively lax enforcement of drinking-driving laws.[38] After passage of a statewide implied consent law, the proportionate difference in number of tests administered, arrests and convictions remained essentially the same. Moreover, after an initial spurt there

---

[35] *New York Times,* May 29, 1969.

[36] Billie J. Watson, "Baton Rouge's Pre-Arrest Breath Test and How It Is Working," *Traffic Digest and Review* 18:4 (April, 1970), pp. 7–9. The Baton Rouge statute was a prototype, developed by the Insurance Institute of Highway Safety.

[37] *Proceedings of the National Highway Safety Bureau Priorities Seminar,* Vol. 2: *Alcohol and Highway Safety Countermeasures* (July, 1969), p. 31.

[38] E. H. Hunvald, Jr., Franklin E. Zimring, "Whatever Happened to Implied Consent," *Missouri Law Review* 33:3 (1968), p. 323.

was no long-term effect on the number of arrests or accident rate. Although, in this case, an effective legislative step "did not change administrative attitudes sufficiently to escalate enforcement where there was a prior low level," we do not know whether the response would have been different with easier procedures—*i.e.*, the pre-arrest and breath screen combination. On the other hand, at Lackland Air Force Base, a sustained increase in enforcement coupled with initiation of more severe penalties led to a continuing decrease in accident rate over an extended period.[39] There were no legal or technical innovations—just more effective enforcement of the old. The greater ease in effecting normative change in this second situation of strong societal control is obvious.

In general, enforcement of drinking-driving laws in the United States has been traditionally lax with the tendency of both judge and jury to go easy on offenders.[40] This seems related to the generally permissive attitudes toward drinking and drinking and driving, and the common conceptualization of the drinking-driving population—everyone drinks and drives, "it could be me" in the witness stand, a few drinks are not detrimental, the real alcoholics are all skid-row bums.

Such general assumptions may explain our failure to pick up the options that the technology provides. For example, if the alcohol level were used as evidence of "intoxication," the law could define the crime in terms of a given alcohol level so that a subject with an alcohol level above the stated limit would be automatically guilty and only the test's validity need be proven in court. Such a move would eliminate some of the current legal problems by limiting individual options to prosecute or not to prosecute, as well as sympathetic jury response.[41]

Part of the difficulty in gaining consensual validation for any effort lies

---

[39] J. E. Barmark and D. E. Payne, "The Lackland Accident Countermeasures Experiment," *HRB Proceedings* 40 (1961), pp. 513–522, referred to in *Department of Transportation Report*, p. 81, and by Roger C. Cramton, "Driver Behavior and Legal Sanctions: A Study of Deterrence," *Michigan Law Review* 67:3 (January, 1969), pp. 421–454.

[40] Among many references to this, see the *Department of Transportation Report*, p. 100, and the AMA *Manual*, chapter 1, or *U.S. News and World Report* (Washington, D.C.), July 16, 1968. The Insurance Institute for Highway Safety was quoted as saying that the "drunken driver has a 50 percent chance of escaping conviction" in this country.

[41] It is of interest that more direct legislation, as exists in other countries, without mention of the driver having given his implied consent, and stating that it would be illegal to drive with a blood alcohol of a certain level, would probably be constitutional. For statements to the effect that such legislation would probably be constitutional, see: Andrew R. Hricko, "British Pre-Arrest Breath Tests—Constitutional in the U.S.?" *Traffic Digest and Review* 17:12 (December, 1969), pp. 1–6; or the *Department of Transportation Report*, p. 118, which states that laws prohibiting driving at specific limits, like England, "probably have no constitutional problems here."

In the United States to date, only Nebraska has passed such a law. (*Department of*

in the fact that we do not have a population clearly defined as deviant, but rather a continuum of abuse—social through chronic drinkers, undifferentiated by both laws and penalties. The current attempt to redefine the problem drinker as the prime culprit seems directed at this very problem;[42] perhaps focusing on the deviant end of the spectrum will create greater societal legitimacy for strict enforcement as well as for more legislation. But it may also prove counterproductive since it tends to obscure the contribution of the social drinker, who, although not "the most lethal subgroup," does contribute to the problem and may in fact be the drinking driver reached by deterrent programs such as the British model.[43]

In the most direct sense the actual deterrent effect of legislation comes from what we *do* with the offender, be it punitive, preventative, or rehabilitative.[44] There seems to be no conclusive evidence that any of the prescribed penalties in common use work, and some indication that they may be ineffective. For example, studies show that a large proportion of drivers with suspended or revoked licenses drive anyway.[45] Although there are other pos-

---

Transportation Report, p. 119.) Similar legislation has been proposed in New York State by Governor Rockefeller at the beginning of several legislative sessions, but has failed to gain sufficient support.

[42] In line with this, concerned organizations such as the National Safety Council have conducted informational and educational campaigns to inform the public about the "true facts," first publicizing the danger of "one for the road," and most recently of the "killer"— the alcoholic. The shift seems in part a response to continuing research on the drinking-driving population, as well as to opinion polls which have shown ignorance of the contribution of the alcoholic driver. (*Department of Transportation Report,* chapter 6.)

However, the image of a generally uninformed public is contradicted by opinion polls which have indicated majority recognition of the dangers of driving and drinking, and support for more severe legislation and penalties. (See *Department of Transportation Report,* chapter 6 for a summary of polls; *New York Times,* December 31, 1968.) Taken in context with courtroom and enforcement patterns, such contradictions may underline the bias of polled opinion toward public support but private sympathy, and point out the weakness of educational programs *per se.*

[43] We tend to forget that both social and problem drinkers contribute substantially to the problem. See Roger C. Cramton, "Driver Behavior and Legal Sanctions: A Study of Deterrence," *Michigan Law Review* 67:3 (January, 1969), p. 444.

[44] Wolf Middendorff, *The Effectiveness of Punishment Especially in Relation to Traffic Offenses* (South Hackensack, New Jersey: Fred B. Rothman and Co., 1968), chapter II. Middendorff discusses the difficulty of getting a general effect through legislation in western democratic countries given the conditions of mobility, anomie, etc.

[45] For example, R. S. Coppin and G. Van Oldenbeck, "Driving Under Suspension and Revocation," Report #18, California Department of Motor Vehicles (January, 1965). They found as many as one-third of the persons whose licenses are suspended, and of those revoked, are known to continue to drive anyway because of subsequent traffic citations.

A survey of U.S. cities and Canadian cities, reported in *Traffic Digest and Review* (March, 1970), pointed out the ineffectiveness of existing programs for detecting and deterring suspended or revoked drivers in 98 percent of the areas.

sibilities, existing societal biases make it difficult to explore some alternatives that might allow for control with less general coercion. Examples are selective licensing (the general feeling is that driving is a right and the recognition of the hardships involved in keeping anyone from driving) and civil penalties such as insurance fines or subrogation (this invokes the fear of allocating more power to the private sector). Even where used (see discussion of Sweden below), these techniques have not been specifically evaluated.

There seems to be a growing awareness that given the diverse nature of the drinking-driving population, varying approaches are necessary. Thus we might deter one group (the so-called casual or social drinkers) and try to keep the smaller but more dangerous sociopathic drinking drivers off the road, or rehabilitate them as we seem to prefer to do.[46] But the general question still remains, Are legal sanctions in fact effective deterrents for drinking-driving? Do we reduce drinking-driving in any permanent fashion, rather than just give more tests, increase arrests, convictions, or achieve shock effects as we rush to more severe legislation, enforcement, and penalties? This question directs us not only to examine more closely Great Britain's experience, but to pull from the range of national policies an example of strict, long-term encompassing regulatory activity regarding alcohol and driving such as we find in Sweden.

SWEDEN—THE TOTAL PACKAGE

Sweden has one of the longest histories of legislation and active regulation, a pattern of increasing severity and control. The significant dates are: 1920—the first legislation against drinking and driving; 1934—mandatory chemical tests for blood alcohol where a crime was involved or if there was suspicion of drunken driving; 1941—regulations defining the crime by alcohol level and distinguishing two levels of impairment (.08–.15 percent, and .15–plus percent) with penalties of fines, jail terms, and license revocation; and 1957—the punishable lower limit was dropped to .05 percent.[47]

Sweden uses almost every known form of deterrence.[48] There are li-

---

[46] In his critique, Cramton discusses the questionable value of resocializing problem drinkers.

[47] Rune Andreasson, "Alcohol and Road Traffic: An International Survey of the Discussions," in *Alcohol and Road Traffic-Proceedings of the Third International Conference on Alcohol and Road Traffic* (London, 1962), p. 9. Also, Rune Andreasson, *Alcohol, Drivers and Traffic Safety* (Stockholm: Ansvar International Insurance Company, Ltd., 1960), pp. 57–59.

[48] The variety of techniques are discussed in several sources: R. Andreasson, *Alcohol*

cense restrictions, fines, jail terms, license revocation. To prevent a convicted driver from buying another car, his registration can be taken and his insurance policy suspended; to discourage his borrowing another car, the owner of that vehicle is assumed responsible and can be penalized. There are strong economic sanctions; the insurance company has the right of subrogation where there has been a drinking-while-driving conviction. When a license has been revoked the driver must be re-tested, and in the meanwhile, he comes under the scrutiny of his local temperance committee and is often plugged into rehabilitative programs. Additionally there are random road-blocks in which qualitative screening tests are given to deter and detect drinking drivers.

Moreover, in Sweden, the drinking-driving problem is part of a much larger context of alcohol control, which includes all aspects of public life and not just driving behavior. This is also a total attack; there is education, rehabilitation, local surveillance by temperance units that deal with the individual and can compel treatment, and legislative and enforcement efforts. We cannot forget that temperance has been a viable movement in Sweden since the nineteenth century, and although the rationing of hard liquor, begun in 1915, was abandoned in 1955, in its place there are now high liquor taxes and continuing restrictions on its sale (selectivity, for example: liquor cannot be sold to those under twenty-one, nor to certain listed persons—17,360 in 1965).[49]

Furthermore, the impetus to the temperance movement and related activities seems to reside in collectivities such as the automobile clubs and insurance companies which have mobilized support for and lobbied for stricter alcohol and auto regulations.[50] Thus there is well-organized, broad-based support for such measures which in turn reflect upward consensual movement and not just downward legislated control. This increased legiti-

---

Drivers and Traffic Safety; Marvin Wagner, "The Scandinavian Approach to the Drinking Driver," *Traffic Digest and Review* 17:12 (December, 1969), p. 7; *Annual Report for 1965,* from the Swedish National Board of Excise, regarding the consumption of alcoholic beverages, cases of drunkenness and driving under the influence of alcohol; *Alcohol and Highway Safety Countermeasures,* Vol. 2 of *Proceedings of the National Highway Safety Bureau Priorities Seminar* (Virginia, July, 1969); Arthur Little Inc. *The State of the Art of Traffic Safety: A Critical Review and Analysis of the Technical Information on Factors Affecting Traffic Safety* (June, 1966).

[49] See Andreasson, "Alcohol and Road Traffic: An International Survey of the Discussions," and Arthur Little Inc., *The State of the Art of Traffic Safety,* p. 231.

[50] Olaf Soderberg, *Motororganizationer i Sverige,* Lund Political Studies, #6, 1966. This study discusses groups, organizations, and political interests involved in motoring and road temperance legislation.

macy through collective mobilization is of interest, particularly when we consider the potential but unused power of our comparable organizations.

Although it is widely assumed that the regulations have been effective in reducing the frequency of drinking and driving, and of alcohol contribution to accidents—particularly serious and fatal—there is a paucity of studies comparable to the controlled American studies.[51] A 1968 review of the evidence on Sweden, by R. Bonnichsen, gives a figure of 10–12 percent as the proportion of fatally injured drivers with significant blood levels (over .05 percent).[52] This is a **lower** proportion than the few earlier controlled studies[53] and certainly stands in dramatic contrast to comparable figures for other countries or for the United States (*e.g.,* 50 percent). However, it would still need to be interpreted with careful consideration of the drinking patterns, alcohol consumption, and extent of the problem in each country.[54]

In addition to a lack of proper controlled research on the incidence of drinking and driving, there is a lack of comparable before-and-after studies of countermeasures, except by using arrests for drinking-driving, which as we have noted is not a satisfactory indicator. Given the large number of alcohol-related inputs—from publicity campaigns to insurance bonuses—it is impossible to isolate the effective weight of the many different preventative and

---

[51] Much of what we do find suffers from the use of contaminated police data. To really gauge the extent of the problem one cannot rely upon accidents investigated by the police (which they have found "suspicious" enough to test), as is done for example by Andreasson, in his assessment of the effectiveness of the legislation. This assumes that drinking and driving arrests are equivalent to the proportion of drinking and driving. Although Andreasson seems aware of the underestimation of the alcohol factor in police and official statistics, and although the police may do better in Sweden than elsewhere, controlled studies are still needed. The best studies include an early 1932–33 study (the year before the 1934 reforms) of all non-fatal accidents reporting to the hospital for injuries in Stockholm. Here BALs were systematically given and 44 percent of the total 113 casualties were found to have consumed alcohol, 29 percent of the 113 had a level over .10 percent. Another excellent study by Sven Wahlgren of 222 Swedish road deaths in 1956 found alcohol involvement to greater or lesser extent in 19.4 percent of the cases. See Andreasson, "Alcohol and Road Traffic: An International Survey of the Discussions."

[52] R. Bonnichsen, "Alkoholens Roll Vid Svenska Trafilkolychor," Sartryc, Up *Alkoholfragen,* 1968.

[53] See footnote 51.

[54] It is hard to get accurate or comparable data on alcoholism. Some Swedish reports cite 8 percent of adults in Sweden and 13 percent of males in Stockholm as "excessive drinkers" (implying one or more arrests for drinking). This seems to imply a much larger problem if we compare it with even the revised estimates for the U.S. For example, a recent survey at George Washington University suggested that the number of hard alcoholics be revised upward by one-third—from 6.5 to 9 million. This is still only about 5 percent although they noted that additionally there are "many millions on the verge"—whatever that means.

punitive measures used retrospectively or to take account of the cumulative effect of such policies on behavior over such a long period time.[55]

The picture we get by comparing international statistics should make us wary of generalizations. Fatality rates can give dramatically different pictures depending upon what base is used.[56] For example, in Table 1, using total population as the base, the United States has a much higher fatality rate than Sweden. However the U.S. has more cars per person, and using the total number of private cars as a base, the U.S. is about equal to Sweden. But this figure still obscures differences in the proportionate distribution of the various types of motor vehicles and their different contribution to fatalities. For example, there are significantly more motorcycles and other two-wheel vehicles in Sweden than in the United States and they contribute more to her fatalities.[57] Fatalities per 100,000 miles would be a good measure except for the unreliability of estimates of mileage, and would also hide different driving conditions, such as the relatively higher proportion of superhighways in the United States.

It has been suggested that the most accurate index would be the measure of risks for each specific group (*e.g.*, pedestrians/population, car occupants/cars registered, motorcyclists/motorcycles.[58] Indeed Sweden, using this type of statistic is a relatively low-risk country compared to most of Europe and the U.S. (see Table 2, line *d*), but does not rank much better than Great Britain, a country which has not taken such stringent measures.

Even internal longitudinal comparison does not allow easy conclusions. The Swedish fatality figures over the last fifty years show fluctuations not necessarily related to any control measures, and the pattern is complicated by the many intervening variables of wars, depression, motorization, alcohol

---

[55] For example we do not find evaluation of short jail terms and fines versus the use of civil penalties, although it is possible that the insurance liabilities have been a significant deterrent. (30 percent of Swedish arrests result from information provided by the public— *e.g.*, wives fearing monetary loss. *Proceedings of the National Highway Safety Bureau Priorities Seminar,* Vol. 2, *Alcohol and Highway Safety Countermeasures.*)

[56] For general discussions of the variation in national rates due to differences in number of road users, types of vehicles, etc., see L. G. Norman, *Road Traffic Accidents* (Geneva: World Health Organization, 1962); Ross A. McFarland, "Significant Trends in Human Factor Research on Motor Vehicle Accidents" in *Proceedings of the 13th Stapp Car Conference* (Boston, Mass., December, 1969); and Office for Economic Co-operation and Development Research Group, *Research on the Effects of Alcohol and Drugs on Driver Behavior* (Paris, 1969), p. 41.

[57] See Andreasson, "Alcohol and Road Traffic: An International Survey of the Discussions."

[58] J. B. Bull, "International Comparisons of Road Accident Statistics," *Journal of the Institution of Highway Engineers,* 15:3 (March, 1968), pp. 15–19.

consumption, etc.[59] Furthermore, some experts have noted some tendency toward patterns—perhaps worldwide.[60]

In summary, some control over the alcohol contribution both to fatalities and to accidents in general seems to have been achieved in Sweden, but this has occurred over a long period of time and with, for a democratic nation, almost maximum control. Sweden is, comparatively, one of the low-risk countries in terms of danger to road users. Because of the long duration of time and the multi-faceted approach, and because this problem in Sweden is subsumed by a larger context of alcohol control, it is not possible to pick out those factors which have been most important in control. Indeed, there may be no single or several primary factors; it may take a decade or two to evaluate the effectiveness of a program, and it may be hard to replace sustained multi-faceted effort, proceeding perhaps inevitably in small incremental steps.

GREAT BRITAIN AND THE ACT

Probably the more relevant case for us is Great Britain which historically and culturally has an alcohol climate more comparable to ours—neither

---

[59] Andreasson, "Alcohol and Road Traffic: An International Survey of the Discussions."

[60] We note, for example, that the deaths for Sweden, U.S., and U.K. from 1958–68, indiced on the 1958 figures point out some of the possible cyclical and regional trends in auto fatalities. We note that in the mid-1960s all the countries showed a dramatic rise in the total number of fatalities. After the Road Safety Act (1967–68), fatalities for the U.K. dramatically fell; however, Sweden experienced an equally dramatic drop at the same time, without any major input as stimulus.

Total Number of Persons Killed and Injured in Road Traffic Accidents 1953–1968
1958 = 100

	Sweden	*U.K.*	*U.S.*
1953	98	85	103
1958	100	100	100
1959	106	109	103
1960	110	117	103
1961	115	116	103
1962	119	112	110
1963	129	116	118
1964	139	131	129
1965	139	133	133
1966	139	134	142
1967	114	123	144
1968	111	114	149

Source: Economic Commission for Europe, *Statistics of Road Traffic Accidents in Europe, 1967* (United Nations Publications), Table 1.

Table 2.   Traffic Fatality Rates, 1966 Expressed Per Million Population, Per Million Private Cars Registered, Per 10 Million Kilometers*

	U.S.	*U.K.*	*Sweden*
a) Total fatalities per million population	265	149	167
b) Total fatalities per million private cars registered	672	837	696
c) Total fatalities per 10 million kilometers (estimate)	355	446	no estimate
d) Fatalities of private car occupants per million private cars registered	448	334	341

* Computations based on statistics from Economic Commission for Europe, *Statistics of Road Traffic Accidents in Europe, 1967* (United Nations Publications).

long-term national temperance activity nor cumulative drinking and driving programs.

The Road Safety Act of 1967 was a major innovation in the context of the previous regulations and attitudes to drinking and driving. It was controversial and found rough going in Parliament due to fears that it would infringe upon the "fundamental rights" of Britons. Some of the more radical proposals (random roadside breath tests) were dropped before the Act finally passed Parliament.[61]

The Act numerically defined the previously vague phrase "unfit to drive" by prohibiting driving when the alcohol level was over .08 percent and allowing the police to require a roadside breath test with reasonable cause (suspicion of accident involvement, of traffic offense, or of alcohol use), and gave the policeman the right to arrest without a warrant on the basis of this rough test, taking the driver to the police station for a required quantitative analysis that would then be used as evidence in court. Penalties were set for refusing the breath screen test and for refusing to give a specimen for quantitative analysis as well as for exceeding the legal limit (fines, short jail terms, plus the loss of a license for a year in the case of conviction).[62]

The law went into effect in October, 1967, and was accompanied by the other major program input of the period—a one-month publicity campaign

---

[61] *The Economist* (London), November 12, 1966. We might note that prior to the law there were favorable attitudes to driving and drinking (see *Traffic Safety,* July, 1965 and *New York Times,* February 14, 1965).

[62] J. S. Dempster, "The Road Safety Act of 1967 and Its Effect on Road Accidents in the United Kingdom," *Traffic Digest and Review* (August, 1969), p. 3.

(September–November, 1967) involving television, radio, press, and leaflets. The new law was also said to have received excellent news coverage.[63]

There was an immediate drop in fatalities and serious injuries after the Act went into effect. For example, the first Christmas there was a 50 percent drop in fatalities compared to the previous Christmas. During the first twelve-month period (October, 1967–September, 1968) fatalities decreased 15 percent, serious injuries by 11 percent and total accidents by 10 percent. During the second twelve-month period (October, 1968–September, 1969) fatalities were down 10 percent, serious injuries 9 percent, and total accidents 10 percent, as compared with the year prior to the Act. (See Table 3.) Furthermore, there is considerable evidence relating the reduction in accident and fatalities specifically to the alcohol legislation and its publicity, and not just to other road safety input during the period, such as new tire regulations. In both years, 70 percent of the loss reduction occurred between 10 P.M. and 4 A.M.—the hours of heaviest alcohol consumption in Great Britain.[64] The greatest gains in safety, as might be expected if we are seeing an alcohol program effect, are for adults. (There is no change and if anything an increase in fatalities and injuries for those under age fifteen.) Since motor vehicle use increased during each period, what we are seeing is not just a reduction in driving.

Further evidence of reduction of the incidence of drinking and driving comes from a survey of post-mortem BALs on all drivers killed in road accidents over age sixteen. This shows an immediate drop in the percentage of BALS over .08 percent—from 28 percent to 15 percent, before and after the Act.[65]

Before-and-after surveys on behavior change (do you ever drink before driving, or if you drink, do you drive yourself home) have shown a decrease in reported drinking and driving of between 10–12 percent.[66] These trends were backed up by initial reports in the press of "major social change" and "new drinking habits."[67] They noted that taverns reported weekend drinking falling off; that drinkers were turning from hard liquor to beer (a false distinction); that night road traffic was diminishing; that 600 new taxis were in service in London; that driving schools were receiving a rush of

---

[63] *Ibid.,* p. 4.

[64] The Ministry of Transport press notice of December 22, 1969, entitled, "Two Years of 'Breath Tests.'"

[65] *Ibid.*

[66] Dempster, p. 5.

[67] For example, *The Spectator* (London), October 20, 1967, "Social Revolution"; *U.S. News and World Report* (Washington, D.C.), June 9, 1969, "New Drinking Habits." Whether or not these effects "lasted" is questioned in some accounts. See *New York Times,* August 25, 1968 and October 5, 1968.

Table 3. Road Casualties in Great Britain: Percentage Change Compared with Previous Year, and with Year Prior to Act

	Fatalities	*Serious Injuries*	*Total Accidents*
a) Year I 1967–68	−15%	−11%	−10%
b) Year II 1968–69	+5%	+3%	+1%
c) Year II compared to Year prior to Act	−10%	−9%	−10%

Source: "Two years of 'Breath Tests,' " Ministry of Transport [Great Britain], press notice (December 22, 1969).

women applicants sent by husbands to learn to drive so that one spouse could drive the drinker home. Although there was no reported decrease in the consumption of alcohol *per se* in 1968, there was evidence from the survey suggesting changes in consumption habits—that less alcohol was consumed in public houses and more privately.[68]

The evidence suggests that the British legislation introducing the pre-arrest breath screen test did reduce fatalities and accidents particularly during the hazardous nighttime drinking hours, and that the problem is open to preventive approaches of this sort. However the Act seems to have had a declining impact. Although the British Road Ministry prefers to publicize its statistics on percentage change for Year II based on the year prior to the Act, if we compare Year I with Year II, we find fatalities up 5 percent, serious injuries up 3 percent, and total accidents up 1 percent (Table 3, line *b*). This raises questions about whether a general deterrent, such as the pre-arrest use of the breath screen, which relies on its psychological effect (increased risk of detection), will be maintained by individuals over time and with experience. For example, *The Economist* reports in November, 1969, that the number of breath tests which are positive has risen from less than 50 percent to nearly 66 percent since the end of 1967. Since the number of tests given has risen, this suggests that "more drunks are back on the roads," leading the writer to wonder if "the novelty has worn off." There have been other expressions of discouragement and speculation on increasing the punitive measures.[69] We note similar patterns elsewhere.

---

[68] Dempster, pp. 7–8.

[69] Certain observers are discouraged, apparently, in that the "Breath Act" is not an answer in itself. See Colin McIver in *The Guardian* (Manchester, England), October, 1968; and Alfred Friendly, *The Washington Post,* December 6, 1969.

For example, strict legislation with severe penalties was introduced in Germany in 1965, followed first by a sharp reduction in BALs and six months later by a return to prior levels.[70] If there is in fact a "habituation effect,"[71] perhaps one must continually up the ante to maintain credibility of threat (as Sweden has done over the years). (There is some talk in Great Britain of introducing random road tests.)[72] If this is so, the costs of escalating control must be weighed against the comparative gain in safety.

Secondly, we remain uncertain about who is being affected by this approach. We did not find information or analysis of possible differential effects on subgroups—for example, the chronic versus the social drinkers; young males versus middle-aged, etc. Are the reductions coming from the "social drinkers," theoretically more amenable to this sort of approach, or does it cut across both groups? Is the declining impact coming from one type of drinking driver rather than another? Such information would help us to assess more realistically what percentage of the alcohol contribution we can hope to reach through similar programs and who to direct our programs to. (We note that a recent Department of Transportation–National Highway Safety Bureau Report recommends as number one target the problem drinkers. They may be the more dangerous subgroup but the less reasonable choice.)[73]

The question in summary is not whether we have the technology but whether a given technology can be effectively utilized at a given place at a given time. In this regard there seems to be a cross-national continuum. Thus in Scandinavia, the blood test, required for suspicion of drinking-driving, posed no problems; in Great Britain, the screening kits and procedures survived the courts although with criticism. Given that the United States is the country most wary of redefining as privileges what are popularly considered rights (besides the right to drive a car, the right to carry a gun is another good example), the current state of the technology, juxtaposed against the sense of crisis (currently not very strong), may not suffice to extend legislation and enforcement in this direction.

---

[70] Middendorff, p. 64.

[71] *Ibid.* Middendorff warns we must not confuse shock effect with deterrence.

[72] The *Times*, November 12, 1969, reports that the House of Commons is considering random breath tests. See also *The Economist* (London), November 29, 1969 and *The Guardian* (Manchester, England), November 19, 1969 for a discussion of how to get a bigger effect—the possibilities of playing with penalties, distinguishing different degrees of infringement. Also *The Guardian* (Manchester, England), June 23, 1969.

[73] As C. H. Rolf warned in "The Breathing Act," *New Statesman* (London), October 20, 1967, perhaps it is the ".08 people who will be more careful because the .30 people (chronics) won't change their ways." At any rate, we need evidence of specific alcohol levels before and after, and not just changes in the average level.

OVERVIEW

The identification of major factors in traffic safety has led to high expectations for proposed solutions which range from changing human behavior to the relatively "pure" technological solutions such as the safety car.

What with some 44–60 percent of all drivers involved in fatal crashes having significant alcohol levels, there is no doubt that alcohol is a major factor in traffic safety. It has been proposed that alcohol is *the* major culprit and that by attacking the drinking driver we can halve our highway fatalities. But as the problem is examined, we find it complex and multi-faceted on all levels, and not particularly amenable to unitary solutions or dramatic expectations.

First, the drinking-driving population is diverse, ranging from social drinkers, which may be almost all of us, to the chronic alcoholic who, although a minority, is responsible for a disproportionate number of fatal and serious accidents. Secondly, there is a high incidence of mental illness and sociopathic behavior which cuts across a spectrum of social drinkers and chronic alcoholics suggesting that alcohol, at least for part of the population, may be an epiphenomenon—symptomatic of deep and unmet social needs. Given this range of human behavior, we see the necessity and the wisdom of a multi-faceted approach. An increased level of deterrence might work for most social drinkers, but the alcoholics may have to be prevented from driving, however onerous that would be.

The new technology involving quantitative and qualitative breath tests has made programs of detection and deterrence practicable for the first time. But the effective use of these technological innovations is dependent upon societal constraints. The pattern in America so far has been not to make effective use of the increased possibilities in deterrence. We have been constrained from writing effective legislation for the tests due to fear of encroachment on individual liberties, and beyond that, our basic lack of commitment to the problem; we have not maximized the legislation we have by providing equally effective enforcement. The point here is that legal and social constraints are just as real as any knowledge gap. The recent introduction of the breath screen tests, when used in conjunction with pre-arrest testing, further increases the options—it is cheap, portable and easy enough to encourage effective use. But if there is to be more than transient results by new programs (as may be the case in Great Britain), we must be prepared for long-term sustained efforts to maintain credibility, of which the breath test legislation is only one step, which in turn would require the kind of commitment and consensual support which may account for the relatively greater success of the Swedish model. Furthermore, there must be toleration of less than spectacular results—after fifty years, the drinking driver still remains a major problem in Sweden, although the importance of alcohol as a causative factor may have been reduced.[74]

MULTI-CAUSALITY AND CHOICE

The alcohol problem serves as a paradigm for the entire problem of traffic safety, both for its complexity and for our inability to make optimal use of technology.[75] As the model complexifies, it becomes obvious that intervention at many different points would have some effect on the web of interconnected variables. For example, we could improve our highway design, enforce speed limits, improve emergency ambulance and hospital care, selectively license, and make all roads one-way.[76] This leads logically to cost-benefit analysis: thus even if alcohol is the largest single contributing factor, the best approach may be through other factors—for example, the vehicle.[77]

The United States has been the first country to attempt to improve auto

---

[74] Problem drinkers (registered by local temperance committees) are still 48 percent of the individuals arrested for drunken driving in Sweden between 1955–58. Arthur Little Inc., *The State of the Art of Traffic Safety.*

[75] This view stands somewhat in contrast to the recent editorial in *Science* (69:3948, August 28, 1970) by Robert Morrison who said that unlike other social problems, this one has a solution and that "the alcohol-automobile problem provides a simple model with which to begin."

In contrast, Dr. Seldon Bacon, director of the Center for Alcohol Studies at Rutgers, stated that "very few single causes will be found to provide by themselves sufficient number of accidents to make attack on single causes worthwhile . . . more and more, constellations of multi-cause factors will be required." *The Second Annual Traffic Safety Research Symposium,* March 19–21, 1968, All State Plaza, North Brook, Illinois.

[76] For example, K. A. Stone estimates saving more than 20,000 lives by one-way operation of cars. ("The Single Car Accident Problem," Society of Automotive Engineers, *Progress in Technology,* Vol. 13, 1968.)

The New York City Port Authority, in a one-year test, reduced rear-end accidents among its vehicles by 45 percent by running them with parking lights in the day. (*New York Times,* February, 1969.)

There are estimates that 25 percent of persons permanently disabled in highway accidents would not be crippled with better emergency care. (*Report of the Secretary's Advisory Committee on Traffic Safety,* p. 46.) Also estimates are that a safer container could reduce chances of death or serious injury by 70–80 percent (*U.S. News and World Report,* October 16, 1967). And estimates of savings in lives and injuries are based on better highway engineering. ("The Epidemiology of Road Accidents," *WHO Chronicle,* 20:11, November, 1966.)

[77] The relation between causation and cure is succinctly put by Teasdale who says that even though the ratio of accident initiation is 1:2:17 for vehicles, highways, and driver respectively, we may still have to direct cures at 1 and 2 because it is so hard to change human behavior. Others who have made similar statements include many who have researched the alcohol factor in traffic accidents. See W. Haddon, "Research with Respect to Fatal Accident Causes: Implications for Vehicle Design," Society of Automotive Engi-

safety by controlling technological factors through the issuance of safety standards. On the basis of prior research, it was anticipated that seat belts would drastically reduce injuries and deaths. Some years later, however, studies show that the belts are worn only one-third of the time[78] (and this cautious one-third might not even be the group most likely to get into accidents in the first place).

Besides pointing out our initial magical expectations for a plug-in technology, and underlining the difficulty of divorcing technological from human factors, the seat belt example, in the context of the continuing work on restraint systems, reveals that what technology has uniquely to offer to the solution of complex problems is a kind of option-reducing potential— the possibility of at least removing the decision from the individual (whom we have failed to change time and time again) to the societal level. Such usage far outweighs, for example, epidemiological utility which still calls for profound and complementary individual commitments. This necessitates a distinction between active and passive techniques which we seem to be making. Thus the effectiveness of the seat belt, an active device because it requires participation, is more problematic in contrast to the passive restraint systems, such as the air bag, which protects the driver and even the drunken driver, without his participation or even his consent.[79] Along these lines, the safety car concept of passenger packaging can be seen as a kind of ultimate loss reductive solution and perhaps fantasy.[80]

---

neers, *Progress in Technology*, Vol. 13, 1968; or Julian A. Waller, "Present Knowledge of Medical and Behavioral Factors in Highway Crashes: Options for Loss Reduction," Society of Automotive Engineers, #700197, January, 1970.

[78] B. J. Campbell, "Seat Belt Use among Drivers in Accidents and Drivers in the Population at Risk," University of North Carolina Highway Safety Research Center, January, 1969.

[79] For two good reviews of restraint system development, see C. M. Patrick, "Projected Evolution of Restraint Systems," Society of Automotive Engineers, #690250, January, 1969; and R. G. Snyder, "A Survey of Automotive Occupant Restraint Systems: Where We've Been, Where We are and Our Current Problems," Society of Automotive Engineers, #690243, January, 1969.

[80] Perhaps it is at this point another technological myth, in that closer examination of the problems of translating a set of priorities into design indicate that we may really be talking about a safer, not a safety, car. See R. D. Leis, *et al.*, *The Evaluation of Phase I Reports on the Experimental Safety Vehicles Program* (Columbus, Ohio: February 10, 1970), which states cautiously that "although sufficient art is believed to exist for vehicle application now, a great deal of design ingenuity will be required to incorporate the specified levels of crashworthiness into the near term car in a satisfactory way." Also Dervyn M. Severy, "A Researcher Looks at Traffic Safety Today," *Traffic Safety* (June, 1969), p. 11; and R. A. Wolf, "Overview of Highway and Vehicle Safety Research," Society of Automotive Engineers, #680271, January 8, 1968. Discussing the standards-incremental versus the total approach, Wolf asks whether "By the time safety cars are built and debugged on the proving grounds, would they be 'safer' than cars evolving through the standards approach?"

Although such distinctions are made by professionals in the field, there is a certain illogic to our application of these concepts because it would be possible to introduce passive techniques at an earlier level—*e.g.,* an interlock system on the driver's seat belt so that the car could not be driven when the belt was unlocked, or directly defining intoxication by the technology (*i.e.,* the alcohol level). All of which introduces the following irony: that perhaps we are culturally inhibited from making the best use of our technology—either the alcohol breath test or the seat belt; that given our own norms of individual responsibility, societal control, etc., a given technology before it can be acceptable and utilized (whether restraint system or alcohol tests) must be so unobtrusive, so fail-safe, as to slip in unnoticed—so that the user won't even be aware of the extent to which his options have been reduced.

First, we sought unitary solutions to complex problems. Now giving more weight to complexity, we seem to be looking for package solutions. But awaiting major breakthroughs and dramatic cures we still tend to drop difficult although not necessarily ineffective approaches (one-third seat belt utilization is not insignificant) to switch to different ones in the hope that they will yield more, while continuing to ignore the cumulative evidence that suggests that the problem may be open to present attack in only 5, 10, or 15 percent bits.

4

A TECHNOLOGY
WHOSE REMOVAL "WORKS":
GUN CONTROL[1]

GUN CONTROLS AND VIOLENCE: TWO VIEWS

The enactment of gun controls, or legal restrictions on the private possession of firearms, has frequently been presented as a means of reducing the rates of violent crime and accidental death and injury in the United States. Since guns are more widely owned and less strictly regulated in the United States than in most other industrial countries the question arises as to whether the sheer physical availability of guns contributes in a major fashion to the American rates of murder, suicide, and accidental death. Does the presence of approximately 90 million guns in the country, with one-half of the households possessing at least one firearm and usually more than one,[2] add to the nation's crime and accident rates? Or, on the other hand, are fire-

---

[1] Gun control, in contrast to the other innovations discussed, is a "negative" alteration in the technology of a social problem: the restriction or removal of a preexisting technology. Such procedures might be useful when a developing technology (or the changing context of an existing technology) leads to a widely recognized social problem *and* when that technology is susceptible to control or elimination through legislation. For an extensive review of the lack of effective gun controls in the United States and the consequences of this situation, see Carl Bakal, *The Right to Bear Arms* (New York: McGraw-Hill Book Co., 1966). An examination of recent increases in firearms sales and ownership in the United States and the relationship between gun availability and violence is provided by George D. Newton and Franklin E. Zimring, *Firearms and Violence in American Life:* A Staff Report to the National Commission On the Causes and Prevention of Violence (Washington: U.S. Government Printing Office, 1970). For an account of the struggles in and around Congress over gun control legislation during the last decade, see Richard Harris, "Annals of Legislation: If You Love Your Guns," *New Yorker* (April 20, 1968), pp. 56–155. A discussion of the National Rifle Association's opposition to gun controls is provided by Robert Sherrill, "A Lobby on Target," *New York Times Magazine* (October 15, 1967), pp. 27–132.

[2] Newton and Zimring, *op. cit.,* pp. xi, xii.

arms merely incidental tools only apparently associated with crimes and accidents which would usually occur in other ways if guns were not available?

The opposing sides in the debates arising from attempts to enact legislation controlling the sale or possession of firearms present quite different interpretations of the relationship between firearms and crimes and accidents.[3] Woodson D. Scott, then vice-president of the National Rifle Association (NRA), an organization of firearms enthusiasts who oppose gun controls, has stated, "Firearms are not a factor in crime; if there were no firearms, I suggest people would find other means and methods of doing equal harm."[4] This interpretation of the role of firearms in crime involves two major points: the observation that crime is caused by other, more basic factors than the availability of guns, and the suggestion that potential implements of violence are largely interchangeable. Opponents of gun control legislation have emphasized both of these ideas. The view that basic human drives which can not easily be diverted are involved in murders is reflected in the NRA's widely disseminated slogan "Guns don't kill people, people kill people." The NRA has also reprinted a list of environmental factors which, according to the FBI who originally published the list, "affect the crime rate in any community."[5] Among other factors, the list includes economic status of the population, population density, climate, and standards of law enforcement. The NRA notes in summary that the "FBI list contains no mention of the impact of firearms regulation on crime."[6] If criminal behavior is due primarily to fundamental and slow-to-change factors such as those listed by the FBI, or to a predisposition in human nature toward aggressive behavior, then it seems likely that crime rates would not be seriously affected by the absence of any one implement of violence, such as a gun. Opponents of gun control legislation extend this interpretation by emphasizing the multiplicity and availability of potential means of violence. The NRA's president told a visiting interviewer:

> There are 20 weapons in this office that I could use to kill you, and you won't

---

[3] Gun controls have been suggested to have an impact upon rates of accidental death and injury as well as on rates of homicide and other crimes, particularly robbery. This discussion's focus will shift among these various topics as is required by the data available, however all are of concern throughout. In general the proposition that there are more firearms accidents where there are more firearms will be assumed, and the discussion will focus upon crime rates, and particularly homicide.

[4] Sherrill, *op. cit.*, p. 132.

[5] National Rifle Association, *The Gun Law Problem* (Washington: National Rifle Association), p. 11.

[6] *Ibid.*

find a single gun in the room. This dictating machine. The telephone. That picture frame—I could kill you with any of them if I wanted to badly enough.[7]

Still another expression of this argument is the suggestion frequently offered by critics of gun control that if guns are to be registered so should all other potential means of violence such as knives, baseball bats, tire irons, and hands and feet.

Critics of gun controls also draw on a number of other arguments, however these criticisms usually focus on other matters than the suggested inability of gun laws to do what their proponents claim they will. For instance, it is suggested that the United States Constitution's protection of the state militia's right to bear arms applies to each individual citizen. Additionally it is suggested that, despite the overwhelming power of contemporary military technology, the unregulated and widespread availability of shotguns, rifles, and handguns serves to protect the country from foreign invasion and internal subversion. In general, the opponents of gun controls and more specifically the NRA, in the words of its executive vice-president F. L. Orth, look upon

> the vast majority of bills for firearms legislation as the misdirected efforts of social reformers, do-gooders, and/or the completely uninformed who would accomplish miracles by the passage of another law.[8]

Supporters of gun control legislation have been highly critical of existing firearms control policy in their advocacy of more restrictive control measures. Maryland's former Senator Joseph Tydings, while appealing for the passage of gun control legislation, has observed, "It is tragic that in all of Western civilization the U.S. is the one country with an insane gun policy."[9] Henry Fairlie, a British journalist living in the United States has written:

> History and character cannot be reversed and changed overnight. But this is no excuse for allowing violence such an easy access to the weapons which it not only needs, but which actually encourage it, tempt it, incite it. However much I may love and admire America, its gun laws come near to ruling it out of civilized society.[10]

Proponents of gun control legislation imply that, to a significant degree, the high incidence of violent crime in America is due to the widespread,

---

[7] *New York Times,* June 8, 1968.
[8] Sherrill, *op. cit.,* p. 122.
[9] *Time,* June 21, 1968.
[10] Harris, *op. cit.,* p. 56.

unregulated, availability of firearms. J. Edgar Hoover's observation that "the easy accessibility of firearms is a significant factor in murders committed in the United States today"[11] is often quoted in pro-gun control literature.

It is also suggested that limiting the availability of firearms will lower, not only the rates of utilization of guns in crimes, but also the overall rates of murder and robbery. The National Council for a Responsible Firearms Policy has observed that

> . . . more effective controls over the availability of firearms to the general public are indispensable to effective policies to combat crime—"to insure domestic tranquility, provide for the common defense, [and] promote the general welfare."[12]

This is held to be so in part because, although there are available a number of alternative means of violence, firearms are so effective and easy to use that their ready availability adds substantially to the incidence of violent crimes. This argument notes that firearms are fairly complicated technological devices, specifically designed to kill, like the electric chair, or gas chamber. Thus guns are more efficient at killing than almost all other weapons used in murders. A staff report of the National Commission on the Causes and Prevention of Violence has reported that "the fatality rate of firearms attacks is about five times higher than the fatality rate of attacks with knives, the next most dangerous weapon used in homicides."[13] Accordingly the widespread availability of guns increases the probabilities of violent arguments ending in fatalities. As Detroit Police Commissioner Ray Girardin has put it: "When people have guns, they use them. A wife gets mad at her husband, and instead of throwing a dish she grabs the gun and kills him."[14] Similarly Elmer H. Johnson, author of the criminology text *Crime, Correction and Society,* has indicated that the availability of weapons "may spell the difference between aggravated assault and homicide."[15] Not only are gunshot wounds more deadly, guns also have a special capacity to be effective at a distance that can lead to fatalities in situations where other weapons would not. Marvin Wolfgang, a noted criminologist, has observed that a potential murderer, lacking a gun, might

> . . . use a knife to stab, or fists to beat his victim to death. On the other hand,

---

[11] *For Firearms Policies in the Public Interest* (Washington: National Council for a Responsible Firearms Policy, Inc.).

[12] *Ibid.*

[13] Newton and Zimring, *op. cit.,* p. 41.

[14] *Time,* June 21, 1968.

[15] Elmer H. Johnson, *Crime, Correction and Society* (Homewood, Illinois: Dorsey Press, 1964), p. 268.

small physical size or the offender's physical repugnance to engaging in direct physical assault by cutting or stabbing his adversary, may mean that in the absence of a firearm no homicide occurs.[16]

Additionally, it is often noted that because of the emotional, impulsive nature of most American murders, the availability of such efficient weapons as firearms tends to raise the overall homicide rate. Wolfgang has divided "normal" homicides into two groups: "a) premeditated, felonious, planned, and rational murder; and b) slaying in the heat of passion, or killing as a result of intent to do harm, but without a specific intent to kill."[17] The "premeditated and rational" murder by the so-called "hardened" criminal would appear to be least affected by gun control laws reducing the availability of guns. Clearly, this type of homicide is most susceptible to the argument that if guns were outlawed for all citizens, criminals would find some means of getting guns, or would use other weapons instead. While the total prohibition of firearms would make it more difficult for the criminal to get guns (*e.g.*, even inquiring about guns may raise police suspicions), even that restriction would not eliminate this category of homicide.

The irrational, "impulsive" type of homicide is, however, another story and quite an important one. FBI statistics show that 82 percent of all murders were committed within the family unit or among acquaintances (31 percent within the family, 51 percent among acquaintances) and the people involved frequently have no previous involvement with the police. Moreover, over 60 percent of the killings within the family involved the use of guns and 57 percent of the killings outside the family involved guns.[18] What this suggests is that most homicides are not committed by the "hardened" criminal who would seek out a gun or other lethal weapon, whether or not it was legal, but rather by ordinary, "law-abiding" citizens who kill on impulse rather than by intent. In terms of Wolfgang's classification, over 95 percent of all homicides would fit into the general "unpremeditated category."[19] Several studies by noted criminologists may be cited in which the "unplanned, rage" killers constituted the largest group.[20] J. L. Gillin, in an analysis of ninety-six Wisconsin murders, found that most of these killings were "crimes of passion, explosive reactions to difficult situations." Alcohol

---

[16] Marvin E. Wolfgang, *Patterns in Criminal Homicide* (Philadelphia: University of Pennsylvania Press, 1959), p. 79.

[17] Marvin E. Wolfgang and Franco Ferracuti, *The Subculture of Violence* (New York: Tavistock Publications, 1967), p. 189.

[18] *Uniform Crime Reports—1963*, Federal Bureau of Investigation (Washington, D.C.: U.S. Government Printing Office, 1963), pp. 6, 7.

[19] Wolfgang and Ferracuti, *op. cit.*, p. 189.

[20] The following studies are cited in Wolfgang and Ferracuti, *op. cit.*, pp. 189–191.

was considered particularly important in homicides of this type. In the cases studied by Wolfgang in Philadelphia, 64 percent of the homicides showed the presence of alcohol in either the victim or the offender. James Calder came up with similar results in a study of Puerto Rican offenders. In Gillin's Wisconsin study, alcohol was present in one-third of the cases.

Experiments conducted by L. Berkowitz and A. LePage of the University of Wisconsin have shown that the sight of a gun can act as a "last straw" responsible for illiciting otherwise uncharacteristic, aggressive behavior. Specifically, they found that the actual presence of a weapon, especially in a case when anger was present between the individuals, may yield an aggressive act that would otherwise not occur.[21] Studies of this sort give greater weight to the view that "guns kill people" in the sense that the presence of guns escalates a conflict from a quarrel to a homicide.

Thus overall, advocates of gun controls generally argue that a reduction in the availability of guns is the most effective and direct means of reducing violent crime in America. While discussing ways of reducing violence in America, Berkowitz has suggested, in addition to reducing the frustrations of social groups and maintaining peoples' inhibitions against violence, a third approach.

> The third possibility, reducing the number of aggressive stimuli people encounter from day to day, is probably the easiest one to effect, and the fastest. This may seem a surprising statement—deciding to remove aggressive stimuli from American life is a little like setting out to clean the Aegean stables. But the task seems more manageable when one realizes that most aggressive stimuli fall into only a few large categories, one of the largest of which bears the label "Guns." Guns not only permit violence, they can stimulate it as well. The finger pulls the trigger, but the trigger may also be pulling the finger.[22]

Finally, Wolfgang has expressed similar views about the desirability of sharply limiting the availability of guns:

> I am one of those persons who believe that violence and instruments of violence breed violence. Legislation which makes more restrictive the manufacturing, sale and distribution, and licensing of firearms is I think, desirable in almost any form. If pushed to the wall, I would probably support the Japanese ruling that no one except a police officer should be allowed to possess or carry a pistol.[23]

---

[21] *New Society*, No. 292 (May 2, 1968), p. 645.
[22] Leonard Berkowitz, "Impulse Aggression and the Gun," *Psychology Today*, Vol. 2, No. 4 (September, 1968), p. 22.
[23] Harris, *op. cit.*, p. 67.

As we see it, *both sides have presented largely monistic interpretations of the causes of homicide, and accordingly of the consequences of reducing the availability of guns.* The opponents of gun controls have conceived of murder as being due primarily to fundamental, environmental, cultural and psychological factors and accordingly view the removal of firearms as being of no serious use in the reduction of homicide and violent crime. The advocates of gun control basically have not replied to the arguments that murders are caused by a variety of difficult-to-change fundamental factors, and that many weapons can be used to murder. Instead advocates of gun control have focussed upon the logically persuasive argument that due to the efficiency of guns and the impulsiveness of people, the availability of guns causes more homicides than would otherwise occur. By focussing their attention primarily upon these additional gun-caused homicides and downplaying, or ignoring the other causal factors, their discussions tend to suggest that the availability of guns is the primary cause of violent crime and homicide, and that the removal of guns is largely a means of ending such violence.

While both of these stances may have some utility in the recurrent political struggles over the enactment of gun control laws, their analytic utility is limited. It seems more probable that *both* the economic, social and psychological causes of homicide referred to by opponents of gun controls, and the availability of guns are major influences on rates of violent crime and homicide. Further, in view of the frequently abstract and hypothetical nature of the discussion to this point, *it is not clear what shares of relative influence can be assigned to the two factors,* the social-psychic and the technology of violence. Accordingly it will be useful now to examine some empirical materials bearing on the relationship between these two variables. Data from two major areas will be considered. Initially, comparative information on gun laws, socio-economic influences, and crime statistics from cities, states, and regions within the United States will be presented. Subsequently, international comparisons will be reviewed. Of the two sets of data, the international comparisons seem likely to provide a more adequate reflection of the influence of variations in the availability of firearms upon rates of violent crime. Several problems hamper our perception of the influence of varying gun availability in domestic geographical comparisons. Initially there is very little variation between most regions of the United States in the suggested causal factor—the availability of firearms. American laws formally impose only a very limited range of restrictions upon the availability of firearms and even this limited possible influence is considerably reduced since most gun laws are easily and widely circumvented. International comparisons involve a much greater range of gun availability, since many nations have much more restrictive gun laws—approaching conditions of domestic disarmament in several cases. Secondly, domestic comparisons

are hampered by variations in the economic and social-psychological characteristics among regions which provide additional influences upon crime rates
and confuse our evaluation of the influence of gun availability. This problem is somewhat greater in international comparisons than in domestic
comparisons, however data on these factors are examined in an effort to adjust or control for their influences in both types of comparison. Thus domestic comparisons are limited in value both by the presence of confounding
variables and the absence of much variation in the suggested causal factor—
the availability of firearms. Attempts to evaluate the confounding variables
occur during both kinds of comparison, however major variations in gun
availability can only be observed in the international comparisons and thus
this is the context in which we can expect the impact of gun availability
upon violent crime rates to be most evident. In the final section, the implications concerning the influence of firearms availability, drawn from the
international comparisons, are applied to the domestic context in a consideration of the potential benefits and costs of various types of gun control for
the various categories of American gun owners.

AMERICAN COMPARISONS: CITIES, STATES, REGIONS

The reviewed data is divided into two major parts: initially several
comparisons of the gun laws and crime statistics of various American cities,
states, and regions; and secondly, a comparison of the crime statistics for a
number of selected industrial nations.[24] In each section, the analysis will proceed in the following way: 1) a review of the gun laws in the various areas
and the basis on which they may be ranked according to restrictiveness; 2)
a comparison of the crime statistics drawn from the different areas, and
particularly the total homicide rate and the percentage of these deaths attributable to firearms use; and 3) an examination of the intervening variables whose possible influence must be accounted for if a valid causal relationship between gun legislation and crime statistics is to be shown.

The fundamental criteria for distinguishing among gun laws is whether
or not they prohibit all gun use or simply regulate gun use. Regulation
measures may be further subdivided according to the effect of the laws on
the availability of firearms—how much do they diminish gun sales and possession, for which groups and what purposes, etc. Thus, one can draw a
continuum of laws from the most restrictive to the most lenient: at one end,
there is total prohibition plus implementation which effectively means a
domestic disarmament; in the middle of the range of laws are regulatory

---

[24] The discussion in this chapter is primarily based upon data available by June 1971.

measures which bar specific guns from specific categories of individuals; and finally, at the other end, are regulatory measures which are either so limited in their range of application or so lenient in their effect as to be of little consequence in curbing gun use. American laws, both state and federal, are in the last category; most of the gun laws of the foreign industrialized states discussed below fall into the stricter sectors of the continuum.

Two general statistical measures of crime are examined as indications of the effect of the gun laws of the various regions on violent crime: the percentage of gun homicides and the total homicide rate. If the percentage of gun homicides "declined" markedly from a region with lenient gun controls to a region with stricter controls while the total homicide rate were roughly the same, then it could be claimed that the overall crime situation was relatively unchanged by gun laws, and that people were simply utilizing other weapons in place of the more difficult to obtain guns. However, if in most cases, the overall homicide rate declined as well, it could be inferred reasonably that the laws were effective in reducing a wholly different category of homicide—impulsive, unplanned homicides.

Clearly, the direct comparison of homicide rates under differing regional laws is apt to be a fallacious procedure; the assumption that two ostensibly similar laws will have the same effect in two different areas is not justified, since each area may have other factors—intervening variables—influencing the local homicide rate. A list of such factors would include: density and growth of population, economic level, and expenditure on police force.[25] Data on these factors will be obtained for each area studied and an attempt will be made to interpret the variations in crime rates, along with the variations in gun law severity, in the light of the suggested intervening influences. The goal here is not rendering one area's homicide statistics precisely comparable to those of another by weighing and compensating for the probably biasing factors. Rather, the goal is to aid the identification of reductions in the homicide rates corresponding to the elimination of many of the "impulsive" homicides, which can be attributed to the influence of the gun laws alone. One might say that the characteristics of each city or state or nation provide a prism through which a gun law's effects may be felt, and the specification of the intervening variables is intended to aid in estimating the amount of diffraction involved. Additionally, at a later point, data bearing on crime rates in two cities before and after the enactment of gun restrictions will be reviewed. Such comparisons are particularly useful since they minimize the problem of intervening variables.

---

[25] *Uniform Crime Reports—1963,* p. ix.

CITIES

The cities discussed in this section are: New York, New York; Philadelphia, Pennsylvania; Newark, New Jersey; Detroit, Michigan; Los Angeles, California; Chicago, Illinois; Phoenix, Arizona; Dallas, Texas, and Jackson, Mississippi. Since in each of these cities the gun laws are concerned with regulation, not prohibition of firearms, the laws will be categorized as moderately lenient to very lenient, the entire range falling into the permissive sector of the continuum. This ranking is based in part on the scope of the laws—the presence or absence of provisions regarding: 1) the possession of a handgun; 2) the purchase of a handgun; and 3) the carrying of a handgun. The control of handguns is particularly crucial since they are the weapons used in most gun-assisted crimes.[26] Few American jurisdictions restrict the possession of long guns in any way. Clearly a moderately restrictive gun law would require a specific license or permit for each step—buying a firearm, owning a firearm, and carrying a firearm. Where the law only refers to the buying of handguns, it has little supervision over a handgun which someone purchases and then gives or privately sells to another. Where the law only deals with the carrying of handguns (generally, such regulations refer to the carrying of concealed handguns on one's person), it provides little information about or control over who owns or purchases a gun and keeps it in the glove compartment of his car, or beside his bed at home. The cities ranked here as having "moderately lenient" (as opposed to "very lenient") gun laws generally regulate the purchase and carrying of handguns; additionally, they may also regulate the possession of handguns. The stringency of the licensing requirements further distinguishes the cities included in this moderately lenient category. Indications of stringency are the length of the waiting period required between purchase and delivery of handguns, the requirement of a license to sell handguns at retail, a minimum-age provision for handgun purchasers, and a statement of appropriate purposes for which licenses will be given (the effect of permit requirements for the possession or carrying of firearms is seriously diluted if most permits are granted simply for "personal protection"). In cases of the cities with very lenient laws, either permits are not required for the purchase of handguns and control of their sale is left to the decision of the dealer, or permits are so easily obtainable that the requirement is nearly meaningless. In this context of very weak controls any restrictions on the carrying of handguns alone can do little to regulate the handgun traffic.[27]

---

[26] Newton and Zimring, *op. cit.*, p. 49.

[27] Reviews of state gun laws many be found in Bakal, *op. cit.*, Appendix II, and in Newton and Zimring, *op. cit.*, Appendix G.

The gun laws of New York City and Philadelphia are among the most restrictive of all examples of gun control legislation in the United States. New York State's Sullivan Law, passed in 1911, requires a permit for the buying, carrying, and owning of a handgun.[28] New York City requires a waiting period between the purchase and delivery of a handgun (that time consisting of the time required for the granting of the permit to purchase the gun), reporting of all handgun sales to the police, possession of a license to sell guns at retail, minimum age to buy or receive a handgun, and the possession of a permit to carry a gun "openly on person" or "concealed on person." In addition, in 1967, the City of New York passed a law requiring the registration of all rifles and shotguns as well. New York City is also among the few areas of the state requiring periodic renewal of licenses, and where applicants are screened particularly carefully. There are only 17,087 valid licenses in the city, roughly one per 470 persons, while there are 750,000 handguns or one per 16 people in the state.[29]

Philadelphia's 1965 gun control law has also made its municipal gun law considerably less lenient than the state law of Pennsylvania. Philadelphia requires a license for the purchase or possession of all firearms. The city also requires a permit for an individual to carry a handgun concealed on his person, a forty-eight-hour waiting period, the reporting of all handgun sales to the police, a license for the retail sale of guns, and a minimum age (eighteen) for the purchase of a handgun. However, most licenses applied for are approved; of the 6,890 applications filed since 1965, 97 percent have been approved.[30]

The firearms laws of Newark, Detroit, and Los Angeles are considerably weaker, as they do not regulate the possession of handguns. Newark requires a license only for the purchase of a handgun and the carrying of a concealed handgun. The waiting period required before the handgun purchase is completed consists of seven days, the time required for granting the permit. The remainder of its requirements are similar to those of New York and Philadelphia. Detroit also requires a license to purchase handguns and to carry them "concealed on person" in addition to a waiting period (the time required for granting the permit), the reporting of handgun sales to the police, licenses for retail sale, and a twenty-one-year-old age requirement for the purchase of a handgun. Los Angeles requires all of the above with

---

[28] U.S. Congress, Senate Committee on the Judiciary, Subcommittee to Investigate Juvenile Delinquency, *Hearings, Interstate Traffic in Mail-Order Firearms,* 88th Congress, 2d Session, Vol. 137, p. 3674.

[29] Bakal, *op. cit.,* p. 158.

[30] U.S. Congress, Senate Committee on the Judiciary, *Hearings* (July 10–August 1, 1967), pp. 343–345.

the addition of a seventy-two-hour waiting period and an eighteen-year-old minimum age for a handgun purchase.[31] In Los Angeles, 8,324 pistols were purchased legally out of a population of 2 million. One person out of every 250 has a gun legally, while in New York with 8 million people, 17,000 individuals, or one person out of 470 has a handgun legally. Chicago's firearms laws may be considered the weakest of all the cities in the "moderately lenient" law category. While Chicago, unlike the rest of Illinois, requires a license for the purchasing of a handgun, and also enforces the statewide prohibition on the carrying of a handgun "on or about the person," the city does not require a license for the retail sale of handguns, the reporting of handgun sales to police, nor a waiting period between purchase and delivery of a handgun.[32]

The cities with "very lenient" gun laws provide a distinct contrast. Phoenix regulates nothing but minimum age; the prospective buyer or recipient of a handgun must be at least eighteen (or younger if accompanied by the consent of a parent). The Arizona state law prohibits persons convicted of crimes of violence from possessing handguns or persons under the age of eighteen from having handguns transferred to them without their parents consent, otherwise the purchase or sale of firearms is unrestricted. The state law also prohibits the carrying of all concealed and loaded firearms. Dallas and the state of Texas require only a license for retail sale and prohibit sales to "minors" (a categorization decided upon at the discretion of the dealer),[33] and the carrying of all handguns except by persons who are "traveling."[34] Similarly, Jackson requires a license for an individual to carry a concealed handgun and to sell handguns retail; and in the state of Mississippi "minors," "students on campus," and "intoxicated persons" may not be sold handguns (categories again being defined by the dealer).

Thus the cities may be ranked according to the restrictiveness of their gun control laws in two main groups, with the "moderately lenient" law category containing, in roughly decreasing order of legal restrictiveness, New York, Philadelphia, Newark, Detroit, Los Angeles, and Chicago; and the "very lenient" category containing Phoenix, Dallas, and Jackson.

The general homicide rates (defined as the number of murders per 100,000 in the population) for 1963, 1965, and 1969 as reported by the FBI for the cities just discussed are shown in Table 1:

---

[31] *New York Times,* June 8, 1968.

[32] U.S. Congress, Senate Committee on the Judiciary, *Hearings,* 88th Congress, 2d Session (March 26–April 25, 1964), pp. 3649, 3691.

[33] Bakal, *op. cit.,* Appendix II, footnote 14.

[34] *Ibid.,* footnote 22. While discussing this provision, Bakal adds, "Hence every Texan is a traveler," p. 14.

Table 1

Cities by Category of Legal Restrictiveness	Homicide Rate		
	1963[a]	1966[b]	1969[d]
Moderately Lenient			
New York	5.2	6.4	9.4
Philadelphia	3.8	5.3	7.5
Newark	4.7	5.1	7.3
Detroit	4.4	6.8	13.0
Los Angeles	4.7	5.8	9.7
Chicago	6.7	9.0	11.6
Very Lenient			
Phoenix	6.4	7.2	7.2
Dallas	10.1	11.4	18.1
Jackson	NA	13.1 (1968)[c]	12.9

Sources: [a] U.S. F.B.I., *Uniform Crime Reports for U.S. & Its Possessions . . . –1963,* Table 4, pages 67–86.
[b] U.S. F.B.I., *Uniform Crime Reports for U.S. & Its Possessions . . . –1966,* Table 5, pages 78–90.
[c] Computed on the basis of information derived from *Uniform Crime Reports . . . –1968* and the *County and City Data Book–1969.*
[d] U.S. F.B.I., *Uniform Crime Reports . . . –1969,* Table 5, pages 74–88.

This computation of homicide rates is based on the "Standard Metropolitan Statistical Area" which includes not only the municipal unit proper but many of the surrounding counties as well.

Five of the six cities with "moderately lenient" laws had lower homicide rates than two cities with even weaker laws. The comparatively poor showing of Chicago may be related to the fact that, as was previously noted, Chicago's gun laws are among the weakest of the moderately lenient cities with which it is grouped. Furthermore, Chicago is located within a state with quite weak gun controls. The rise in Detroit's homicide rate from 4.4 in 1963 and 6.8 in 1966 to 13.0 in 1969 coincides with a rise in gun ownership in the city following extensive rioting during the summer of 1967. This case is examined later in greater detail (pp. 130–131).

The figures in Table 2 show the percentage of homicides involving the use of guns in 1963. It seems clear from these figures that two of the cities categorized as having the weakest gun control laws, namely Dallas and Phoenix, had the highest percentage of homicides committed with a gun. The cities with moderate gun laws, New York, Philadelphia, Detroit, Los Angeles, and Chicago, had notably lower percentages (even Chicago with the highest percentage of gun homicides of the moderate-law group was nearly 20 per-

Table 2

Cities by Category of Legal Restrictiveness	Gun Homicide Percentage (1963)
Moderately Lenient	
New York	25.0
Philadelphia	36.0
Newark	NA
Detroit	40.0
Los Angeles	43.5
Chicago	46.4
Very Lenient	
Phoenix	65.9
Dallas	72.0
Jackson	NA

Source: Congressional Quarterly Weekly Report, Vol. 23, No. 23 (June 4, 1965), p. 1061.

centage points below Phoenix and nearly 26 points below Dallas). New York, the city with the most restrictive gun control law in 1963 (Philadelphia's law not having been enacted at this time), also had the lowest percentage of murders by gun. Compared with the nine next largest cities, New York had the fifth-lowest assault rate, and the lowest robbery rate.[35]

It may reasonably be argued that "moderate" cities' gun control laws alone may not be responsible for the observed low homicide rates and low rates of homicide by guns, and instead, other factors having nothing to do with gun laws may better account for the crime statistics. A high crime rate has been found to be associated with densely populated areas, fast-growing populations, poor economic conditions, uneven distributions of wealth, and small expenditures on police relative to the total government expenditure.[36] Classifying the cities on this basis gives results found in Table 3.

In addition to very weak gun control laws, Jackson, Phoenix, and Dallas had several other factors—rapidly growing population and relatively low income—frequently recognized as predisposing them to crime. On the other hand, there are three cities, which according to several indications other than gun laws "should" have high crime rates, but in fact, do not. Detroit, Newark and Philadelphia have dense populations with high poverty rates and low incomes; yet, in 1963, Philadelphia had the lowest homicide rate (4.9) and

---

[35] Harris, *op. cit.,* p. 73.
[36] *Uniform Crime Reports–1963,* p. 3.

Table 3

City	Pop. Per Sq. Mile (1960)	Pop. Change (1950–1960)	Median Family Inc. (1960)	% Under $3,000	% Over $10,000	City Government Finances 1964/65 ($1,000)	Expenditure On Police 1964/65 ($1,000)	% of City Finances Spent On Police 1964/65
New York	25,940	−1.4	6,091	15.2	18.5	3,358,852	268,652	.08
Philadelphia	15,584	−3.3	5,782	17.1	14.2	328,180	44,598	.14
Newark	16,814	−7.6	5,454	18.9	12.1	109,980	15,876	.14
Detroit	12,103	−9.7	6,089	19.0	17.8	238,908	37,911	.16
Los Angeles	5,447	25.8	6,896	14.4	25.1	295,855	64,049	.22
Chicago	16,014	−1.9	6,738	13.6	21.3	401,029	92,137	.23
Phoenix	2,344	311.1	6,117	16.8	16.8	49,567	6,679	.13
Dallas	2,676	56.4	5,976	18.4	18.9	77,177	10,075	.13
Jackson	3,106	47.0	5,216	26.1	14.4	19,747	2,712	.14

Source: Department of Commerce, *County and City Data Book, 1967* (Washington, D.C.: U.S. Government Printing Office), Table 4, pp. 464–573.

the next lowest percentage of gun homicides (36.0), while Detroit had the third-lowest homicide rate (5.5) and third-lowest percentage of gun homicides (40.0). (As was noted earlier, Detroit's homicide rate was considerably higher in 1969, but this may have been related to a rise in gun ownership following riots in the summer of 1967.) Newark also has several characteristics which seem to predispose it to a high crime rate—dense population, second-lowest income (only Jackson is lower); yet according to the FBI's statistics, only two cities had lower homicide rates in 1963. In 1968 none of the other cities had a lower homicide rate, and in 1969 one city did. Additionally, Los Angeles, the only city in the "moderately lenient" gun law category with a growth rate comparable to those of Phoenix, Dallas, and Jackson had a considerably lower homicide and gun homicide rate.

STATES

The states whose gun laws and criminal statistics are to be compared are: New York, New Jersey, Massachusetts, Rhode Island, Pennsylvania, Arizona, Texas, Mississippi, Nevada, and Florida. These states have been chosen to provide jurisdictions with a range of degrees of gun law severity and to include examples from a variety of regions in the country. On the basis of the previously discussed means of ranking gun control legislation, the following states will be classified as having "moderately lenient" gun control laws: New York, New Jersey, Massachusetts, Rhode Island, and Pennsylvania. The states of Florida, Arizona, Texas, Nevada, and Mississippi will be classified as having "very weak" gun control laws. In the first category, the laws of New York State are clearly the most restrictive. On the next level, New Jersey (whose statewide laws are similar to those of Newark) and Massachusetts can be considered "moderately restrictive." In Massachusetts, for example, a license is required to purchase a handgun, the waiting period is the time required for the granting of the permit, handgun sales are reported to the police, a retail sales license is required for guns, the minimum age for gun possession is eighteen, and a license is required to carry a gun openly or concealed. On the "least restrictive" level within the group of moderate-law states, Rhode Island and Pennsylvania have the weakest requirements. While both states' laws include all of the above requirements (although Pennsylvania requires a forty-eight-hour waiting period and has an eighteen-year-old minimum age, and Rhode Island has a seventy-two-hour waiting period and a twenty-one-year-old minimum age), neither state requires a license for the purchase of handguns. However, despite this fact, the limitations each state sets on the purchase of handguns ("applications to purchase" are required) are sufficient to warrant their placement in the moderate-law group.

Arizona's, Texas's, and Mississippi's very lenient gun controls were discussed in the previous section. Nevada's and Florida's laws are equally weak, requiring only a minimum age for handgun purchases (for Nevada it is eighteen and in Florida, sixteen) and a license to carry a concealed handgun (Florida also regulates the carrying of a handgun openly).

Table 4 lists the total rate of murders per 100,000 population for the years of 1963, 1966, and 1968 in each of the ranked states:

Table 4

States by Category of Legal Restrictiveness	Homicide Rate		
	1963	1966	1968
Moderately Lenient			
New York	3.8	4.8	6.5
New Jersey	2.8	3.2	5.1
Massachusetts	1.9	2.4	3.5
Rhode Island	1.4	2.1	2.4
Pennsylvania	2.3	3.2	4.0
Very Lenient			
Arizona	6.0	6.1	6.3
Texas	7.3	9.1	10.6
Mississippi	7.2	9.7	9.9
Florida	8.2	10.3	11.9
Nevada	7.9	10.6	5.5

Sources: Federal Bureau of Investigation, Uniform Crime Reports—1963 (Washington, D.C.: U.S. Government Printing Office), Table 3; Federal Bureau of Investigation, Uniform Crime Reports—1966 (Washington, D.C.: U.S. Government Printing Office); U.S. Bureau of the Census, Statistical Abstracts of the United States—1968 (Washington, D.C.: U.S. Government Printing Office).

In 1963 and 1966, all the states with moderate gun laws may be seen to have considerably lower overall homicide rates than all the states with weak gun laws. Even the state with the highest homicide rate among the moderate-law states, New York with 4.8 homicide rate in 1966, does markedly better than the state with the lowest homicide rate among the weak-law states, Arizona with 6.1 as a homicide rate. The general relationship between the homicide rates of the two categories of states reappears in the 1968 data, although New York's homicide rate exceeds those of two states in the "very lenient" gun law category.

The absolute figures on the number of gun accidents, suicides by guns, and homicides by guns occurring in each state in 1963, 1964, and 1967 are listed in Table 5.

Table 5

State	Year	Accidents		Suicides		Homicides	
		Total	Gun	Total	Gun	Total	Gun
New York	1963	7,346	61	1,621	370	705	201
	1964	7,482	81	996	319	852	254
	1967	4,488	65	900	270	1,076	424
New Jersey	1963	2,582	30	584	130	193	73
	1964	2,749	34	513	74	191	63
	1967	2,909	41	486	146	307	142
Massachusetts	1963	2,229	6	438	166	100	23
	1964	2,227	11	434	93	64	26
	1967	2,664	24	408	84	169	75
Rhode Island	1963	341	3	65	9	13	2
	1964	357	6	81	13	12	4
	1967	367	3	38	14	28	9
Pennsylvania	1963	5,282	73	1,122	444	297	136
	1964	5,369	67	1,091	433	398	154
	1967	5,646	81	1,071	418	465	202
Arizona	1963	933	34	210	129	81	50
	1964	1,321	21	194	127	80	47
	1967	1,144	46	145	105	111	65
Texas	1963	6,009	164	988	662	775	516
	1964	6,284	185	1,009	694	848	574
	1967	6,601	150	1,049	717	1,170	851
Mississippi	1963	1,592	83	127	97	263	167
	1964	1,623	85	159	127	253	173
	1967	1,928	119	160	126	253	184
Nevada	1963	318	9	71	46	31	20
	1964	378	10	92	43	37	25
	1967	328	9	100	58	42	26
Florida	1963	3,386	96	739	356	518	327
	1964	3,530	103	772	399	544	355
	1967	3,910	119	824	466	763	519

Sources: U.S. Bureau of Census, *Vital Statistics of the United States 1963,* Vol. II (Washington, D.C.: U.S. Government Printing Office), Tables 1–24; U.S. Bureau of Census, *Vital Statistics of the United States 1964,* Vol. II (Washington, D.C.: U.S. Government Printing Office), Tables 1–26; U.S. Bureau of Census, *Vital Statistics of the United States 1967,* Vol. II (Washington, D.C.: U.S. Government Printing Office), Tables 1–26.

The percentages for gun homicides for each of the states are shown in Table 6. The gun homicide rates parallel the split observed between "moderately lenient" and "very lenient" law states in the total homicide rates. All of the moderate-law states have lower gun homicide rates than all of the "very

Table 6

States by Category of Legal Restrictiveness	Gun Homicides %		
	1963	1964	1967
Moderately Lenient			
New York	29	30	39
New Jersey	38	33	46
Massachusetts	29	41	44
Rhode Island	15	33	32
Pennsylvania	46	39	43
Very Lenient			
Arizona	62	59	58
Texas	67	68	73
Mississippi	63	68	73
Nevada	65	68	62
Florida	63	65	68

Sources: U.S. Bureau of Census, *Vital Statistics of the United States 1963,* Vol. II (Washington, D.C.: U.S. Government Printing Office), Tables 1–24; U.S. Bureau of Census, *Vital Statistics of the United States 1964,* Vol. II (Washington, D.C.: U.S. Government Printing Office), Tables 1–26; U.S. Bureau of Census, *Vital Statistics of the United States 1967,* Vol. II (Washington, D.C.: U.S. Government Printing Office), Tables 1–26.

weak" gun law states. As was the case with the total homicide rates the size of the gap is considerable; the highest gun homicide rate of the "moderately lenient" law states for 1963 is 16 percentage points below the lowest rate of gun homicides among the "very lenient" gun law states. Up to this point the analysis would suggest that gun controls had sharply lowered overall homicide rates in the states in which they have been enacted.

As was the case with the cities selected in the previous section, other explanations may be advanced for the lower homicide rates and percentages of gun homicides in states with moderate gun control laws. Here again, population density, population change, median income, amount of poverty, and police expenditure are possible factors accounting for homicide rates, rather than the availability of firearms. Tables 7 and 8 present some of the statistics for these variables for the states we have considered.

States with the fastest-growing populations (with the exception of New Jersey) had the highest homicide rates. The states with the highest homicide rates were also poorer than the states with the lowest homicide rates (except Nevada and New York in 1968) and the states with the highest homicide rates also had the most poverty. With the exception of New York and Massachusetts, the states with the lowest police expenditure had the highest homicide rates. States with the lowest population density (Florida, Mississippi, Texas, Arizona, and Nevada) generally had the highest homicide rates.

Table 7

State	Total Population	Pop. Per Sq. Mile	Pop. Change (1950–1960)	Median Income $	% Under $3,000	% Over $10,000
New York	16,782,304	351	13.2	6,371	13.8	19.9
New Jersey	6,066,782	806	25.5	6,786	11.4	22.0
Massachusetts	5,148,578	657	9.8	6.272	12.4	17.0
Rhode Island	859,488	817	8.5	5,589	16.8	11.7
Pennsylvania	11,319,366	251	7.8	5,719	16.8	13.9
Arizona	1,302,161	16	73.7	5,568	21.3	14.4
Texas	9,579,677	36	24.2	4,884	28.8	11.8
Mississippi	2,178,141	46	00.0	2,884	51.6	5.2
Nevada	285,278	3	78.2	6,738	12.4	21.9
Florida	4,951,960	92	78.7	4,722	28.4	11.1

Source: U.S. Bureau of the Census, *County and City Data Book, 1967* (Washington, D.C.: U.S. Government Printing Office).

Table 8

State	Government Expenditure (1962) $s	Expenditure on Police	Percentage of Government Expenditure for Police
New York	5,497,114	307,781	5.6
New Jersey	1,476,277	93,332	6.3
Massachusetts	1,283,460	68,563	5.3
Rhode Island	135,032	9,164	6.2
Pennsylvania	1,986,740	100,059	5.0
Arizona	315,081	13,190	4.2
Texas	1,761,364	75,452	4.3
Mississippi	319,813	8,140	2.5
Nevada	98,727	5,456	5.5
Florida	1,053,487	58,892	5.6

Source: U.S. Bureau of the Census, *County and City Data Book, 1967* (Washington, D.C.: U.S. Government Printing Office).

These observations suggest the possibility that the observed homicide statistics are less a consequence of the presence· or absence of gun control laws than of the economic level of the area (*e.g.*, in poorer states money spent on police protection is lessened, and there is more economic motivation for violent crime) and of other environmental factors (such as the western states having a "violent heritage" and "frontier traditions").

However, despite the fact that one may outline all the factors predisposing a given state or region to violence, one is still justified in pointing out the extent to which the ready availability of firearms exacerbates the situation; the differences in the percentage of homicides involving the use of guns are especially instructive in this regard. In Pennsylvania, the median family income is relatively low ($5,719), income is poorly distributed, and the gun homicide percentage in 1963 was 46 percent and the general homicide rate was 2.3. Nevada, where median income was higher ($6,736) and better distributed (there were more upper incomes), had a 65 percent rate of gun murders in 1963 and 7.9 homicide rate. Similarly Arizona, with a median income slightly lower than Pennsylvania ($5,568) and with a poorer pattern of income distribution, had a 62 percent gun homicide rate and an overall homicide rate of 6.0 in 1963. Additionally, Texas and Mississippi had population growth rates comparable to those of the "moderately lenient" law states and still had the high homicide and gun homicide rates characteristic of the "very lenient" gun law states.

If Texas, a state with a high overall homicide rate and gun homicide rate, had New York State's law, and, further, if Texas' homicide rate should even come close to New York's (from 9.1 to 4.8) 4.3 lives per 100,000 (or 464 of the 10,869,000 Texans in 1967) might be saved. Or, using an even stronger model, England, one could estimate that approximately 8.4 lives per 100,000 in the population (or 907 Texans in 1967) might be saved if Texas' homicide rate approached England's (.7). These estimates are presented to indicate the number of lives that would be saved if gun laws and gun availability accounted for *all* the variance between different areas' homicide rates. However economic and social-psychological factors certainly do influence the varying homicide rates and thus it will be necessary to discount the above estimates according to one's impression of the extent of that influence.

While it is unlikely that Texas' overall homicide rate would ever near New York's or England's because of the intervening and alternate causal factors discussed previously, still one may talk realistically of reducing the percentage of homicides by guns. For instance, one could determine how many firearms murders were committed by those under sixteen in Texas, by those with criminal records, by the insane, etc.; in each of these instances the perpetrator would have been less likely to have access to a handgun in New York and the subsequent homicide might have been avoided. Applying the nationwide figures for the percentage of murders by handgun (44 percent) to Texas yields 331 homicides, a good proportion of which might have been avoided if Texas restricted handguns as severely as does New York. Moreover, assuming that 82 percent of southern murders occur within the family or among acquaintances, as is the case nationally, there would be 803 such murders in Texas. English law, by substantially reducing the number of privately owned guns, could reduce the murders as well, and even a 50 percent reduction would save 400 lives.

REGIONS

Regional comparisons particularly tend to highlight the probable influence of the intervening variables on homicide rates. The northeastern section of the country, whose overall homicide rate and percentage of gun homicides is lower than the rest of the country, is generally wealthier, and has a more equitable income distribution. Thus many New England states have been singled out as illustrations of the inadequacy of arguments for gun control; states like New Hampshire and Connecticut have quite lenient gun control laws and still have low homicide rates: Connecticut, 1.3 (1963); New Hampshire, 2.4; the 1963 total for New England (including Maine, Massachusetts, Rhode Island, Vermont, Connecticut, and New Hampshire) was 1.9. The total Mid-Atlantic region (New York, New Jersey, and Pennsylvania) homicide rate was 3.1.[37] Similarly the Midwestern states (classified in the FBI reports as East and West North Central) whose laws are as lenient as those of the South (South Atlantic, East and West South Central) have relatively low homicide rates; regional totals for the West North Central area is 2.6 and for the East North Central 3.5, while the South Atlantic's rate is 7.7.[38] Once again the median income is higher in the midwestern areas than in the southern and there is less poverty.[39]

Nevertheless, the observation that certain areas of the country are particularly prone to violent crimes due to factors other than the degree of gun control does not lead to the conclusion that nothing significant can be done to ameliorate the situation, and that gun control legislation will have little or no effect. Regional breakdowns of the use of firearms in homicides provide evidence to the contrary: a firearm was used in 37 percent of the killings in the Northeast where there are moderately restrictive gun controls, in 53 percent of the killings in the western states, in 56 percent in the northern central states and in 64 percent in the southern states where there are less restrictive gun controls.[40]

Overall then, we have compared various American cities, states, and briefly, regions in terms of, first, their having enacted gun control laws of various moderate degrees of restrictiveness or no seriously restrictive laws at all, and secondly, in terms of the various areas' homicide and gun homicide rates. In most instances we have found an apparent relationship be-

---

[37] *Uniform Crime Reports–1963*, p. 48. The 1966 figures are similar: Connecticut 2.0, New Hampshire 1.9, New England 2.1, Mid-Atlantic 4.1. *Uniform Crime Reports–1966*, p. 60.

[38] *Ibid.*, 1966 figures are West North Central, 3.1; East North Central, 4.9; South Atlantic, 9.1.

[39] *County and City Data Book, 1967*, Table 1.

[40] *Uniform Crime Reports–1967*, p. 7.

tween the presence and severity of gun control laws and lower homicide and gun homicide rates. However, we are prevented from drawing the inference that the observed lower crime rates are a consequence of the enacted gun laws because of the presence of other likely causes of the lower crime rates. The extent of poverty and the rate of population growth, along with other environmental, demographic, and cultural factors have been suggested to be intervening factors influencing crime rates. While not all of the suggested intervening factors are open to ready measurement (*e.g.*, it is difficult to specifically measure the "violent heritage" or "frontier traditions" which are suggested to influence rates of violence in some regions of the country), enough of these suggested variables have been measured to provide, within a broad range of possibilities, some specification of the probable relationship between gun controls, intervening variables, and crime rates. Initially however, the most general observation is that in most of the instances in which they have been specified the intervening factors have covaried with crime rates and with the restrictiveness of gun laws (*e.g.*, crime-promoting factors, weak or nonexistent gun controls, and high crime rates have generally occurred together). This situation, by itself, provides little basis for evaluating the relative influence of either type of causal factor. And despite the logical persuasiveness of the argument for the effectiveness of gun controls, in the absence of some empirical support for the independent impact of gun laws, it would be particularly difficult to interpret a situation in which all three factors (gun controls, intervening factors, and crime rates) varied together as providing a demonstration of the effectiveness of gun controls, since many of the suggested intervening variables have previously been empirically observed to covary with crime rates.

However, in a few of the comparative examples, crime rates have been observed to covary with the gun laws largely independently of the intervening variables (*e.g.*, crime-promoting variables, restrictive gun laws, and low crime rates have occurred together). These instances are of particular interest because they provide empirical indications that gun laws do indeed affect crime rates, and thus suggest that both gun controls and the intervening factors may be significant influences upon the observed crime rates.

NO ECOLOGICAL SEGREGATION: MAIL-ORDER AND INTERSTATE GUN SALES

One major reason why most of the preceding geographic comparisons do not provide a clear demonstration of the influence of moderately restrictive gun control laws on crime rates may be that *these laws do not significantly restrict the availability of firearms.* As was indicated in the earlier discussion of the means by which a gun law might affect homicide rates, reducing the physical availability of guns is the crucial step which would force the large number of impulsive murderers to use less deadly weapons or calm down without killing anyone. However, several factors have tended to reduce the effect of the regulations upon the availability of guns. Frequently a city or state with moderately stringent gun laws borders on several other jurisdictions which have considerably more lenient regulations, or none at all on the purchase of firearms. Thus even moderately restrictive local gun laws are often largely vitiated by the ease with which guns can be obtained in an adjoining jurisdiction. There are a great many instances in which the guns involved in homicides within states with comparatively strict laws were purchased from dealers in neighboring states. In the 1965 Senate Hearings on the National Firearms Act, Attorney General Katzenbach reported that: a) in 1964–65 a hardware store in Chillum, Maryland made 58 percent of its sales to Washington, D.C. residents, 40 percent of whom had criminal records; b) a trading post in Suitland, Maryland made 40 percent of its gun sales to Washington residents, 23 percent of whom had criminal records; c) in Massachusetts, six of the last seven police killed or wounded were victims of guns from other states; and d) in 1963, Massachusetts State Police in a two-month check of three dealers in an adjacent state found thirty-nine Massachusetts residents who bought handguns of whom only four could qualify under Massachusetts law. A 1965 study conducted by the Commissioner of the Massachusetts Department of Public Safety reported that only six guns out of 4,506 recovered from criminals in Massachusetts during the previous eight years had been stolen, but 87 percent of the weapons had been purchased in "over-the-counter" fashion in Maine, New Hampshire, and Vermont.[41]

Additionally, until recently and during the period covered by our comparative data, the mail-order sale of firearms eliminated even the need to cross a border in order to circumvent a local gun regulation. In many of the cities with strong gun control laws, much of the crime committed with guns involved guns purchased from out-of-state mail-order firms. A 1964 study by Chicago police revealed that, of 4,067 Chicago residents who had purchased guns from three mail-order firms, 948 (25 percent) had arrest records, and would not ordinarily have been able to purchase guns within the city. In Philadelphia, of 300 mail-order guns that were spot-checked, 54 of the owners had police records and 15 of these had been arrested for crimes involving firearms.[42] In Newark 80 percent of the guns confiscated from

---

[41] Harris, *op. cit.*, p 70.

[42] U.S. Congress, House Committee on Ways and Means, *Hearings on Proposed Amendment to the National Firearms Act and the Federal Firearms Act,* 89th Congress, 1st Session (July 12–28, 1965), p. 7.

criminals had been bought outside the state.[43] In Los Angeles, police found that 72 percent of the rioters arrested in Watts with guns in their possession had criminal records; in Detroit 90 percent of the revolvers and automatic pistols confiscated from rioters were the cheaper foreign models widely imported and sold by mail-order firearm concerns.[44] Another investigation revealed that 61 of 154 guns sold and shipped to New Jersey by two California suppliers were not registered or authorized by state permits; and furthermore, 26 of the customers had criminal records.[45] Thus the effects of existing American gun laws upon the general availability of firearms have been largely dampened by mail-order sales and the accessibility of jurisdictions with few, if any, restrictions on the sale of guns.

"BEFORE AND AFTER" CASE STUDIES: PHILADELPHIA AND TOLEDO

Another approach to the problem of controlling the influence of the intervening causal variables so that even the "dampened" effect of gun control laws may be observed has somewhat more success. Analyses of variation in the crime rate of a single city before and after the enactment of gun control legislation have provided some indications of the efficacy of such laws. An ordinance was passed in Philadelphia in 1965 which tightened the previously existing firearms ordinance primarily in two ways: first it included under the rubric of "firearm" any pistol, revolver, rifle, gun or shotgun, thus the licensing requirements it provided extended beyond handguns; and secondly, it provided that no one may obtain or transfer a firearm in the city unless a license had been obtained. The previous gun law had not limited transfers of guns into Philadelphia when the gun transferred was not to be resold.[46] The greatest omission of the new law was the fact that it did not cover firearms already owned by citizens when the law was enacted. Furthermore, even with the supposedly strict requirement of police review and approval of all permits, few people were actually denied permits. In the first six years since the ordinance was passed, 779 applications out of 27,858 were denied (primarily because of previous criminal records).[47] It is not known at this point what portion of these individuals subsequently purchased guns

---

[43] Harris, *op. cit.*, p. 70.

[44] *Ibid.*, p. 150.

[45] U.S. Congress, House Committee on Ways and Means, *op. cit.*, pp. 70–72.

[46] U.S. Congress, Senate Committee on the Judiciary, *Hearings* (July 10–August 1, 1963), pp. 345–346.

[47] Carl Bakal, "The Failure of Federal Gun Control," *Saturday Review,* Vol. 54 (July 3, 1971).

Table 9

CRIMINAL HOMICIDES (MURDER) IN PHILADELPHIA*

Year	Criminal Homicide (murder)	Number Involving Guns	Percent Involving Guns
1964	188	62	32.9
1965	205	88	42.9
1966	178	69	38.7

Source: FBI and Philadelphia police.

* In 1969, guns were involved in 44 percent of all criminal homicides in Philadelphia, only a slight increase over the 1963 figure of 43 percent. In contrast, the national average for 1969 was 65 percent, an 8 percent rise in the number of homicides involving guns since 1965. (From Bakal, *op. cit.*)

GUNS INVOLVED IN CRIMES, 1963–66

	1963	1964	1965	1966
Criminal homicides by gun	48	62	89	69
Aggravated assaults by gun	460	464	490	441
Armed robberies by gun	550	622	653	634
Arrests for violation of State Firearms Act and city ordinance	473	599	1,088	1,254
Total	1,531	1,747	2,320	2,398

Source: U.S. Congress, Senate Committee on the Judiciary, *Hearings* (July 10–August 1, 1967), pp. 354, 356, 704.

in the five surrounding counties in which regulations were considerably more lenient.

Yet despite these drawbacks, statistics comparing the years prior to the enactment of the law with those after enactment reveal a drop in the homicide rate. Between 1963 and 1965 there had been a rise in the number of aggravated assaults by gun, and the number of armed robberies by gun; between 1965 and 1966 the numbers in each case decreased markedly.[48] Clearly these statistics are not conclusive; the time period involved is too short, and the homicide reduction, though readily apparent, is not overwhelming. One can say, however, that there are indications that the new ordinance has had a considerable impact on Philadelphia's crime.

---

[48] U.S. Congress, Senate Committee on the Judiciary, *Hearings* (July 10–August 1, 1963), pp. 345–346.

In August of 1968, Toledo, Ohio enacted an ordinance prohibiting anyone from keeping or obtaining a handgun without a license from the police. While the law's scope was broad, since it included handguns obtained prior to the enactment of the ordinance, its restrictiveness was limited, as the police were required to issue licenses to all applicants except minors under twenty-one years of age, fugitives, people who had been convicted twice in the past year of crimes involving force, certified mental cases, narcotics addicts, and habitual drunks. Out of more than 16,000 applications, 100 were rejected. However, there were visible efforts to enforce the law. Thirty-seven people were jailed for an average of ninety days for violations of the law (mainly possession of an unlicensed handgun) during the first year and a quarter of its operation.[49] And, as was the case in Philadelphia, crime statistics released by the FBI (in November of 1969) indicated sharp drops in Toledo's rate of violent crime. While the national average rate for homicide, assault, robbery, and rape rose 9 percent from the first six months of 1968 to the first six months of 1969, Toledo experienced a 31.5 percent drop in these crimes. While Toledo's gun control ordinance was only one part of a crime-reduction campaign, including an expanded police force, altered probation procedures, and better street lighting, still municipal officials have suggested that the new gun law was a major factor causing the decrease in violent crimes.[50] While, again as is the case with the Philadelphia data, it will take time to clarify the long-term effect of the gun legislation and the actual causal relationships involved in the initially reported drop in crime statistics, still the cases suggest that gun laws may contribute significantly to reductions in rates of violent crime. Additionally these indications occurred in a setting where the sort of intervening variables which complicated and obscured the geographic comparisons are essentially held constant.

GUN AVAILABILITY AND VIOLENCE

A somewhat different approach to the problem of investigating the impact of gun control upon crime and violence rates is provided by a staff report prepared for the National Commission on the Causes and Prevention of Violence.[51] Focussing not upon the presence or absence of gun laws, but upon the degree of availability of firearms, the report provided several comparisons indicating that rates of firearms possession in an area are paralleled by the amount of gun-related violence in the same area. This approach has

---

[49] *Wall Street Journal,* October 7, 1969.
[50] *Ibid.*
[51] Newton and Zimring, *op. cit.*

both advantages and problems. On the one hand, the approach is particularly useful because it bypasses the problem of evaluating the restrictiveness and efficacy of gun laws. On the other hand, however, by focussing upon the rates of gun-involved violence and not upon overall rates of violence and crime the empirical analyses stop short of clearly demonstrating a connection between the availability of guns and the general level of crime and violence (*i.e.,* the suggestion that absent guns will be replaced by other weapons is not empirically confronted). This truncation of the empirical analysis short of demonstrating changes in the overall rates of violence is dealt with in two ways. At one point the decision to focus primarily upon rates of *gun* violence is viewed as a means of avoiding the confounding effects of varying intervening variables by simply comparing proportions of gun violence across regions with varying overall violence rates.[52] Although this approach, taken by itself, would evade the important practical question of whether a reduction in the availability of guns would lower overall rates of violence, it is supplemented in the report by an effort to strengthen the logical, if not empirical, connections between rates of gun violence and overall rates of violence. Several empirical studies were conducted which indicated that gun wounds are five times more apt to be fatal than knife wounds, and that similar circumstances surround both gun and knife attacks, suggesting that the deadliness of gun attacks is not due to differing degrees of motivation on the part of the attacker, but to the effectiveness of the weapon itself.[53] These studies strengthen the logical connection between rates of gun violence and overall rates of violence by indicating that a given number of gun injuries will simply produce more fatalities than a similar number of injuries by alternate weapons. Thus, although the report's studies focus upon rates of gun violence, a significant connection between these rates and overall violence rates is suggested to exist.

While the Task Force on Firearms conducted several comparative studies of the relationship between the availability of guns and rates of gun violence, the analysis that most clearly links gun availability to overall violence rates is a case history of Detroit, Michigan, from 1965 to 1968. Michigan law requires that anyone desiring to purchase a handgun apply for a permit from the local police. During 1965, 4,876 permits for handgun purchases were issued in Detroit and 6,416 were issued in 1966. In 1967, a year during which extensive rioting occurred in Detroit during the summer, 10,872 new permits were issued and the following year, 1968, 17,760 permits were issued, almost four times as many as in 1965. While these figures do not

---

[52] Newton and Zimring, *op. cit.,* pp. 124, 182.
[53] *Ibid.,* chapter 7.

reveal out-of-state purchases or illegal acquisitions of weapons, there were indications that "the illegal acquisition of firearms followed similar trends . . . the number of guns stolen in the 5 months following the July, 1967 riot was approximately 70 percent greater than the number of thefts reported in the five months preceding the riot."[54] Data on homicides in Detroit indicated both a rise in the proportion of gun homicides over the four-year period, and also a marked increase in the total number of homicides. In 1965 there were 140 homicides, 39 percent of which involved guns; in 1968, 389 homicides occurred, and 72 percent, or 279, homicides were committed with guns.[55] Handgun sales had increased by approximately 400 percent from 1965 to 1968, and over the same period the proportion of gun homicides also increased 400 percent. Homicides committed with weapons other than guns increased 30 percent over the four years. A roughly similar pattern occurs in the rates of increase in robberies, with and without firearms. Robberies without firearms increased from 100 in 1965, to 218 in 1968, while robberies with firearms increased from 100 to 378 over the same period.[56] Finally, as might be expected, the rapid rise in the ownership of firearms led to a tripling of the accidental deaths due to firearms (10 deaths in 1965 and 32 in 1968).

Two further atemporal geographic comparisons are provided by the Firearms Task Force's report: the first indicates that the percentage of gun use in homicide and aggravated assault varies along with the ownership of guns in the four major regions of the country. Additionally, a 1968 Harris Poll of a national sample of 1,175 men and women indicated that 33 percent of the households in the northeastern section of the country possess one or more guns, while 51 percent do so in the Midwest, 49 percent in the West, and 59 percent in the South. These variations in gun ownership from region to region are paralleled by variations in the rates of homicide and aggravated assault in which guns are used. Finally, an examination of the rates of firearms use in homicide, robbery, and aggravated assault reported by the police departments of eight cities indicates both that cities with the highest rates of gun crime are in the regions of high gun ownership, and also that high rates of gun use in one crime within a city tends to be paralleled by high rates of gun use in the other crimes, even though "only a small proportion of those who commit homicide are known also to commit robbery."[57]

Thus by bypassing the topic of gun laws, and focussing upon the ques-

----

[54] Arnold Kotz, "Firearms Violence and Civil Disorders," Stanford Research Institute, July, 1968, pp. 44–45, quoted in Newton and Zimring, *op. cit.*, p. 70.

[55] Newton and Zimring, *op. cit.*, p. 73.

[56] *Ibid.*, p. 74.

[57] *Ibid.*, p. 77.

Figure 1.   Gun Ownership and Percentage Gun Use in Homicide and Aggravated Assault by Region

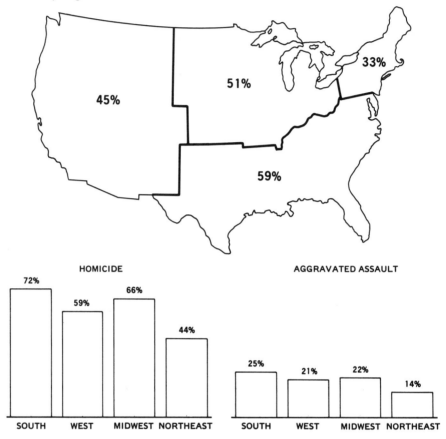

Source: George D. Newton and Franklin E. Zimring, *Firearms and Violence in American Life,* p. 75. A Staff Report to the National Committee on the Causes and Prevention of Violence (Washington, D.C.: U.S. Government Printing Office, 1969), p. 75.

tion of the consequences of differing degrees of availability of firearms, the Firearms Task Force was able to illustrate in three different contexts (Detroit, four national regions, and eight cities) that an increase in weapons availability has led to an increased use of guns in crime and, inferentially in two instances and directly in the other, that this increase in gun violence led to higher overall violence rates.

Overall then, the question of whether a reduction in the availability of firearms will achieve significant savings in reduced numbers of crimes, deaths, and injuries has been approached four times now, once on an abstract analytical level, and three times in terms of empirical data. While consideration of the varying abstract prognoses of the utility of reducing the availability of guns did suggest, and strongly, the effectiveness of a restrictive system of gun control, the reviews of empirical data were much less clear cut and interpretable. The first set of three comparisons of areas with differing gun laws was hindered both by the weakness of the equation of gun laws with gun availability (*i.e.,* a moderately restrictive gun law did not, for several reasons, lead to a comparably moderate restriction in the availability of guns) and by the difficulty of isolating the effect of the reduction in the availability of guns on the crime rates from the influence of other possible factors acting upon the examined crime rates (*i.e.,* the intervening variables). The results of the comparative studies as a consequence, while not incompatible with the initial hypothetically predicted results (*i.e.,* fewer guns will lead to lower homicide rates), were, nonetheless, rather foggy and inconclusive. However, a second type of data, two case histories of cities that had enacted gun controls (Philadelphia and Toledo) provided clearer indications of the utility of gun laws for reducing crime rates, though the data here was less widely based and more illustrative in nature than the comparative studies. Finally, several analyses prepared by the Task Force on Firearms approached the question of the possible savings associated with a reduction in the availability of firearms somewhat obliquely, leading to empirical statements of greater definitiveness than the previously discussed studies had, but with less direct impact on the practical question of the utility of gun control laws. While the Task Force's analyses indicated that variations in the availability of guns are paralleled by variations in the rates of gun violence, the studies did not attempt to empirically demonstrate similar covariations in the overall crime rates (*i.e.,* confront the problem of intervening causal factors). Instead the Task Force chose to make this connection by presenting, and to a degree empirically supporting, the logical argument (efficient guns and impulsive people result in more deaths) indicating that higher gun-homicide rates will directly increase overall homicide rates. Thus an empirically clear demonstration that variations in the availability of guns will produce parallel alterations in total crime rates is not provided, although a reasonably close approximation is presented.

In view of the considerable persuasiveness of the logical argument for the utility of reducing the availability of guns which was reviewed at the beginning of this discussion and was used to bolster the Task Force's argument, what factors might account for the difficulties that have hampered these differing approaches to empirically evaluating the hypothetical interpretation of the utility of gun control; why all the waffling and side-stepping, particularly with regard to the influence of the intervening causal variables? One possible interpretation of this situation has already been alluded to, but not fully enunciated. This is the possibility that the amount of variation in the access to guns that is empirically present in the United States is quite limited (despite the presence or absence of "gun laws") and the amount of variation in other variables (*e.g.,* population growth, poverty) so comparatively high that only in occasional, illustrative instances (often temporal case histories which essentially hold constant many of the environmental, demographic variables) is a clear indication of the effect on crime rates of variation in availability of guns easily discernible.

Figure 2.   Amount of Variation in Firearms Availability and Other Factors Affecting Crime in Geographical Crime Rate Comparisons

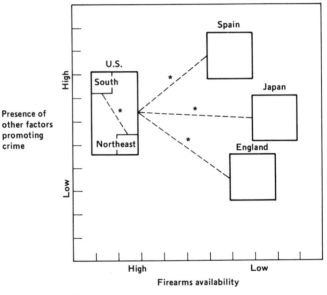

*Statistical comparisons

Graphically depicted, in the form of a four-fold table with the two postulated causal dimensions being conceived of as continuous variables, it is suggested, first, that most of the comparative studies of American data focus on the relations between points or sequences of points within an area containing causal variation primarily in terms of the alternate and intervening variables, with considerably less variation present in the hypothesized causal variable, the availability of guns (area "U.S." in Figure 2). Additionally, it may be suggested that some of the more simple and facilely arrived at demonstrations of the desirability of gun control may have derived their apparently persuasive evidence from the confounding of the effects of their overtly announced causal variable, the enactment of gun controls, with covertly present intervening variables. A simple comparison of the American Northeast, as an area that has enacted many gun laws, with the South, as a region that generally has not, could produce such a demonstration (area "S" to area "NE" in Figure 2). It should be noted, however, that this does not mean gun controls have not significantly affected crime rates in these areas; it seems fairly likely that they have. The danger is that such comparisons claim too much for their data and fail to confront the actual problems in the situation.

The major utility of this perspective, however, is not that of suggesting why American comparisons tend to have so much trouble with intervening variables, but rather that of suggesting that the major range of variation along the gun-control continuum does not even enter the American discussion. The amount of disarmament attributable to the weak and circumventable American gun laws represents a very small movement along the gun-control continuum from a society with widespread and easy access to firearms toward a society with effective civilian disarmament. And this variable, the postulated reduction in the general availability of firearms, was the critical element in the abstract explanation of the saving to be achieved through gun control. Quite possibly if the empirical investigation of the benefits that may be derived from gun control is to achieve any clarity, it will have to occur in the area of international comparisons. For despite the difficulty of dealing with the increased number of intervening variables that are involved in international comparisons, this *is* the comparative field within which significant variation occurs in the domestic availability of firearms.

INTERNATIONAL COMPARISONS

This section will consider the following countries: the United States, France, England and Wales, Switzerland, Belgium, West Germany (excluding West Berlin), Spain, Italy, the Soviet Union, Canada, and Japan. Each of the other nations discussed in this section has gun laws that are considerably stricter than any of the laws of the American areas mentioned previously. The laws range from those which essentially provide for total disarmament (*e.g.,* those of the Soviet Union and Japan) to laws whose licensing and registration requirements are strict enough to very effectively limit the firearms traffic in the nation.

The Soviet Union and Japan are at one end of the spectrum; in both countries private ownership of guns is effectively prohibited. In Japan, this is particularly true of handguns; in all of Japan only 50 pistol permits have been issued.[58] In the Soviet Union, the ban on firearms applies only to rifles and handguns, as shotguns may be bought in most of the country (in the far north and in Siberia they require a special permit and also must be registered with the police).[59]

On the next level of strictness of gun control are those countries which require a permit to buy or own a firearm (with restrictive criteria for granting these permits) and/or strict provisions for the registration of firearms that effectively limit their ownership and use. In Britain, it is illegal to buy or own any firearm without a permit certificate from the local police chief. Firearms permits are not granted by right to anyone who wants one, but only for specific purposes and after the police chief has satisfied himself "that the applicant is not by reason of a criminal record prohibited from possessing a firearm, and is not in any other way likely to endanger the public safety or peace."[60] Furthermore, all transactions involving guns and ammunition are registered with the local police. Since few people can give valid reasons for wanting guns (protection of persons or property is not seen as a valid reason), the only people normally armed are those assigned to protect members of the royal family and the prime minister.[61] In London, with a population of over three million, there are only 15,584 certificate holders.[62]

In France, the law requires that individuals have police permits to buy or own handguns and rifles, the granting of which involves a background investigation that may take as long as six weeks. Here again all gun sales are registered and in addition, no mail-order sales are permitted. The carrying of weapons is restricted by law to police and licensed guards only; private persons with properly licensed handguns cannot carry them under any circumstances.[63] As a result, in Paris and its suburbs, with five million people, only 700 permits for "special purchase" weapons have been issued.[64]

In Spain and Switzerland, the administration of permits and registration laws severely controls the traffic in firearms. In Spain, a purchase permit is required from the director general of security, who may deny it without giving a reason. If the purchase permit is granted, the applicant must register his gun with the Civil Guard and subsequently receives a "guia," or guide, which must be carried along with the license whenever the weapon is used;

---

[58] *New York Times,* October 5, 1967.

[59] *New York Times,* June 13, 1968.

[60] *Ibid.*

[61] U.S. Congress, Senate Committee on the Judiciary, *Hearings* (July 10–August 1, 1967), p. 347.

[62] *Ibid.*

[63] *New York Times,* June 13, 1968.

[64] U.S. Congress, Senate Committee on the Judiciary, *Hearings* (July 10–August 1, 1967), p. 1958.

furthermore, only fifty cartridges may be purchased at once, and the transaction must be recorded in the "guia."[65] In Switzerland, although the nation's defense system requires that each citizen militiaman keep his weapon at home between tours of training duty, the requirement that each gun be registered with military authorities and that each *round* of ammunition issued be accounted for effectively amounts to strict gun control laws.[66]

Italy, West Germany, Belgium, Sweden, and Canada require an individual to obtain a permit to buy a firearm, which is subject to the approval of the police or of equivalent authority. These nations also record all gun transactions; the police maintain records of both the gun owner and the gun itself.[67] Overall homicide rates for these countries are presented in Table 10.

As these figures clearly show, the United States leads all other advanced industrial nations both in the homicide rate for the two years listed and in the rate of increase between those two years. The United States also heads the list of all other advanced industrial states in terms of the proportion of homicide deaths due to firearms, proportion of suicides by firearms, and proportion of accidental deaths due to firearms. Sixty percent of all homicides in the United States involve the use of guns, as compared with 10 percent in England and Wales. During a three-year period, of the 400,000 criminals arrested in England and Wales, only 159 were carrying guns.[68]

These differences were particularly apparent in a study conducted by Dr. Donald James West, a criminologist at Cambridge. The study compared murder statistics for London and Manhattan and revealed that 5 percent of London murders involved the use of guns, while 36 percent of Manhattan murders involved guns. Moreover, in Manhattan, 46 percent of the murderers had more than two previous convictions, of which 50 percent had been for violent crimes; in London only 22 percent of the murderers had more than two previous convictions, and 14 percent of these had been convicted of violent crimes. The study, however, did not connect the incidence of crime by previous offenders to the varying availability of weapons to those with criminal records in Manhattan and London.[69]

It is clear that when an international comparison of gun laws is attempted, basing causal inferences upon a simple contrasting of crime statistics from two countries is most suspect. On the international level in particular, a large number of alternative explanations may be advanced to account for differences in homicide rates. However, as was pointed out in

---

[65] *New York Times,* June 13, 1968.

[66] Bakal, *op. cit.,* p. 281.

[67] *New York Times,* June 17, 1968.

[68] *New York Times,* July 5, 1968.

[69] *New York Times,* July 5, 1968.

Table 10

Country	Year*	Homicide Rate	Year**	Homicide Rate
United States	1963	4.9	1965	5.5
France	1963	.8	1965	.8
Sweden	1962	.6	1966	.7
Japan	1963	1.5	1965	1.4
Canada	1963	1.3	1965	1.3
England and Wales	1963	.7	1965	.7
Switzerland	1962	1.0	1964	.8
Belgium	1962	.6	1964	.6
West Germany	1963	1.2	1964	1.2
Italy	1962	1.1	1964	.9
Spain	1962	.2	1963	.1
Soviet Union		NA		NA

Sources: *United Nations, *Demographic Yearbook,* 18th ed. (Lake Success, 1966), Table 20. Copyright 1966, United Nations. Reproduced by permission.
**United Nations, *Demographic Yearbook,* 16th ed. (Lake Success, 1964), Table 22. Copyright 1964, United Nations. Reproduced by permission.

Table 11.   Deaths Due to Firearms in 16 Countries of the World
Total Number and Rate per 100,000 Population

Country	Homicide Number	Homicide Rate	Suicide Number	Suicide Rate	Accident Number	Accident Rate
United States, 1963	5,126	2.7	9,595	5.1	2,263	1.2
Australia, 1963	61	.56	336	3.1	87	.80
Belgium, 1963	24	.26	64	.69	10	.11
Canada, 1963	99	.52	556	2.9	150	.80
Denmark, 1962	6	.13	59	1.3	15	.32
England and Wales, 1963	24	.05	161	.34	77	.16
France, 1962	584	1.3	777	1.7	265	.56
German Federal Rep., 1962	68	.12	438	.80	93	.17
Ireland, 1963	—	—	7	.25	15	.53
Italy, 1962	351	.70	362	.73	181	.36
Japan, 1962	37	.04	93	.10	90	.09
Netherlands, 1963	3	.03	11	.09	4	.03
New Zealand (excl. Maoris), 1962	4	.17	39	1.7	6	.26
Scotland, 1963	3	.06	20	.38	13	.25
Sweden, 1963	8	.11	163	2.1	27	.36
Switzerland, 1962	—	—	—	—	26	.46

Source: Carl Bakal, *The Right to Bear Arms* (New York: McGraw-Hill Book Co., 1966), Appendix IV.

the previously mentioned study, the incidence of a crime by firearms is affected both by the readiness to use weapons, a characteristic that is often "culture bound" and by the availability of firearms. Here, as in the case of the inter-state comparisons, the argument that one nation has several factors pre-disposing it to violent crime does not detract from the position that certain types of gun control laws may exacerbate the situation. The treatment of intervening variables that has been utilized throughout this discussion is primarily an illustrative approach to the problem; a much more elaborate analysis, isolating and measuring a considerable number of the possible rele-vant variables would be necessary in order to closely specify the relative influence of these factors and that of gun availability upon rates of violence. However, what must be shown here is that these "predispositional" factors do not completely account for the substantially different homicide rates of the United States and the other advanced industrial states.

Table 12

Country	Population Per Sq. Kilometer 1961(a)	Population Per Sq. Kilometer 1963(b)	GNP ($Millions) 1957 (c)	Pop. (1,000) 1963 (e)	Income Distribution Before Taxes: GINI Index of Inequality (d)
United States	20	20	443,270	189,417	.397
France	83	87	41,563	47,854	
Sweden	17	17	10,166	7,604	.399
Japan	254	259	27,844	95,899	
Canada	2	2	32,291	18,925	.390
England and Wales	217	212	61,379	47,028	.366
Switzerland	133	140	7,305	5,770	
Belgium	301	304	10,748	9,290	
West Germany	217	224	49,906	55,430	.473
Soviet Union	10	10	121,920		
Italy	164	168	25,003	50,641	.403
Spain	61	62	8,630	31,077	

Sources: [a] United Nations, *Statistical Yearbook 1962* (Lake Success, 1963), Table 1, pp. 26, 34–35. Copyright 1963, United Nations. Reproduced by permission.
[b] United Nations, *Demographic Yearbook 1964*, 16th ed. (Lake Success, 1964), Table 4, pp. 120–130. Copyright 1964, United Nations. Reproduced by permission.
[c] Mikoto Usui and E. E. Hagen, *World Income 1957* (Cambridge, Mass.: Center for International Studies, M.I.T. c/59–25), pp. 11–18.
[d] Based on Bruce M. Russet, *et al., World Handbook of Political and Social Indicators* (New Haven: Yale University Press, 1964), Table 71, p. 245.
[e] United Nations, *Demographic Yearbook 1967*, 19th ed. (Lake Success, 1967), Table 1, p. 97. Copyright 1967, United Nations. Reproduced by permission.

The United States has the highest homicide rate and gun homicide rate of all the listed countries. All but three of the countries being compared have denser populations than the U.S. At least these three have greater degrees of economic inequality. Seven countries (Italy, West Germany, Belgium, Switzerland, France, Japan and Spain) had greater increases in density of population per square kilometer than the United States, and also had lower homicide and gun homicide rates. Italy, in particular, has several characteristics that would predispose it toward high homicide rates—fairly dense population and poorly distributed income—yet its homicide and gun homicide rates are considerably lower than that of the U.S. In addition, Canada had a frontier tradition and despite this had a rate of .52 firearms homicides in 1963 compared to 2.7 in the United States.

Homicide rates, particularly in such places as Latin America, are often correlated with "political instability." In the context of the following study, political stability is defined in terms of deaths from domestic group violence. The United States, according to this listing, is among the most "stable" countries of the world. At the same time in terms of murder statistics, and particularly murders by firearms, it outdistances even the most unstable of the industrial states listed here.

Similar to this analysis is the study by Ted Gurr, a Princeton University political scientist, who ranked 114 nations on the overall violence in their societies for 1961–65. The United States was ranked as number forty-two. Overall violence included the number of homicides, insurrections, riots, strikes, political terrorism, and civil war. Among the fifty nations he classed as functioning democracies (in order to separate out "authoritarian" states

Table 13

Country	Deaths from Domestic Group Violence per 1,000,000 Population (1950–1962)
Belgium	.9
Soviet Union	.7
France	.3
Italy	.2
Spain	.2
Japan	.1
West Germany	.02
United States	.01

Source: Based on Bruce M. Russet, *et al.*, *World Handbook of Political and Social Indicators* (New Haven: Yale University Press, 1964), Table 29, pp. 99–100.

where violence is checked by repression) fifteen ranked as more violent than the U.S. in total civil strife.[70] Here again, the stability of the U.S. according to these measures contrasts markedly with the evidence of its homicide statistics.

Thus, when we turn from comparisons within the United States, where variation in the availability of guns is quite limited, to international comparisons where the variation in the availability of guns is considerable, the view that the presence of guns significantly influences homicide and gun homicide rates receives much more persuasive support.

GUN OWNERS AND GUN CONTROL

By clearly indicating that variations in the availability of guns do significantly influence overall rates of homicide as well as gun homicides, the international comparisons suggest that the high rate of gun-caused injury and death in the United States is not primarily a consequence of environmental or cultural factors and only coincidentally associated with extremely lenient gun-ownership policies. On the contrary, the American rates of gun-caused injury and death are indicated to be a cost deriving in large measure from the maintenance of those gun policies—a cost which should be reviewed in terms of the utility of guns to their owners and either intentionally accepted, or reduced by reducing the availability of guns.

Such an analysis requires a detailed examination of the varying ways in which firearms are presently being used in the U.S., and of the costs and benefits that would be associated with restricting these uses in various possible degrees, up to and including domestic disarmament. The categories of domestic gun owners to be considered are: those people who keep guns for protection of their homes and businesses, hunters, police and habitual criminals, target shooters, and gun collectors. These groups will be considered roughly in order of their numerical size, and in each case the approximate rates of gun-caused injuries and deaths associated with the particular category of gun use will be noted, and the possible effect of three increasingly severe forms of gun control upon these casualties and upon the group's gun use will be discussed. While the particular form of the three possible levels of gun control to be discussed will vary somewhat, they will generally include: first, general registration of all firearms, with only a few categories of people prohibited from owning guns; second, an intermediary form of restrictive licensing, the prohibition of domestic ownership of handguns; and finally, domestic disarmament, under which arrangement only a few

---

[70] William M. Carley and Earl C. Gottschalk, Jr., "How Violent Are We?" *The Wall Street Journal* (June 25, 1968).

categories of people other than the military will possess firearms. Although these forms of gun control are among the more commonly discussed possibilities, they have been selected essentially arbitrarily from among the extensive range of possible gun control arrangements, in order to serve as illustrations of a continuum of increasingly restrictive components of gun control systems, and not to suggest their adequacy as total patterns of gun control.

With regard to the benefits to be derived from gun control it will be useful to consider both the absolute size of the various categories of gun users and indications of the degree to which they contribute to gun-caused death, injury, and crime rates. The costs of gun control to be considered are primarily the inconvenience or deprivation which each type of gun user would experience as a result of the imposition of the varying degrees of gun control.

FIREARMS AS PROTECTION

A 1968 Harris Survey indicated that approximately one-half of the 60 million households in the U.S. have at least one gun, and of these households, 6 million have four or more firearms.[71] While guns are kept in households for many reasons (*e.g.,* storage of hunting and target-shooting weapons as well as for protection of the household), a 1966 poll indicated that two out of three of the 30 million householders with guns list "protection of the household" as one of the reasons for having a gun. Additionally, a 1968 poll indicated that guns are kept for protection in 26 percent of retail business establishments.[72] While a certain proportion of the "protection" weapons may be long guns, primarily intended for hunting or target shooting, it can be assumed that most of the handguns kept in homes are intended as means of protection since these weapons are difficult to use in target shooting and are of little use for hunting. Of the estimated 90 million guns in civilian hands, somewhat more than two-thirds are rifles and shotguns (35 million and 31 million respectively).[73] These long guns are owned more often by rural than urban residents. Less than a third of the civilian guns are handguns (24 million) and these are spread fairly evenly across rural and urban areas, with a slightly higher rate of possession in small towns and large cities.[74]

What costs and benefits would the variously restrictive systems of gun

---

[71] Newton and Zimring, *op. cit.,* p. 9.

[72] *Ibid.,* p. 61.

[73] *Ibid.,* p. 6.

[74] *Ibid.,* p. 11.

control entail for those 20 million homes where guns are perceived as providing protection? Perhaps the basic element to be considered in estimating the "costs" of gun control with regard to the use of guns as household protection is that it is widely agreed that, in general, firearms do not provide the household with protection. Intrusions into the home by burglars or robbers are rarely prevented by firearms. Burglars usually do not encounter the homeowner, often entering the premises in his absence, and robbers who confront their victims generally give the homeowner little chance to use his weapon successfully. The large majority of intrusions into the home are burglaries[75] and weapons in the home are much more apt to be stolen (and possibly converted to criminal use) than they are to prevent a burglary or robbery. An examination of Detroit police records indicated that "not more than two in a thousand burglaries in Detroit are foiled by shooting the burglar."[76] Similarly, firearms have not been successful in preventing home robberies and it is estimated that "perhaps two percent of home robberies appear to result in the firearms death or injury of the robber."[77]

An extended version of the viewpoint that guns provide the individual with protection is evident in the behavior of various militant groups (*e.g.*, the Minutemen, and the Black Panthers) who suggest that they can promote their interests more effectively as a consequence of being heavily armed. As is the case with home protection firearms, while this behavior may have some symbolic, psychological value for the participants, it has little practical utility (as these armed groups do not begin to threaten the power of the state), and its immediate consequence is a heightened possibility of gun accidents and homicides.

The question of the usefulness of protection weapons in businesses in high-crime areas is somewhat more ambiguous. While the owner is still at a great tactical disadvantage compared to the robber, and is risking his life to prevent what is often only a moderate loss, fewer tangential risks are incurred than is the case in the home and the gun may serve as a deterrent to some degree.

Since no significant benefit is derived from the availability of firearms for protection of the home, the primary impact of their presence upon the household's actuarial profile is a considerable increase in the likelihood that those who live there will be injured or killed. Sixty percent of the country's firearms accidents occur in the home.[78] Approximately 14,000 firearms accidents occur annually in or around American homes, leading to 1,600

---

[75] *Statistical Abstract of the United States 1968*, p. 143.
[76] *Ibid.*, p. 63.
[77] *Ibid.*
[78] *Ibid.*, p. 30.

deaths.[79] Eighty-six percent of the women and 84 percent of the children accidentally killed by guns die in the home. Additionally a significant proportion of the 82 percent of the total homicides that take place among relatives and acquaintances may be presumed to occur in or around the home.

Accordingly, for the owners of home-protection firearms, the primary consequences of the establishment of a system of gun control will be a decrease in the risks of death, injury, and involvement in an unpremeditated homicide. Additionally these risks may be expected to decrease roughly in the degree that the restrictions eliminate all firearms from the home.

The establishment of the most lenient form of gun control, essentially unrestrictive registration of all firearms, can be expected to have practically no impact on the risks generated by home-protection firearms. However, an intermediary program, the restrictive licensing or prohibition of civilian handgun ownership, would seem to decrease the probability of a "heat of anger" gun homicide since handguns are involved in a high proportion of such murders. However, the major decrease in the risks of death, injury, and involvement in an unpremeditated homicide would seem to occur only when all firearms, both those primarily intended for home defense and those available for this purpose although primarily intended for other uses, are removed from the household—essentially a state of domestic disarmament.

HUNTERS

Hunters constitute the largest single, clearly defined category of gun users, numbering between 19 and 25 million.[80] Both the rate of ownership of hunting weapons and the proportions of the population who hunt are higher in the southern and western sections of the country than in the Northeast[81] and higher in rural areas (42 percent of rifles and 53 percent of shotguns are owned by rural residents) and small towns than in cities and suburbs.

The National Safety Council has estimated that hunting leads to an average of 9,000 casualties each year, of which 700 are fatal. In the majority of these cases the injured individual is shot by someone else.[82] Examination of the circumstances of hunting accidents in Minnesota and New York suggest the possibility that more rigorous licensing procedures for hunters could reduce the accident rate. Extensive case studies, involving a three-hour

---

[79] *Ibid.*, p. 32.

[80] Bakal, *op. cit.*, p. 69.

[81] Richard E. Snyder, "Guns in Today's Economy," *The World of Guns*, E. B. Morgan, ed. (Skokie, Illinois: Publishers Development Corporation, 1964), p. 26.

[82] Bakal, *op. cit.*, p. 237.

Figure 3.   Percent of U.S. Households Owning Various Firearms, by Region. (United States, 1968).

Source: George D. Newton and Franklin E. Zimring: *Firearms and Violence in American Life.* A Staff Report to the National Commission on the Causes and Prevention of Violence (Washington, D.C.: U.S. Government Printing Office, 1969), p. 10.

interview and the administration of the Minnesota Multiphasic Personality Inventory (MMPI) were conducted on 93 of the 130 hunters who had been involved in accidents in Minnesota in 1953.[83] Of the seventy-four hunters who had been involved in major accidents, 77 percent were found to have faulty vision, two-thirds of these having poor depth perception. Sixty percent of the hunters who had killed or wounded other hunters while

---

[83] Bakal, *op. cit.*, pp. 243–244.

mistaking them for deer were color-blind. All of the men who were mistaken for deer and shot had been wearing red clothing. On the basis of the hunters admitting to previous accidents, the study also found that "the shooter who has caused one accident is 100 times as likely to cause another as the average hunter is to have his first accident."[84] The older New York report suggested that 80 percent of the 130 hunting accidents analyzed were in part caused by poor eyesight.[85]

These observations suggest that hunters confront two rather distinct sources of danger. One is the sort of danger, which given the nature of the activity, is probably endemic to hunting; traveling through fields and forests intent on shooting other animals, hunters will probably always shoot one another and themselves. These are the sort of accidents emphasized in the NRA's Uniform Hunter Casualty reports, where either human failings which are presumably ineradicable in some portion of most groups of men, such as carelessness or ignorance, cause hunters to shoot someone while moving a loaded rifle over a fence or out of a car or unpredictable tricks of fate, such as a rifle's trigger being caught by a bush, lead to accidents. The other sort of danger, referred to in the two reports mentioned above, is due to human failings that presumably can be easily and accurately detected in most groups of men, such as color blindness, faulty depth perception, poor general vision, or a history of previous firearms accidents.

Overall it seems possible that gun control laws of three differing degrees of severity could achieve three different kinds of savings in terms of deaths and injuries caused by hunters' firearms. Initially, relatively mild restrictions on who would be licensed to own a gun (ideally coupled with even stricter provisions for hunting licenses) in terms of physical condition, including vision, and previous record, including firearms accidents, would seem likely to eliminate some of the more predictable casualties due to hunters who are demonstrably accident prone or physically deficient. Public opinion polls have repeatedly indicated that not only the general public, but also gun owners favor stricter gun laws, including the registration of all guns and the prohibition of certain categories of people from possessing them.[86] Accordingly the savings associated with such a system of licensing could be achieved with practically no widely perceived sacrifices by hunters.

A second, and considerably more severe form of gun control for hunters, associated with a general civilian disarmament, is the establishment of depositories for firearms, maintained by hunting and sporting clubs. Members would be allowed to sign out their weapons for appropriate purposes but

---

[84] Quoted in Bakal, *op. cit.,* p. 243.
[85] *Ibid.*
[86] *New York Times,* June 9, 1968; April 23, 1968; *Gallup Poll,* September 14, 1966.

would be required to return them to the depository. The storage of hunting weapons in depositories, and not in the home, as an adjunct to a general domestic disarmament, with its potential saving of 14,000 accidental firearms casualties a year, seems likely to be a more widely acceptable arrangement than a total domestic disarmament.

Another intermediary possibility, that of banning handguns, and its limited impact on hunting has already been discussed. A variety of other intermediary restrictions are also possible, such as the banning of high-powered rifles with their capacity to kill and wound far beyond the hunter's field of vision.

The final, and most complete form of gun control—domestic disarmament—would terminate firearms-inflicted hunting accidents along with gun hunting. However, from the hunter's viewpoint, the savings offered by halting gun hunting have not to date been perceived as justifying the cost. In part this decision may be seen as equitable, since to a considerable extent hunters in the field threaten one another rather than uninvolved bystanders. However, the youth of many of the victims of hunting accidents (45 percent involve teen-agers)[87] raises the question of the degree to which they are experienced enough to evaluate and accept the risks involved in hunting.

Overall, however, the use of depositories for hunting weapons in conjunction with a domestic disarmament seems to offer the highest net return by permitting the household to be disarmed without ending hunting.

POLICE AND CRIMINALS

Another significant category of gun users are those individuals whose means of making a living involve the use of threats of force against other people. Such groups would include police officers and armed guards, and alternatively, those criminals whose regular activities involve the threat of violent assault upon others—particularly armed robbers.

In 1966 there were 437,000 police officers employed by all levels of government, 369,000 of these being employed by local governments.[88]

With regard to criminal activity our concern here is not with the situationally induced or impulsive criminal act (the role of firearms as a facilitating or precipitating factor in a large number of homicides has already been discussed), but rather with more calculated, or habitual criminal activities in which guns play a major role, most notably with armed robbery. While estimates of the number of individuals involved are difficult to obtain, there

---

[87] Bakal, *op. cit.*, p. 239.
[88] *Statistical Abstract of the United States 1968*, p. 149.

were 153,000 robberies recorded in 1966[89] approximately 36 percent of which were armed robberies committed with guns.[90] In New York City from 1965 to 1968 firearms robberies led to fatalities at a rate of 5.5 per 1,000 robberies. Additionally, of course, firearms are involved in a variety of other criminal acts.

With regard to the possible application of gun controls to police, it should be noted that although discussions of gun control have occasionally involved reference to police shooting bystanders and observations that British police are able to operate without firearms, it does not seem likely that American police would be asked to abandon their weapons until evidence was available of a major reduction in the use of firearms by criminals. Such a development seems unlikely under any arrangement short of an effective domestic disarmament.

Less stringent forms of gun control, however, can be predicted to have an impact upon the ease with which criminals can obtain and utilize firearms. Even a minimally strict form of gun control, the requirement that all firearms and particularly handguns be registered and that certain categories of persons, including those with criminal records, cannot possess them would both partially inhibit criminal access to guns and, perhaps more significantly, facilitate the ability of police to prevent criminal activity. While a criminal legally prohibited by such a law from obtaining a gun would no doubt succeed in circumventing the law, his illegal possession of the weapon provides a basis for the police to take action against him, quite possibly before he uses the weapon in a more serious crime, or when his present participation in a more serious crime cannot be easily demonstrated. This function of a firearms registration law was pointed out in 1934 by a defender of New York State's Sullivan Law:

> One benefit to be derived from this type of firearms legislation is that it provides a basis for easily convicting gun-carrying gangsters when witnesses have been intimidated or when there is not sufficient evidence to prove guilt beyond a reasonable doubt for a major offense. Proving that a gunman possessed a gun without a license is a simple matter compared with proving that he participated in a bank robbery. It is a type of "public enemy" statute, simple in operation.[91]

A more stringent form of gun control which could be expected to lead to a notable drop in criminal firearms use, and very probably to an associated drop in some overall crime rates is the prohibition, or extremely re-

---

[89] *Statistical Abstract of the United States 1968*, p. 143.

[90] Newton and Zimring, *op. cit.*, p. 46.

[91] John Brabner-Smith, *Law and Contemporary Problems* I (1934), quoted in Bakal, *op. cit.*, pp. 154–155.

strictive licensing, of handguns. The characteristics of handgun use in the U.S. make these weapons a particularly apt site for the use of gun controls to reduce both the criminal use of guns and overall crime rates. Handguns have few legitimate domestic uses; they are neither good hunting weapons, nor easily or widely used target guns. Their use as protection weapons, already discussed, tends to be ineffective, providing instead an illusion of protection while actually entailing increased risks of death and injury for those "protected." Additionally they constitute a relatively small proportion (somewhat more than a quarter) of privately owned firearms. However, handguns figure centrally in the criminal use of guns, constituting 96 percent of the guns used in robberies, 86 percent of the guns used in aggravated assaults, and 76 percent of the guns used in homicides. While prohibition of domestic handgun ownership would take time to become effective, it could be expected to eventually lead to a significant reduction in criminal handgun use. Additionally, the requirements of criminal gun use suggest that the missing handguns could, in most instances, not be replaced by the still legal long guns. The visibility and awkwardness of long gun possession and use would prevent their use in many criminal activities. The Task Force on Firearms concluded with regard to this question, "even though such a system [restrictive handgun licensing] would not reduce long gun ownership, it would not appear to risk a massive shift to the use of long guns in crime."[92] Finally the absence of handguns might well reduce the overall incidence of certain types of crimes. Homicides have already been discussed. With regard to robbery, a psychiatric investigator, reporting to the Firearms Task Force on a series of interviews with criminals, noted:

> Robbery appears to be a crime made infinitely more possible by having a gun. To rob without one requires a degree of strength, size and confidence which was lacking in many of the men with whom I spoke. . . . For the most part the men involved in robbery were not very large and not very strong. Some were not very aggressive. Some of these men could not possibly carry out a robbery without a gun. In short, there was a clear reality element in the need for a gun once a man made the decision to rob. . . .[93]

Thus overall, the prohibition of handguns would seem to be an effective way of limiting crime through fairly stringent gun controls.

Finally, essentially total domestic disarmament could reasonably be expected to eliminate most forms of criminal gun use, and achieve the goals mentioned in association with the prohibition of handguns in an even more secure manner. For, in a situation in which there are still legitimate uses for firearms, individuals can attempt to circumvent the existing laws

---

[92] Newton and Zimring, *op. cit.,* p. 127.
[93] *Ibid.,* p. 47.

without necessarily calling attention to their purposes. However, in a condition of domestic disarmament the difficulty of obtaining or utilizing firearms is multiplied many times, for in such circumstances it would be very hard to suggest that any activity or inquiry related to firearms was innocently or conventionally motivated.

TARGET SHOOTERS AND GUN COLLECTORS

Target shooters and gun collectors are two other categories of gun owners whose relationship to gun control or disarmament should be briefly considered. Although the formal sporting organizations, the Amateur Trapshooting Association, a group of 500 local clubs, and the National Skeet Shooting Association, a group of 450 clubs, are indicated to have memberships of only 25,000 and 10,500 respectively, the number of less formally organized target shooters are estimated to be much greater, perhaps as high as 4–5 million.[94] Although target shooters do suffer or inflict injuries on occasion, particularly when firing informally on unsupervised ranges, in general they do not seem to have accidents in the field at anything like the rate that hunters do. While their safety record in the field may be paralleled by greater than average caution about the handling of guns in the home, it still seems likely that target shooters and their weapons contribute substantially to the rates of gun-inflicted accidental deaths and injuries which occur in American households. Accordingly, it seems likely that increasingly stringent gun controls would not reduce accidents due to target shooters until these restrictions led to the removal of firearms from the household. Similarly, it seems likely that little further reduction in death and injuries due to target shooters would be forthcoming even if all domestic firearms were banned altogether. Thus, even more strongly than was the case with hunters, the use of depositories to store target-shooting weapons would seem to be the level of gun control restrictiveness productive of the greatest savings accompanied by the least cost to the target shooters.

Since the 750,000 to 1,000,000 gun collectors in the United States do not, in general, fire their weapons enough to pose a notable safety problem, their primary relevance to a possible system of gun control lies in the fact that most of these individuals (85 percent)[95] collect handguns. However, if the guns were both rendered incapable of firing and registered, the danger of their being illegally used, or stolen, would be greatly reduced, without fundamentally altering their value to the collectors.

Thus we have examined a number of categories of firearms owners with regard to the uses they put their guns to and the risks associated with the

---

[94] Bakal, *op. cit.*, p. 72.
[95] Koller, *Hand Guns*, p. 128.

differing forms of gun possession. The results have suggested a mixed pattern of gun controls. In several instances (home-protection weapons and handguns), the pursuit of a total disarmament seemed a desirable course. The current use of the weapons was either generally ineffective or undesirable, and their prohibition seemed likely to reduce both criminal and accidental casualties. In some other categories of gun use, however (hunting and target shooting), an intermediate form of gun control, the use of depositories, seemed preferable as it would achieve significant savings in casualties in the home without severely hampering the groups' legitimate use of their weapons. Finally, the needs of one category of gun owner, the gun collectors, posed few inherent risks and were sufficiently compatible with safety procedures (disarming and registering the weapons) so that only minimal interference with the gun owners' activities was suggested.

SUMMARY

Overall then, we have approached the question of the usefulness of gun control and domestic disarmament from two perspectives. Initially we investigated the general proposition that a decrease in the availability of firearms will lead to lowered rates of violent injury and death. This involved, first, a consideration of the arguments advanced by the advocates and opponents of gun control legislation concerning the main causal factors leading to variation in homicide rates, and secondly, the examination of data from both American and international comparative studies in an effort to clarify the relative importance of these differing causal factors and thus to arrive at an estimate of the potential utility of gun control measures. The American comparative data did not seem to provide an adequate basis for arriving at a conclusion because one of the two causal factors being compared, the availability of guns, only exhibited a small range of its possible variation in this context. The international comparisons, however, did include wide variation in both forms of causal variable, and in this context it was implied that variations in the availability of firearms have a significant independent effect upon homicide rates, and that gun control—especially domestic disarmament—can reduce the American rates of death and injury.

Secondly, oriented by this general indication of the utility of gun control measures, we turned to the specific categories of gun use in the United States, and considering the probable cost and benefits of varying degrees of gun control in terms of each group's form of gun use and its associated dangers, we arrived at the conclusion that since complete domestic disarmament would achieve the maximum savings in lives, injuries, and decreased crime rates, but also maximize the cost to legitimate gun users, the adoption of a varied, but still highly restrictive approach to the different categories of gun user could achieve largely the same benefits, with much lower costs.

5

CONCLUSIONS

THE "DEPTH" OF SHORTCUTS

We have traced in some detail how a variety of technological shortcuts can contribute to the solution or reduction of a number of domestic problems. We have been concerned both with the effects of the use of technological shortcuts, and with the quality of the data reporting those effects. Up to this point this dual concern (imposed by the necessity of evaluating the adequacy of the information bearing on the technologies' effectiveness) has been fused in our discussion. Turning now from the specific cases of technological remedies to a more abstract and general consideration of technological shortcuts, we will be able to separate these two issues. Initially, in the context of a number of other approaches to guided social change, we will consider reasons why technological shortcuts may be particularly useful. Next we deal with factors hampering the acquisition of information about remedial social programs and about the technology that could be used by these programs. Subsequently the two concerns fuse again as we discuss tailoring technological shortcuts to differing portions of the target populations. This is a means of increasing the effectiveness of the technological remedies that is particularly hampered by inadequate information. We conclude with a discussion of the influence of the governmental context on the development of technology, and of the normative questions raised by the impact of technology on society.

In each of the cases studied and in many others not reported here, we encountered an argument, often used by the opponents of accelerated solutions of particular social problems, which suggests that the proposed shortcuts deal only with the symptoms of the problems and do not get at its fundamental causes, that they are only illusory solutions and cannot really handle the problems. Occasionally this is viewed as almost a matter of definition. The word "shortcut" evokes an image of superficiality, of nonstructural, illusory solutions. However, these connotations are misleading; no such implication is included in either our technical use of the term, or in its common dictionary definition. A shortcut simply means a shorter way of getting to the same place. Or, viewed more abstractly in terms of costs, the use of fewer resources, less psychological strain, and less effort to achieve a stated goal. The correct image is of a path across a field which, if one chooses to take, obviates traveling over a long, circuitous road leading to the same place. Shortcuts may entail some adaptive changes, some redistribution of resources compared to previous approaches to the problem, but not an alteration of the goal. Of course shortcuts may be false; offering no saving, or leading to lesser goals. This would argue for *true* shortcuts—not against all shortcuts. Surely we deal here with true economics in costs and pain. Also, it might be useful to compare technological shortcuts not to ideal and unattainable alternatives, but to available strategies. Hence, before reviewing a number of the ways in which technological shortcuts can profitably contribute to the solution, or alleviation, of domestic problems, it will be useful to review briefly the major alternate approaches to the handling of social problems.[1]

FOUR ALTERNATIVE APPROACHES

The four alternate approaches to domestic problems which primarily compete with the shortcut approach are the liberal reformist approach, the psychotherapeutic approach, the rationalistic social planning approach, and the revolutionary approach.

The Liberal Reformist Approach. One widely held view is that there is nothing basically wrong with the existing approaches to our social problems as practiced by the Office of Economic Opportunity and the state and local welfare administrations and school systems, and that instead, what is missing is the necessary resources. It is suggested that given the necessary billions of dollars one could renovate and significantly improve the schools, and also provide sufficient welfare and medical services. This is, for instance, the main idea behind the famous "Title I" Act under which resources are provided to schools in order to service disadvantaged children, in the hope that by giving them more classrooms, books, and teaching aids they will become able to "catch up" with middle-class children. The same basic "resource" view is also behind the new welfare plan of the Nixon administration, which emphasizes increases in income as the primary tool in the war against poverty rather than psychotherapy or other attempts to change people's personalities or their social groupings.

However, the many adherents of this view are confronted with the following situation: the resources needed to transform the "basic conditions"

---

[1] This concluding chapter, prepared later than the substantive chapters, contains some material published after the data reviewed there.

in contemporary America are unavailable and unlikely to be available in the near future. The resources now available to the cities for the service of their needs are only a small fraction of those needed to adequately handle them. To put one patrolman, around the clock, on each city block of New York City could be done—at the cost of $25 billion a year.[2] Mayor John V. Lindsay testified before Congress that he needed $100 billion to rebuild New York's slums; at the present rate, it would take forty years before such an amount would be available to eliminate *all* American slums. With regard to all needs, a study by the National Planning Association calculated that if the United States sought, by 1985, to realize the modest goals specified by the Eisenhower Commission on National Goals, it would (assuming even a 4 percent growth rate in GNP) be at least $150 billion a year short. When President Johnson signed the 1968 Housing and Urban Development Act, he sought the elimination of substandard housing within the next ten years. However, others have observed that if this "part of the program is to be realized, the Government will have to subsidize 10 times more units than it did in the last decade."[3] George A. Christie, chief economist of the McGraw-Hill Information Systems Company, has suggested that the elimination of substandard housing units (6 million in all) would cost over $100 billion for the ten-year period.[4] Similarly the development of mental health facilities in local communities illustrates the significant gap existing between available resources and the funds needed for adequate functioning. The National Institute of Mental Health has estimated that the average cost of constructing one local center is about $1.3 million; and the construction of the requisite 2,000 centers would cost $2.6 billion. Operating expenses are estimated to run about $1.2 million per year for one center, making a total of $2.4 billion per year for the operation of 2,000 centers. However, President Johnson's budget for the 1967–68 fiscal year provided only $50 million for the construction of community mental health centers.[5]

But even if the economic resources were available, and the political will to use them for social improvement were present, we would still face other severe shortages, principally professional manpower. In the United States in 1965 there were an estimated four to five million alcoholics, approximately 575,000 patients in mental hospitals, and 1,071,000 out-patients receiving psychiatric services.[6] To serve them there were about 1,100 psychoanalysts and 7,000 certified psychotherapists. If each therapist could treat fifty

---

[2] *New York Times,* June 3, 1969.

[3] *New York Times,* March 16, 1969.

[4] *Ibid.*

[5] Frank Leonard, "Shortchanging the Mentally Ill," *The New Leader* (August 28, 1967).

[6] Statistics based on information from the National Institute of Mental Health.

patients intensively, a staggering figure by present standards, this would still leave most alcoholic and mental patients without adequate treatment. Today most of those in mental hospitals are not treated at all: only 2 percent of the hospital staffs in 1964 were psychiatrists, only 10 percent were professionals of *any* sort; most of the staff are "attendants," more than half of whom have not completed high school and only 8 percent of whom have had any relevant training. The manpower shortage is not limited only to the professionals. George Christie has estimated that the construction industry would need 4.5 million workers to meet the building demands in 1978. A net gain of nearly 1.25 million construction workers is needed in order to maintain the projected level of housing.[7] Furthermore, Sterling E. Sonderlind has pointed out that "setting high priorities for the housing and urban development goals [listed by the President's Commission on National Goals in the early 1960s][8] would demand increases in many skilled crafts at rates far above the recent growth in these occupations."[9] The Center for Priority Analysis of the National Planning Association has reported that the urban development goal alone would require 7,000 more carpenters each year than are currently trained. Moreover, during the period 1957–1965, the United States experienced a decrease of 50,000 carpenters.[10]

The community mental health center program would also create an excessive demand for trained personnel, who do not exist at the present in the requisite numbers. If the program is implemented, the centers will "require 100,000 psychiatric nurses and 40,000 other professionals. Yet the President's budget for 1967–68 allows 110 fewer fellowships in the mental health field than were given the previous year."[11] Other health areas presently faced with shortages of trained personnel will be under much more severe pressure if future demands are to be met. A shortage of doctors, nurses, and dentists may prevent attainment of the goal of adequate health services for the majority of Americans. Some 18,000 new doctors are needed each year; and since American medical schools are expected to produce only 8,700 doctors annually, a growing deficit results, one which is not likely to be covered by the immigration of foreign physicians. Similarly, only about 3,200 dentists a year graduated during the 1960s; and on the basis of present projections, at least 5,000 dentists a year will have to be added to the professional manpower pool.[12] Areas such as social welfare are also seen as

---

[7] *New York Times,* March 16, 1969, p. 7, "Business and Finance."

[8] *Wall Street Journal,* July 7, 1969.

[9] Sterling E. Sonderlind, "The Outlook," *Wall Street Journal* (July 7, 1969).

[10] *Ibid.*

[11] Frank Leonard, "Shortchanging the Mentally Ill," *The New Leader* (August 28, 1967).

[12] Sonderlind, *op. cit.*

calling "for an average growth of nearly 20,000 social workers through 1975, compared with yearly increases of about 5,000 in the recent past."[13] The Department of Housing and Urban Development (HUD) is encouraging city planning, but there are few city planners.

More immediately the projections for the next few years suggest that a relatively small amount of the total available resources will be shifted to domestic priorities. The defense budget has already been cut and no major additional cuts are expected.[14] While it has been widely hoped that after the Vietnam involvement diminishes, major resources will become available for domestic use, a number of facts suggest that this belief is quite optimistic. The funds which will actually be available are of a much smaller order. It was argued by some that, once the war in Vietnam was ended, the nation could transfer the $24.5 to $32.5 billion now spent each year on the war (estimates of the costs vary) to the treatment of its domestic problems. Pessimists pointed out that Congress could not be expected to transfer all of these funds to the domestic front and suggested a deal: part of the funds would be absorbed by reduced taxes (to satisfy the conservatives) in exchange for allocation to the domestic front of $15 billion, of which $10 billion at the least would be devoted to new domestic efforts.

As the 1968 elections drew nearer, however, the press reported that task forces working for the two major presidential candidates were estimating that, for the present, the defense budget would have to remain more or less at its present level even if the war effort was reduced considerably. First, the Pentagon has convinced many people that stocks of war material depleted during the Vietnamese war would have to be replenished. Second, the Department of Defense has maintained that several urgent military needs, especially in the area of technological development, which had not received attention during the war, will require investment in the post-Vietnam period. In short, we could expect only a few billions of dollars to be diverted from military to domestic programs in the near future even if the war were ended immediately. Some increase in federal revenues due to an increased gross national product is expected, but much of this is already committed in the short run for items such as increased salary of government employees, veterans' benefits, and costs due to inflation and other factors. Charles L.

---

[13] *Ibid.*

[14] Although during the 1972 campaign, presidential candidate George McGovern suggested the defense budget could be considerably reduced from the Republican administration's request of $78.3 billion in fiscal 1973 to $58.8 billion. McGovern's reduced budget involved bringing home American troops from Indochina and Korea, cutting troop levels in Europe by one-half, and eliminating a number of defense projects. No attempt is made to evaluate these proposals; we merely note that they have been advanced. [Information gathered from *Facts on File* (January 23–29, 1972), p. 57.]

Schultze analyzed the "fiscal dividend" as "the difference between the automatic rise in federal revenues that accompanies economic growth and the unavoidable expansion in federal expenditures that stems from increasing wages and prices and from other factors. It measures the budgetary resources that will become available without explicit policy decisions."[15] A Brookings Institution study, *Setting National Priorities: The 1973 Budget*, indicates in that year, the excess of revenues over expenditures will be only $1 billion; in 1975, a negative fiscal dividend, or an excess of expenditures over revenues, will come to $17 billion, and in 1977, there will be a $5 billion excess of revenues over expenditures.[16]

One of the factors contributing to this low or negative level of dividend is that a series of tax reductions between 1963 and 1969 have lowered the potential federal revenues. Another factor is that a large part of the revenue growth will be absorbed by built-in expenditure increases. A built-in increase is included in the budget to cover the price raises that occur on the goods and services purchased by the government. Schultze's 1968 projection included "an $11 billion built-in rise in federal civilian outlays between fiscal years 1969 and 1971, excluding social security. Another $8 billion of built-in increases are likely for the succeeding three years."[17] Expenditure items include: federal employees' pay; public assistance and Medicaid; expenditures to "catch-up" to program levels; highway grants; housing subsidies; workload increases; interest on the public debt; price increases; and other general increases.

The defense budget has proved to be the greatest consumer of the available resources. The size of the defense budget depends on a variety of factors, including attempts to project "non-Vietnam military spending on the basis of currently approved military postures, force levels, and commitments." Schultze notes that "the projections have been made on a conservative basis; they assume a significant stretch-out and deferral of a number of existing weapons system procurement programs."[18] There are in process a great number of weapons systems, which will require sizable expenditures over the next few years. These weapon systems include: a new Minuteman II/III program (at an estimated expenditure of $4.6 billion); the installation of the new Poseidon submarine-launched strategic missile; the deployment of the Sentinel "thin anti-Chinese" antiballistic missile system (at a cost of

---

[15] Charles L. Schultze, "Budget Alternatives After Vietnam," *Agenda for the Nation*, ed. Kermit Gordon (Washington, D.C.: The Brookings Institution, 1968), pp. 18, 19.

[16] Charles L. Schultze, Edward R. Fried, Alice M. Rivlin, and Nancy H. Teeters, *Setting National Priorities: The 1973 Budget* (Washington, D.C.: The Brookings Institution, 1972), p. 63.

[17] Schultze, *op. cit.*, pp. 22–23.

[18] *Ibid.*, p. 30.

$5.5 billion). Furthermore, a large Navy shipbuilding program is also getting under way. This would include four nuclear-powered aircraft carriers at a cost of $3.2 billion. A major construction program for conventional destroyers is also being considered. In addition to these programs, there are many new weapons systems about which procurement decisions will have to be made. These include:

> . . . a new main battle tank for the army (being developed jointly with West Germany), a new Navy attack aircraft (VFX–2), a new antisubmarine plane (VSX), a new undersea long-range missile system, a sea-based ABM, and a long-range missile system for surface ships. In addition there will be substantial pressure to expand the existing "thin anti-Chinese" ABM to cover other contingencies.[19]

From the testimony of William W. Kaufmann, Professor of Political Science at the Massachusetts Institute of Technology, certain definite limits seem to emerge as to the size of the defense budget.[20] Reviewing alternative suggested post-Vietnam defense budgets, he found most experts in agreement about the continued high level of defense spending. Charles L. Schultze, a former Director of the Bureau of the Budget, estimated a defense budget of $76 billion by fiscal year (FY) 1974; Cary Kaysen, Director of the Institute for Advanced Study and former aide to President Kennedy, has recommended a budget of $50 billion for 1974 after expenditures for the war in Vietnam have ceased and a strategic arms control agreement with USSR has been reached. Kaufmann has suggested a budget around $60 billion; however, this figure is indicated to be highly variable, with all the variance inclining toward a yet larger budget. Thus in light of the existing evidence, it seems probable that the post-Vietnam defense budget will continue to consume large portions of the federal budget. Edwin L. Dale, Jr. has noted that the surplus, remaining after the defense expenditures, has already been effectively taken up by the expansion of just federal programs alone; the Johnson Cabinet committee "found authoritative proposals, task-force reports, studies and the like 'costing out' various nondefense outlays that added up to $40 billion a year." Already enacted programs in such areas as education would require an outlay of $6 billion to bring them up to their authorized levels. The $40 billion figure "did not include any of the newer ideas, such as a 'negative income tax' to raise the incomes of the poor."[21]

---

[19] *Ibid.*, p. 32.

[20] William W. Kaufmann, *Testimony from Hearings before the Subcommittee on Economy in Government of the Joint Economic Committee*, 91st Congress (June, 1969), pp. 163–179.

[21] Edwin L. Dale, Jr., "What Will We Do With All That Extra Money?" *New York Times Magazine* (February 16, 1969), p. 64.

"In summary . . . over the next two years, from fiscal 1973 to fiscal 1975, expenditures under existing and currently proposed programs are likely to run substantially ahead of full employment revenues. Barring some change either in current policies or in tax laws, a sizable full employment deficit will be forthcoming. Over the subsequent two years the growth of expenditures under existing programs will be somewhat less and the rise in revenues may be higher than expenditures projected under current and proposed programs, but by a very modest amount, well within the range of error inherent in such projections."[22] It is obvious that there simply is not enough surplus to meet all the demands made on the Federal government. Some set of priorities will have to be established and unless some shortcuts to the treatment of the nation's social problems are found, these problems are not likely to be effectively treated in the foreseeable future.

The Psychotherapeutic Approach. Western cultures in general, and Americans in particular, are highly optimistic about man's capacity to change in response to education. It is widely believed, especially by liberals and social scientists, that the human personality is highly pliable; that a young child can be educated to become lower or middle class; and that mental patients can be, at least in principle, rehabilitated. Specifically there is a great belief in the American society, recently revived with the wave of therapeutic groups, sensitivity training, and similar activities, that people can be made to act "humanly" toward each other, and be psychologically "liberated." There is a relatively high level of belief in American society, compared to others in the efficacy of psychotherapy. This faith is evident not only generally among the public and the policy-makers, but in specific remedial programs. It is, for instance, a major tenet subscribed to by most social workers and welfare program workers.

Those who do not adhere to this general view of human malleability include the conservative philosophers and a few social scientists (*e.g.*, Edward Banfield). Additionally, there are those social scientists who assign genetic factors an unusually high degree of significance in influencing human behavior (this movement recently received an added impetus in the work of Arthur Jensen and his followers). Also there are those who believe that many of our domestic problems simply cannot be solved, that people's behavior cannot be significantly altered, that human nature is essentially unchangeable. Additionally over the last five years, after the evident failure of many of the remedial programs begun during the Johnson Administration, some of the reformers, who do not attribute their failure to low funding, do see some genuine difficulties in changing human behavior. Thus overall there has been some increase in pessimism about human malleabil-

---

[22] Schultze, *et al., op. cit.,* p. 48.

ity, but this has been only a limited and comparative increase. Basically, the American leadership and public still remains much more optimistic in its orientation than most Europeans.

Available data, however, seriously impugns this view, at least in regard to psychotherapy. The general American attitude of commitment to, and emphasis on, psychotherapy almost completely disregards the overwhelming evidence about its general ineffectiveness. Most psychotherapists, psychoanalysts, and social workers refuse to treat alcoholics because of the low anticipation of success (in addition to other reasons such as the low prestige of such treatment and the dangers of physical abuse). Similarly, heroin addiction has not been effectively treated by traditional psychotherapeutic methods. More generally, Berelson and Steiner have concluded:

> There is no conclusive evidence that psychotherapy is more effective than general medical counseling or advice in treating neurosis or psychosis. Strictly speaking, it cannot even be considered established that psychotherapy, on the average, improves a patient's chances of recovery beyond what they would be without any formal therapy whatsoever.[23]

However due to the involved methodological difficulties as well as the generally negative results of attempts to evaluate the overall effectiveness of psychotherapeutic treatment, in recent years investigators have turned to documenting more specific changes that occur during the course of psychotherapy. One example of this concern is the study of changes in sexual behavior and attitudes. In these limited areas, some success has been reported. Berelson and Steiner note that "changes toward a more positive attitude regarding sexual activity and toward freer, more enjoyable sexual activity than the patient was previously capable of having are reported as correlates of psychotherapy from several camps."[24] However, they feel that the chances of a patient finishing and benefiting from psychotherapy depend on the presence of certain conditions: the higher the individual's social class and level of education, and the more psychologically sophisticated he is, the more effective his treatment seems to be. Psychotherapy apparently works for those who are less seriously ill and positionally approximate the therapist's own position.

One of the severest critics of psychotherapy has been Hans J. Eysenck.[25] After an extensive review of evaluative studies he states that the effectiveness of psychotherapy is very limited. Reviewing the results obtained from

---

[23] Bernard Berelson and Gary A. Steiner, *Human Behavior: An Inventory of Scientific Findings* (New York: Harcourt, Brace, and World, Inc., 1964), p. 287.

[24] *Ibid.*, p. 290. Research findings in greater detail are reported in Joseph Wolpe, *Psychotherapy by Reciprocal Inhibition* (Stanford: Stanford University Press, 1958).

[25] Hans J. Eysenck, *The Effects of Psychotherapy* (New York: International Science Press, Inc., 1966).

the Cambridge-Somerville Youth Study, he concluded, along with the investigators, that the therapeutic treatment administered to the subjects did not prevent delinquency. This particular study occupies a special place in the history of studies attempting to ascertain the effectiveness of psychotherapy. Eysenck notes:

> It is the only experiment known to us which made use of a properly chosen control group, which used large enough numbers of cases to make the results statistically convincing, which carried on both treatment and follow-up over a sufficiently long period to make the results meaningful, which used objective methods of acknowledged social significance to assess the final outcome, and which investigated the process of therapy itself in an unbiased and properly controlled fashion.[26]

Other studies covered included: the Brill-Beebe Study (1955) of war neurosis; the Barron-Leary Study (1955) of psychoneurotics; the Barendregt Study (1961); and the Lang and Lazovik Study (1964), among many others. On the basis of the findings in these studies, Eysenck concluded that:

> 1. When untreated neurotic control groups are compared with experimental groups of neurotic patients treated by means of psychotherapy, both groups recover to approximately the same extent.
> 2. When soldiers who have suffered a neurotic breakdown and have not received psychotherapy are compared with soldiers who have received psychotherapy, the chances of the two groups returning to duty are approximately the same.
> 3. When neurotic soldiers are separated from the Service, their chances of recovery are not affected by their receiving or not receiving psychotherapy.
> 4. Civilian neurotics who are treated by psychotherapy recover or improve to approximately the same extent as similar neurotics receiving no psychotherapy.
> 5. Children suffering from emotional disorders and treated by psychotherapy recover or improve to approximately the same extent as similar children not receiving psychotherapy.
> 6. Neurotic patients treated by means of psychotherapeutic procedures based on learning theory, improve significantly more quickly than do patients treated by means of psychoanalytic or eclectic psychotherapy, or not treated by psychotherapy at all.[27]

Overall, the results from the studies show that the effects of psychotherapy are likely to be extremely small; the studies additionally reveal that "all

---

[26] *Ibid.*, p. 12.
[27] *Ibid.*, p. 39.

methods of psychotherapy fail to improve on the recovery rate obtained through ordinary life experiences and non-specific treatment."[28]

Eysenck's critics have pointed out that the spontaneous recovery which was observed might not constitute recovery in a broader sense of that term. As Dr. Elizabeth R. Zetzel has noted, spontaneous recovery need not "imply genuine improvement in respect to emotional maturity or realistic achievement."[29] Studies exist indicating psychotherapy to be successful in treating certain types of neuroses, personality disorders, and alcoholism.[30] Jerome Frank has found some improvement among psychotherapeutically treated neurotics.[31] However, in a longer review, Frank has noted that:

> . . . about two-thirds of neurotic patients and 40 percent of schizophrenic patients are improved immediately after treatment, regardless of the type of psychotherapy they have received, and the same improvement rate has been found for patients who have not received any treatment that was deliberately psychotherapeutic.[32]

Furthermore, about 70 percent of the neurotic patients in state hospitals are released, although they have only received custodial care; about the same percentage of neurotic patients who were treated by private physicians have also returned to work. The existing follow-up studies do not reveal differences in long-term improvement associated with different types of treatment. The more severe disturbances show even less of an effect being made by psychotherapy:

> Indeed, with hospitalized psychotics, although certain procedures such as electroconvulsive therapy seem able to accelerate improvement of certain illnesses, no procedure has been shown to produce five-year improvement rates better than those occurring under routine hospital care.[33]

Overall, the effectiveness of psychotherapy is seriously doubted.

The Rationalistic Social Planning Approach. In addition to the approaches to social reform based on the ideas that individuals can be psychologically altered or that we already have the means for societal transforma-

---

[28] *Ibid.*, p. 41.

[29] *Ibid.*, p. 48.

[30] For a review, assembled explicitly to reply to criticisms of psychotherapy's effectiveness, of studies indicating psychotherapy's efficacy in treating neuroses, personality disorders, and alcoholism, see Julian Meltzoff and Melvin Kornreich, "It Works," *Psychology Today,* Vol. 5 (July, 1971), p. 57.

[31] *Ibid.*, pp. 52–54.

[32] Jerome Frank, *Persuasion and Healing* (New York: Shocken Books, 1963), pp. 13–14.

[33] *Ibid.*, p. 14.

tion only we have not committed the resources, there is an approach that hopes to solve domestic problems by altering society on a broad scale. Behind the war on crime, the war on poverty, the idea of changing the relations among races, and the notion of establishing peace among nations, behind all these lies the idea of rational societal planning; the assumption that one can intentionally reorganize society in a major fashion. This orientation is epitomized by rationalistic models of decision-making.

Rationalistic models about how decisions are and ought to be made are widely held. An actor becomes aware of a problem, posits a goal, carefully weighs alternative means, and chooses among them according to his estimates of their respective merit, with reference to the state of affairs he prefers. Criticism of this approach focuses on the disparity between the requirements of the model and the capacities of decision-makers.[34] Social decision-making centers, it is pointed out, frequently do not have a specific, agreed-upon set of values that could provide the criteria for evaluating alternatives. Values, rather, are fluid and are affected by, as well as affect, the decisions made. Moreover, in actual practice, the rationalistic assumption that values and facts, means and ends, can be clearly distinguished seems inapplicable. In addition, information about consequences is, at best, fractional. Decision-makers have neither the assets nor the time to collect the information required for rational choice. While knowledge technology, especially computers, does aid in the collection and processing of information, it cannot provide for the computation required by the rationalist model. (This holds even for chess-playing, let alone "real-life" decisions.) Finally, rather than being confronted with a limited universe of relevant consequences, decision-makers face an open system of variables, a world in which all consequences cannot be surveyed.[35] A decision-maker, attempting to adhere to the tenets of a rationalistic model, will become frustrated, exhaust his resources without coming to a decision, and remain without an effective decision-making model to guide him. Rationalistic models are thus rejected as being at once unrealistic and undesirable.

A less demanding model of decision-making has been outlined in the strategy of "disjointed incrementalism" advanced by Charles E. Lindblom

---

[34] David Braybrooke and Charles E. Lindblom, *A Strategy of Decision* (New York: Free Press, 1963), pp. 48–50 and pp. 111–143; Charles E. Lindblom, *The Intelligence of Democracy* (New York: Free Press, 1965), pp. 137–139; Jerome S. Bruner, Jacqueline J. Goodnow, and George A. Austin, *A Study of Thinking* (New York: John Wiley, 1956), chapters 4–5.

[35] Kenneth J. Arrow, "A Strategy of Decision," *Political Science Quarterly*, Vol. 79 (1964), p. 585; Herbert A. Simon, *Models of Man* (New York: John Wiley, 1957), p. 198; Aaron Wildavsky, *The Politics of the Budgetary Process* (Boston: Little, Brown and Co., 1964), pp. 147–152.

and others.[36] Disjointed incrementalism seeks to adapt decision-making strategies to the limited cognitive capacities of decision-makers and to reduce the scope and cost of information collection and computation. Lindblom summarized the six primary requirements of the model in this way:[37]

1. Rather than attempting a comprehensive survey and evaluation of all alternatives, the decision-maker focuses only on those policies which differ incrementally from existing policies.

2. Only a relatively small number of policy alternatives are considered.

3. For each policy alternative, only a restricted number of "important" consequences are evaluated.

4. The problem confronting the decision-maker is continually redefined: Incrementalism allows for countless ends-means and means-ends adjustments which, in effect, make the problem more manageable.

5. Thus, there is no one decision or "right" solution but a "never-ending series of attacks" on the issues at hand through serial analyses and evaluation.

6. As such, incremental decision-making is described as remedial, geared more to the alleviation of present, concrete social imperfections than to the promotion of future social goals.

Thus, the incrementalists do not see the availability of either the intellect or the information or the resources needed to allow us to plan the reorganization of a whole society, or even the alteration of any major aspect of it. It is suggested that we had best proceed by pursuing a limited alteration; if it works, then the change is extended; if it fails, some other option is explored.

It does not assume a need to know or plan the entire course to a major goal. One can start by identifying a major component of the problem and attempting to focus in on it and handle it, or one can begin the other way around and ask what new effective tools have become available and see if they can be used to cut off a major segment of the social problem without worrying too much about other aspects which you can not immediately handle.

The Revolutionary Approach. The revolutionary approach basically suggests that shortcuts to social change will not work because it is not possible to change social structures one aspect at a time or in part since the components of a social structure hang together, are "interrelated." A complete recasting of the entire social structure is viewed as a necessary condition for handling most, if not all, domestic problems.

---

[36] Charles E. Lindblom, "The Science of 'Muddling Through'," *Public Administration Review*, Vol. 19 (1959), pp. 79–99; Robert A. Dahl and Charles E. Lindblom, *Politics, Economics and Welfare* (New York: Harper and Brothers, 1953); Arrow, *op. cit.*; and Lindblom, *The Intelligence of Democracy*.

[37] Lindblom, *The Intelligence of Democracy*, pp. 144–148.

The question that the revolutionary approach raises with regard to the feasibility of remedial shortcuts is *not* whether or not there are system linkages in society, or whether its parts make a genuine whole; on the contrary, one should take these linkages for granted quite independently of subscribing to the revolutionary approach. The useful question concerns *how tight* the linkages are and in what manner fundamental structural transformations are achieved. If the linkages are not completely tight, if there is leeway and play, then one can approach part of a problem without necessarily dealing with the whole. The leeway may be relatively small or quite considerable, and may differ from one societal sector to another.

The whole issue is related to the continuing debates about the relationship between family institutions and the modern work structure. Social scientists used to hold that you cannot develop a modern urban industrial sector in a country unless the traditional extended family has first been sharply curtailed. As Professor W. J. Goode has pointed out, the older Chinese family, with its nepotism, its clan system, and its cult of ancestors was a definite hindrance to Chinese industrial development. However, he further noted that the Western conjugal family is not the most useful family form either. There is a lack of "fit" between the values of the conjugal family and the requirements of the industrial order.

> What is needed . . . is that the choice of industrial personnel be made purely on the basis of achievement. But this type of choice runs against deep family values: It is ultimately *individual* in character, for talents and skills are individual, not family, traits. By contrast, members of the conjugal family are obligated to help one another because they are *kin* and love one another. A system which sets the goal of a most rapid industrialization, or of a most efficient utilization of its members, would therefore strive to reduce the scope of family ties as much as possible.[38]

Goode points out that the form of the family is not directly linked to the society's degree of industrialization. Family variables have independent effects, and a knowledge of a society's economic and technological conditions does not provide adequate grounds for making accurate predictions about the family structure in the society. The structure and functions of the family are not easily reduced or curtailed even by as fundamental and pervasive a process as industrialization.

Overall, there seems to be considerable "play" in societal structure, with extensive modernization being compatible with traditional family patterns. Only limited adaptations on the family side are adequate to permit tradi-

---

[38] William J. Goode, *World Revolution and Family Patterns* (New York: The Free Press, 1963), p. 24.

tional family structures to continue to operate in the modern situation (*e.g.,* the many studies indicating that extended kinship relations continue to be found in industrialized societies), conversely, a modern industrial system can be, by relatively limited modifications, made to coexist with a quite traditional family structure (*e.g.,* contemporary Japan). So if we qualify the limited social structural relationship highlighted by the revolutionary theory, and allow for considerable leeway in the linkages, then we raise the possibility of very important shortcuts—especially during periods when revolutions are not practical possibilities.

The popular image of revolution is of one clearly discernible traumatic event. Up to the point at which this event, "the revolution," occurs, the society is seen as falling apart, or deteriorating, as Russia was up to 1917; then comes the scene of the masses in the streets, after which the revolutionary forces take over. Actually few serious revolutionary theoreticians think this way. All serious revolutionaries recognize that most historical situations are not ripe for revolution, and accordingly if one wishes to deal with domestic problems in non-revolutionary situations—which may last centuries—then various adaptations are called for and shortcuts have a useful place. And in fact many revolutionary changes in society, or wholly new alternatives, are introduced without distinct, obvious revolutions, as in the development of societies such as England, Scandinavia, and the United States, from agrarian, feudal social systems to industrial, urban, pluralistic societies. In these societies, deviance and innovation created significant, partially new alternatives which then were widely adopted and became the dominant patterns of social interaction while the previously dominant options became subsidiary styles of life. This sort of change amounts to a holistic or revolutionary change in the social structure. Additionally this kind of change seems much more common, and in this sense, much more consequential than the dramatic, revolutionary uprisings. And, even these dramatic uprisings are, without exception, prepared and followed by gradual, partial, accumulative changes. Again it can be seen that by introducing partial, sectoral changes, we can take steps toward the holistic reorganization of social structures. Hence, while it is true that the partial social changes that shortcuts aim at are by definition non-revolutionary, shortcuts and preparation for fundamental changes of society are not mutually exclusive.

The Symptom-Cause Analogue Revised

What we are concerned with here are shortcut approaches which do *not* assume the availability of a very large amount of new resources; which utilize means of solving problems other than psychotherapy; which do not require total planning; and which can be advanced without a revolution.

Symptoms and Partial Changes. Conceiving of social problems as an illness, and of shortcut remedies as the treatment of symptoms of this illness, provides a way of introducing some distinctions which may help considerably in reaching a more subtle definition of the issue at hand. The medical analogue will be retained and an attempt will be made to move from it to insights other than the common, rather superficial observation which distinguishes "basic" causes from "superficial" symptoms and suggests that treating the symptoms is of no merit, as it does not get at the source of the illness.

The dangers of treating the symptoms without attempting to eliminate the underlying processes of the disease itself has been discussed by Dr. Howard Rusk. As he notes, an aspirin may relieve the symptoms of a fever, but also may allow an associated disease to destroy vital organs. This same logic is applied to social disorders as well:

> So it is with social sickness. Too often the focus is on the disturbing symptoms of social unrest, unhappiness and conflict. Today, the symptoms are the use and abuse of various drugs.[39]

By this view the fundamental questions to be clarified with regard to the reduction of drug addiction are not those concerned, for example, with the addictive or non-addictive properties of drugs; rather the fundamental problem is the recognition and removal of the conditions which prompt individuals to use drugs. Accordingly the main purpose of any investigation of domestic problems should be the discovery of the social conditions that give rise to these symptoms of disturbance.

Another expression of the "underlying problem" orientation toward social reform appears in discussions of mental illness in America. While the number of patients in state mental hospitals has dropped from 535,540 in 1960 to 373,984 in 1969,[40] the underlying conditions associated with mental illness have remained the same. As Frank Leonard has noted, this drop "has not been due to any increased commitment to the mentally ill, however. It is the result of the more or less chance discovery of tranquilizing drugs, which do not 'cure' mental illness and have often been called 'chemical strait-jackets.' "[41] Leonard views the tranquilizers as useless because although they permit the individual to return to his community, there are few services available which help to reintegrate or further treat the patient.

---

[39] Howard A. Rusk, M.D., "Hallucinogenic Drugs: II," *New York Times,* October 29, 1967.

[40] National Institute of Mental Health. Figures based on number of residents for end of year.

[41] Frank Leonard, *The New Leader* (August 28, 1967).

This orientation toward the treatment of symptoms constitutes a primitive theory in the form of a medical analogue. Both because it is so widely subscribed to, and because it lends itself to the development of a more sophisticated theoretical position, we shall stay with the analogue. Accordingly, taking the example of a patient who has a headache and a high fever and is given an aspirin, "everybody knows" that aspirin will provide no basic cure and may just temporarily reduce the pain and perhaps lower the temperature. And unless something is done to cure the illness the patient will not be helped by the aspirin. While there are no exact analogues to such a situation on a societal level, as the continued existence of a society is only rarely threatened, still if we refer to the relative effectiveness of the social system in the handling of its problems, and to the society's realization of its values, then we can identify the same difference between societal aspirins, which have an immediately alleviating effect, and remedial actions of more basic significance. For instance, if a city that regularly experiences a crime wave during the summer provides summer camps, sports events, and other such distractions for the community, and by this means prevents a shooting, looting riot, this procedure does prevent or alleviate that particular, extreme expression of social tension *and its costs* without dealing with underlying problems.

The same general fears of the consequences of treating symptoms that occur with regard to the treatment of a sick individual are also expressed when the use of social palliatives or "social aspirins" is proposed. It is suggested initially that as a consequence of relieving the distress of the overt symptoms of the disorder it will become possible to ignore the underlying problems and accordingly they will receive less treatment than they would otherwise. The societally minded reader is apt to suggest that the treatment of symptoms—the summertime riots—will delay treatment of the basic problems of poverty, discrimination, and alienation. However, there is little evidence to support this proposition. *There is little evidence that those cities which provided summer distractions provided fewer winter reforms than the cities which provided no such distractions.* On the contrary, on impressionistic grounds, it seems that the more responsive cities provided first a summer palliative and then a measure of winter treatment, while the more unresponsive cities provided neither. Of course one may argue that even more would have been achieved in the relatively responsive cities had the summer "cooling out" not been resorted to; but there is no evidence to support this proposition.

Moreover, the possible reform-accelerating effect of allowing the riot fever to run uncurbed has been largely overstated. Up to a point riots and tensions may lead to some token reforms; after a while they tend to lead to a conservative reaction. Accordingly, while one can say that permitting the riots to occur (*i.e.*, not treating the symptom) may lead to a basic change more rapidly, it is possible that the ensuing change would not be favorable to those who riot and would further inhibit remedial action. Thus it is not evident that the use of social palliatives or social aspirins necessarily inhibits more basic remedial actions.

Additionally it is possible in many instances that "symptomatic treatment" may be a *necessary prerequisite* to a more basic attack on the problem. Thus, for instance, if a patient were running a high fever it might be necessary to reduce the fever with a drug in order to prepare the individual for more basic remedies (*e.g.*, surgery). Alcoholics, after long exposure to the illness, are often mentally and physically debilitated. They are frequently unable to function socially and thus are not ready to begin rehabilitation. Tranquilizers are used to quiet alcoholic patients to the point they can be reached.[42] Even if antabuse has no value as a treatment for the underlying causes of alcoholism, for some patients it seems to be effective in keeping them off liquor long enough to allow their bodies to begin to recover and for psychotherapy to be initiated. Similarly for heroin addicts, methadone, by permitting the individual to avoid involvement in the illegal drug acquisition process, may open the door for rehabilitation and psychotherapy.

Another criticism directed at the treatment of symptoms is that even though such treatment may eliminate one expression of the system's disorder, until the basic problem is removed other symptomatic expressions of the disorder will appear. This "hydraulic" conception of the dynamics of a functioning system's disorders seems particularly relevant in the context of human interaction, characterized as it is by intentional behavior and the use of symbols for the review and selection of alternative means to satisfy more or less consciously perceived needs. Thus while symptomatic treatment of a medical disorder may suppress most overt symptoms (other than the final consequence of the course of the underlying disorder), symptomatic treatment of a human behavioral problem is somewhat more apt to lead to the appearance of an alternative, overt expression of the underlying difficulty. Accordingly it is often suggested that when social disorders are treated symptomatically "all" that is achieved is to shift the expression of the problem to some other location and thus the whole effort is futile. However, even on this model level the conception is not complete. One of the assumptions underlying the preceding statement is that all the alternate symptoms are equally dysfunctional. However, the opposite proposition seems more probable: *that functional alternatives are not functional equivalents.* Thus, for

---

[42] National Institute of Mental Health, *Alcohol and Alcoholism*, Superintendent of Documents, No. 5011 (Washington, D.C.: U.S. Government Printing Office, 1969), p. 32.

instance, if an alcoholic who is in danger of destroying his liver and who, because of his drinking, is not able to function socially (*e.g.,* by staying employed, keeping a family, and participating in the activities of his community) is able to liberate himself from liquor by taking antabuse, and instead begins over-eating (a phenomenon common among cigarette smokers when they take Nico-Ban and stop smoking), this still is a significant gain. An overweight person's life seems likely to be considerably less endangered than the alcoholic's. Additionally, he is able to participate in a more meaningful and productive life during those years and he is not apt to be a burden on the community. The various possible symptomatic expressions of fundamental social disorders may be seen to vary considerably in the personal and social costs they entail. It seems likely that the first two drinks a day have few detrimental consequences, while the first three cigarettes may have a larger margin of disutility. Similarly, the use of a little heroin may well lead to the use of a lot of heroin, while the use of a little marijuana seems considerably less dangerous.

Some of the symptomatic expressions involve illegal behavior, while others are legal; in some cases the law may be obsolescent, in some cases it is not. In some shifts in symptomatic expression the personal costs may not decline while the social costs are reduced, and in other substitutions different combinations of cost reallocations may occur. There are of course a large set of complex issues involved here. We do not presume to make here such value judgments. We only seek to point out that no two symptoms are apt to be totally equivalent and hence "merely" shifting things around in some sub-category of conditions could well result in substantial decreases in personal and/or social costs. Accordingly, symptomatic treatment can be extremely useful when, as is very frequently the situation, the basic illness cannot be treated, or at least until it is treated.

Furthermore, the hydraulic analogue assumes that no intensity of expression is "lost" in the process of transferring from one symptom to another, that in no way does the shift itself affect the scope and intensity of the problem. Actually, there is no evidence that we are aware of for or against this "perfect hydraulic system" proposition. Our hunch is that the ease with which alternate means to a blocked end are selected is not unlimited, that the process does entail some friction. Accordingly, some losses or gains in personal tensions and pain, and in social costs, are apt to be incurred. Thus if criminals driven off the streets by improved street lighting or more police patrols shift their activities to the buses and the subways, and are driven out of there, some of them may simply quit the life of crime in the process and not necessarily adapt to the symptomatic treatment by resorting to crime in different areas, say the suburbs. Hence one reason some symptomatic shifts may be desirable is not only that the resulting expressions of the underlying problem are more acceptable in social or personal terms, but also that the total amount of expression once the illness has been shifted from one symptom to another is a lower one.

Another reason the outcome of such shifting among symptoms may be a genuine improvement, even if we accept the "frictionless hydraulic" assumption, is that it might lead to *dividing the problem among various symptoms*. This development is by no means undesirable. When a person has a severe symptomatic problem it may be particularly difficult to deal with because he is overwhelmed by it. The same may be the case with some social problems.

Next, it should be noted that the distinction between the symptomatic treatment and basic cures (*i.e.*, the idea that domestic problems are uniformly constituted of very fundamental causal factors, such as physiological, psychological, or social structural disorders which are made evident by comparatively superficial symptoms, such as a rising rate of robberies in the streets) is too drastic a distinction. *Actually there are differences of degree in basic causal conditions themselves and in symptoms.* Some "symptoms" may be relatively fundamental and some basic illnesses relatively superficial. So rather than dividing the world into very light problems which it is felt can be easily handled, although doing so is essentially useless, and very deep problems which can be handled occasionally and then only through major surgery or revolution, it is useful to recognize that both problems and symptoms range all the way from one end to the other.

For instance, some problems are completely "symptomatic" in that they have no structural root. There is a school of social analysts which insists that many of our social problems are chiefly a matter of definition. Those working in the tradition of W. I. Thomas, George Herbert Mead, John Dewey, and Alfred Schutz have explained the existence of societal order in terms of a common "definition of the situation." As Peter McHugh has noted:

> They imply, by their use of the phrase "definition of the situation," that there is no one-to-one correspondence between an objectively real world and people's perspectives of that world, that instead something intervenes when events and persons come together, an intervention that makes possible the variety of interpretations which Schutz calls "multiple realities."[43]

The implication of these observations for the interpretation of "mental illness" is of interest. The case of the individual who has defined the situation in an atypical manner and has acted on the basis of this definition could

---

[43] Peter McHugh, *Defining the Situation: The Organization of Meaning in Social Interaction* (New York: The Bobbs-Merrill Company, Inc., 1968), p. 8.

very well be the case of the person who is perceived to be mentally ill. For this reason Thomas J. Scheff, among others, has stressed the need to establish the context in which the abnormal behavior occurs. Laing and Esterson report that seemingly schizophrenic behavior becomes understandable if the context in which it is embedded is considered.[44] While the symptoms viewed by themselves appear to be those of a pathologically disturbed person, on further investigation it seems that it is often the families, rather than the patients, who are really disordered and that "the symptoms of the patients are only normal reactions to very unusual situations."[45] Laing and Esterson, in their five-year study of the families of schizophrenic patients, discovered that often normal behavior (or at least that appropriate to the situation in which the subject found himself) was classified as abnormal both by the patients' families and the psychiatrists. Laing and Esterson describe their view of the schizophrenic:

> He is someone who has queer experiences and/or is acting in a queer way, from the point of view usually of his relatives and of ourselves. Whether these queer experiences and actions are constantly associated with changes in his body is still uncertain . . . That the diagnosed patient is suffering from a pathological process is either a fact, an hypothesis, an assumption, or a judgment.[46]

What happens in the clinical situation is that the psychiatrist, who looks at and listens to the individual in front of him as a patient, comes to believe that he is in the presence of the "fact" of "schizophrenia." Having in effect defined the situation as one in which he is dealing with a schizophrenic, the psychiatrist acts accordingly.

> He acts "as if" its existence were an established fact. He then has to discover its "cause" or multiple "aetiological factors," to assess its "prognosis," and to treat its course. The heart of the "illness," all that is the outcome of process, then resides outside the agency of the person. That is, the illness, or process, is taken to be a "fact" that the person is subject to, or undergoes, whether it is supposed to be genetic, constitutional, endogenous, exogenous, organic or psychological, or some mixture of them all. This, we submit, is a mistaken starting-point.[47]

The unintelligible behavior of the patient is seen as becoming intelligible when the family "nexus" is described. Laing and Esterson found that the family of the "schizophrenic" was as "schizophrenic" as the patient. By

---

[44] R. D. Laing and A. Esterson, *Sanity, Madness, and the Family* (New York: Basic Books, 1964).

[45] T. J. Scheff, *Being Mentally Ill* (Chicago: Aldine Publishing Company, 1966), p. 171.

[46] Laing and Esterson, *op. cit.*, p. 4.

[47] *Ibid.*

considering the context in which the behavior occurs, they concluded that the experience and behavior of schizophrenics is much more socially intelligible than is supposed by most psychiatrists.

Thomas Szasz has been a strong advocate of the view that individuals create the concept of mental illness:

> Since all systems of classification are made by people, it is necessary to be aware of who has made the rules and for what purpose. If this precaution is not taken, there is the risk of being unaware of the precise rules, or worse, of mistaking the product of classification for "naturally occurring facts or things." I believe this is exactly what happened in psychiatry during the past sixty or seventy years. During this period, a vast number of occurrences were reclassified as "illnesses." We have thus come to regard phobias, delinquencies, divorce, homicide, addiction, and so on almost without limit as psychiatric illnesses. This is a colossal and costly mistake.[48]

As the title of his book indicates, Szasz believes mental illness to be a myth, the creation of an arbitrary definition. Furthermore, "psychiatrists are not concerned with mental illnesses and their treatment. In actual practice they deal with personal, social, and ethical problems in living."[49] In a more recent book, he has continued his criticism of the concept of mental illness.[50]

Thomas Scheff has stressed the social definition of mental illness. He feels that psychoanalytic theory leaves out aspects of the social context that are vital in understanding mental disorder. Psychoanalysis is constructed on the disease model, "in that it portrays neurotic behavior as unfolding relentlessly out of a defective psychological system that is entirely contained within the body."[51] Scheff cites instances where the context in which the unusual behavior occurred has been ignored by the psychiatrists involved. This tendency to ignore the context in which the behavior occurs derives from the medical model, in which the nonconforming behavior tends to be seen as a symptom of "mental illness." He notes that:

> The concept of disease, as it is commonly understood, refers to a process which occurs within the body of an individual. Psychiatric symptoms, therefore, are conceived to be part of a system of behavior which is located entirely within the patient, and which is independent of the social context within which the "symptoms" occur.[52]

---

[48] Thomas S. Szasz, M.D., *The Myth of Mental Illness* (New York: Hoeber-Harper, 1964), p. 43.

[49] *Ibid.*, p. 296.

[50] T. S. Szasz, *The Manufacture of Madness* (New York: Harper and Row, 1970).

[51] Scheff, *op. cit.*, p. 14.

[52] *Ibid.*, pp. 174–175.

Scheff advocates that this contextual element be accorded particular attention, since the concept of "mental illness" depends on a societal definition. Ullman and Krasner have gone so far as to say that "because there are no disease entities involved in the majority of subjects displaying maladaptive behavior, the designation of a behavior as pathological or not is dependent upon the individual's society."[53] Thus, in effect, it is the individual's social group which decides that he is "mentally ill."

The varying positions toward the role of symbols in the definition of mental illness can be illustrated by divergent interpretations given to a well-known statement by W. I. Thomas: "If men define situations as real, they are real in their consequences."[54] The statement has a certain ambiguity: some give it a more symbolistic, others a more "objective" interpretation. According to a symbolistic view, the statement can be understood to suggest that what really is out there does not matter because the reaction (and the reaction to the reaction, hence all interaction) is determined by the interpretation of what is there. When a man approaches and extends his hand, a fellow man, in our culture, will shake it if he interprets this as a friendly gesture. He may run away if he views the same gesture as an attack. To stretch the point, a man may try to shake a hand even when none has been offered, as long as he defines the situation as one in which there is a hand out there trying to reach his.

Among the numerous sociologists who refer to Thomas' statement, several come close to such a symbolistic interpretation. For instance, two sociologists have stated:

> Human Behavior can be accounted for only in terms of interplay between attitudes and values . . . subjective desires are what usually determine the way in which (the) individual reacts to external influences.[55]

Another suggests that in Thomas' system:

> . . . the subject may perceive a number of elements in a situation which cannot be demonstrated to exist scientifically; but if they exist subjectively, behavior will depend upon this version of the situation.[56]

---

[53] L. P. Ullman and L. Krasner, *Case Studies in Behavior Modification* (New York: Holt, Rinehart, and Winston, 1965), p. 20, quoted in Scheff, *op. cit.*, p. 21.

[54] William I. Thomas and Dorothy S. Thomas, *The Child in America: Behavioral Problems and Programs* (New York: Knopf, 1928), p. 572.

[55] Meyer Weinberg and Oscar E. Shabat, *Society and Man* (Englewood Cliffs, N.J.: Prentice-Hall, 1956), p. 188.

[56] Edmund H. Volkart, *Social Behavior and Personality: Contributions of W. I. Thomas to Theory and Social Research* (New York: Social Science Research Council, 1951), p. 14; see also p. 5: "It was no longer what actually existed that seemed most important: it was what men thought existed." H. Stuart Hughes, *Consciousness and Society* (New York:

The point these views have in common is that no direct effect of "reality" is explicitly recognized. It is not pointed out, for instance, that a locked jail door has social consequences no matter what meaning the inmates give the fact that the door does not open. In addition, the effect of objective factors on the interpretation is also not made explicit, as if the actor is equally free to impose any interpretation that he chooses (*e.g.,* the door is really open, or being imprisoned is a widely recognized honor).

In contrast, the following treatment of the Thomas dictum takes into account both the symbolic and the mechanical aspects of action: "We may therefore conclude that if people define situations as real, whether or not they are, their behavior will be altered" (*i.e.,* not determined, but affected by the interpretation); and, "we do not suggest, however, that a person's definition of the situation is totally unrelated to the reality of the situation."[57]

An actor may respond to "pure" symbols which have no natural base apart from their carrier. This could mean either that the symbol exists only in the actor's own mind, or that it is shared by at least some of the other actors in the given situation. Or an actor may respond to a symbol that has some objective correlative beyond its mere carrier. In the first case, only the interpretation applies; in the second, both symbolic and mechanical processes affect the action.

An illustration may help to bring into relief this crucial distinction between symbolistic and social interaction. When forces of the Soviet Union shot down an American airplane in 1963 during a period of detente, the event had no effect on United States military or economic capabilities; and, though it occurred in the mechanical world in the sense that bullets ripped the plane, its socio-political consequences were completely dependent on the interpretation given the occurrence (*i.e.,* on what normative symbol was assigned and how this symbol related to other symbols). In this case, the United States government and press first presented the incident as a violation of the detente spirit, which in itself was a symbolic state; later, the

---

Knopf, 1958), p. 66. Thomas D. Eliot paraphrases the dictum as follows: "The way in which people define situations determines their attitudes, their conception of their roles, and therefore their acts under the given conditions." See his "A Criminological Approach to the Social Control of International Aggressions," *American Journal of Sociology,* Vol. 58 (1953), p. 513. A "modernization" and further popularization of Thomas' thesis in a symbolistic interpretation is found in the work of Marshall McLuhan, who sees man as creating communicative tools and thus defining the environment, his perception, and through them, himself. *Understanding Media: The Extensions of Man* (New York: McGraw-Hill, 1964).

[57] Alvin W. and Helen P. Gouldner, *Modern Sociology* (New York: Harcourt, Brace & World, 1963), p. 555. See also Margaret W. Vine, *An Introduction to Sociological Theory* (New York: Longmans, Green & Co., 1959).

incident was reinterpreted as an "honest" mistake, and its effect on the detente was defused.[58] However, had Soviet forces destroyed on the same day four hundred American long-range missiles, the event—whatever the interpretation given to it—would have curtailed United States capacity to act in the world of objects. And, as is often the case when an "objective" change is involved, there would have been less leeway for interpretation, although the interpretation given would still have mattered. In the social realm, the logics of objects and of symbols are coeffective.

Thus, possibly the physiological and medical difference between methadone and heroin is rather small, and the major difference may be that at present in the United States heroin use is considered highly illegal and accordingly its use leads to contact with criminals and the need to raise funds illicitly, while methadone is defined as a treatment drug, the use of which leads to contact with social workers, psychologists, doctors, rehabilitation programs and opportunities for employment. While we are not at all certain that the whole difference between the consequences of using the two drugs is due to their social definitions, we are sure that the difference in the social definitions of these drugs is much greater than the physiological-medical difference. So, even though there may be medical differences, the contrast in the social definitions is very important.

Finally, it can be suggested that symptomatic treatment often has a Hawthorne effect; it shows that someone cares. That is, the very indication of interest in the subject population results in an improvement not as a consequence of the substance of the treatment but as a reaction to the attitude of the treaters. It is usually assumed that the effect of showing interest will wear off once people get used to the new attention, and then the new technology (or new treatment) will no longer be effective. But if we design the program in such a way that it will show a continual indication of interest, of concern, and commitment to the treated persons, this may create a continual Hawthorne effect.

In conclusion, if shortcuts are viewed as non-basic, and in this sense symptomatic, there are nevertheless several reasons, in theory alone, why they should "work"—among others, by reducing the problem, by opening the system to basic treatment, and by reducing significantly the cost of the problem. This is not a suggestion that there are no shortcuts which are "bad" or useless; which look as if they provide a reduction in the problem, but actually do not, and thus delay overdue treatment of the problem. Our purpose is not to imply that all shortcuts, or even most of them, are effective but rather to provide a principle which will allow us to differentiate

---

[58] Amitai Etzioni, "Anatomy of an Incident," *Columbia Journalism Review,* Vol. 3 (1964), pp. 27–31.

between those that are and those that are not, and also to suggest that often a problem can be divided into perhaps five subproblems, and then three or four of those can be handled by shortcuts, and often technological shortcuts.

THE UTILIZATION OF KNOWLEDGE
ON TECHNOLOGICAL EFFECTIVENESS

The Overriding Conclusion

All said and done, what did we find in our examination of specific technological shortcuts? Do the shortcuts we studied work? In view of the preceding analysis, obviously the answer will not be a simple yes or no. The question is: What works for what and whom? Do the technological shortcuts solve the problem? None of the technologies we studied does that. Even if domestic disarmament did take place, there still would be numerous violent crimes. Even if methadone is widely used, those addicts who do not wish to take it and find heroin more attractive will use heroin, and this group may amount to as much as a third, perhaps two-thirds, of the addict population. The same holds true for antabuse and alcoholics. Similarly, it seems to us that there are subjects which cannot be taught effectively by television (a point to which we will return below).

Do the technological shortcuts work for important segments of the problem? Will they sharply reduce the overall personal and social costs and pains of dealing with the problems at hand? It is our considered judgment on the basis of the best available information, that for all systems we studied, antabuse included, the answer is a positive one.

It will be useful to review quickly the main findings. Concerning methadone, it is our estimate that it does allow for the social and perhaps the psychic rehabilitation of heroin addicts; that it is effective for one-third, up to two-thirds, of the addicts; and that it probably allows people to function at least at 80 percent of their capacity, which is much more than heroin allows. However, it still is not established that methadone does not have any undesirable side effects. It is addictive, and in the case of female addicts leads to the birth of infants with an addiction. It also seems to have a tranquilizing effect which may reduce in the long run the social and psychic effectiveness of the people being maintained on methadone. "Reduce" in this context refers to a comparison with fully functioning citizens, not with heroin addicts.

Antabuse lacks both the experimental backing and the popular support that methadone has as these lines are written. Still, we see little evidence indicating that, used in moderate dosages, it could not be similarly effective. There is, however, a significant difference between the uses of methadone and antabuse. Methadone, at this stage, is primarily used as a maintenance drug and only in a few highly experimental programs as a weaning or detoxification drug. Antabuse is primarily used as a weaning drug, a counter-drug to alcohol, and only in a few cases as a maintenance drug. The purpose here is to create a temporary aversion, but not a permanent block to the use of alcohol. Hence the rehabilitative mechanisms assumed to be operating are different. However, both drugs seem potentially effective for large segments of the population.

Another way of examining the effectiveness of these two methods is to compare them to "pure" psychotherapy. This needs to be done because occasionally the two systems are mixed, and when methadone plus psychotherapy is compared to psychotherapy, we contaminate and confuse the comparison. *We suggest that methadone used alone or antabuse used alone is considerably more effective than psychotherapy alone.* The same expectation holds when we compare the effectiveness of the two drugs to that of the punitive approach of jailing alcoholics and heroin addicts. With regard to the mixing of drug treatment with psychotherapy, it appears that the mixed treatment is more effective than are drugs used alone, although we have no clear evidence indicating how much is added by the psychotherapeutic element.

Concerning instructional television (ITV), again there is no question that for many purposes and for many subpopulations this technology can be as effective or more so than live teaching.[59] Here again though, it does seem that combining some live teaching with the televised instruction further increases the effectiveness of the mechanical system.

Gun control, or more specifically domestic disarmament, may reduce serious crimes by 40 percent to 60 percent, indicating that in this context the technology itself is a very powerful, although not the only, controlling factor.

---

[59] For a general introduction to the use of television in instruction, see Judith Murphy and Ronald Gross, *Learning by Television* (New York: The Fund for the Advancement of Education, 1966). An extensive analytic review of the research literature dealing with instructional television is provided by Goodwin C. Chu and Wilbur Schramm, *Learning from Television* (Stanford, California: Stanford University Institute for Communication Research, 1967). Abstracts of more than 330 varying studies of instructional television and film are presented in J. Christopher Reid and Donald W. MacLennan, *Research in Instructional Television and Film* (Washington: U.S. Government Printing Office, 1967). For a detailed survey of the use of television for instruction in the United States, see Lawrence E. McKune (ed.), *National Compendium of Televised Education*, Vol. 15 (East Lansing, Michigan: Michigan State University, 1968). Case studies of the use of instructional television drawn from a number of countries are presented in *The New Media in Action: Case Studies for Planners*, 3 Vols. (Paris: UNESCO and International Institute for Educational Planning, 1967).

The Limits of the Relevant Knowledge and Their Sources

There is a major reservation attached to the statements we have made so far which we will examine more carefully in the following pages: they all should be read as if they were *prefaced* by "as far as available information goes." Accordingly we will consider first a variety of constraints within the knowledge-production process itself, and next the relationship between "basic" research and applied technology.

The great difficulties encountered in reaching a simple decision on any one of the issues before us is in many ways the most important finding of our study. The imagery the public, as well as many academics writing in administrative theory, have concerning the acquisition and evaluation of knowledge about a proposed remedy is basically of a fairly precise, rationalistic, and definitive process. The matters to be decided are considered to be questions of expert opinion, of the empirical judgment, of data. However, what we find occurring is a very different process; a complicated interaction in which rational arguments, empirical evidence, and experts do play a role, but are influenced by, and in turn influencing value judgments, political interests, and other formally extraneous forces. The main point, however, is not that there are nonrational forces to be considered; the main point is that they penetrate and *exist within the very knowledge-producing units and processes themselves.*

Most fundamentally there are limitations in the knowledge-production process itself, even when it is completely untampered with and apparently unconstrained. One of the greatest problems faced by federal agencies is a lack of proper data on which to base social policies. Joseph A. Califano, President Johnson's Assistant for Domestic Affairs, has described this state of affairs:

> ... the disturbing truth is that the basis of recommendations by an American Cabinet officer of whether to begin, eliminate or expand vast social programs more nearly resembles the intuitive judgment of a benevolent tribal chief in remote Africa. . . .[60]

Similarly, Aaron Wildavsky has stressed the need for better policy analysis: "Each area one investigates shows how little is known compared to what is necessary in order to devise adequate policy."[61] He further advocates that analysis should concentrate on major issues rather than on specifics. Analysis on a much higher level of abstraction than now employed in evalu-

---

[60] *Washington Post,* January 7, 1970.

[61] Aaron Wildavsky, "Rescuing Policy Analysis from PPBS," *The Analysis and Evaluation of Public Expenditures: The PPB System,* A Compendium of Papers submitted to the Subcommittee on Economy in Government of the Joint Economic Committee, Congress of the United States (Washington, D.C.: U.S. Government Printing Office, 1969), Vol. 3, p. 835.

ating federal programs is seen as needed. The lack of general evaluations and the absence of basic data on which to base policy decisions have been specifically noted in the federal antipoverty and child care programs. Garth L. Magnum has asserted that: "No manpower or antipoverty program has ever been evaluated. No one really knows what has been accomplished and whether any of these programs has been worth the cost."[62] Magnum contends that effective programs will never emerge "unless administrators have 'their feet put to the fire' by being required to achieve, or at least measure their progress against previously announced objectives. Evaluation's purpose is to determine whether objectives have been achieved and at what costs."[63] Joseph S. Wholey has outlined the difficulties of attempting to cope with child care problems in the absence of the needed information. Because of the lack of information and lack of evaluation of program effectiveness, program planning was extremely difficult. As he notes:

> Without knowledge of the effectiveness of past and present programs, the analyst could not confidently recommend reallocations within the existing maternal and child health budget, nor could the analyst provide definitive conclusions on the relative costs and effectiveness of alternative proposals for new programs. In the absence of knowledge about program effectiveness, what could have been compelling arguments for program changes were reduced to semipersuasive arguments, more convincing to the analyst than to HEW decision-makers committed to their own programs and their own legislative proposals.[64]

Wholey concludes that the federal government is in crucial need of a program evaluation system. Without an evaluation program, "the traditional forces within and outside the Federal Government will continue to shape and reshape Federal programs without benefit of the guidance that well-founded analyses could give."[65]

We suggest that the knowledge available about social processes in the United States in general—either from social science or from various "lay" sources, in particular the government—is overly discrete and insufficiently analyzed. Later we will suggest an empirical procedure to verify this statement. Here we would like to add that analysis is lagging to a very considerable extent. That many more facts are collected than analyzed is not the indication of an analysis gap; some such "over" collection is a necessary

---

[62] Garth L. Magnum, "Determining the Results of Manpower and Antipoverty Programs," *The Analysis . . . The PPB System*, p. 1171.

[63] *Ibid.*, p. 1180.

[64] Joseph S. Wholey, "The Absence of Program Evaluation as an Obstacle to Effective Public Expenditure Policy: A Case Study of Child Health Care Programs," *The Analysis . . . The PPB System*, p. 468.

[65] *Ibid.*, p. 469.

redundancy and an inevitable "waste." An attempt to eliminate this would entail the regimentation of science to the degree that it would be totally destroyed. Reference here is to a much greater lag, to a philosophy of science which stresses facts and underevaluates their analysis, to the abundance of facilities for collecting additional facts and the paucity of facilities for the processing of those we already have, and above all to the procedures of semi-analysis detached from a finalized product and often hindering it. The total effect is for the societal actors to have the information they need but not to know what they need to know, or for their vision to be clear at particular points but blurred whenever they attempt to take in more than a small segment of the societal field at a time.

We distinguish between two positions which are essential and legitimate elements of a philosophy of science; each, though, when pushed to its extreme conclusion, undermines the capacity to know. The *empirical* position is that, in principle, factual statements about the world (including societies) ought to be maintained only if validated by systematically conducted tests, especially those quantitative in nature. The *empiristic* position is that theoretical efforts tend to be useless, that which cannot be measured is meaningless, that facts count while interpretations are speculations which tend to weaken the power of the findings. The *reflective* position is that considerations of the relationships among factors and of the meaning of findings advance one's knowledge. The *reflectivistic* position is that one can advance our understanding of the world best by reflecting about it on the basis of existing data and qualitative insights into oneself or one's environment. If the empiristic position is anti-analytic, the reflectivistic one is against empirical research. On the other hand, the empirical and reflective positions supplement each other to provide for external validity and internal consistency, the two bases of a scientific perspective of the world.

One could test our proposition that the United States societal knowledge system is empiristically oriented in several ways: submit to researchers a questionnaire in which alternative statements describe the four positions defined above and ask them which one most aptly characterizes their position. Or, they may be asked, if given $100,000 to study poverty in city X, which research method they would choose, and how they would divide the funds among the following items: review of literature; preparation of a questionnaire (if any); coding; collection of additional qualitative data; processing of data; semi-analysis; final analysis; writing of final report. And, finally, how much time they would allow for each item. The pattern obtained may be compared to that of researchers in a less empiristic culture or subculture. We expect that empiristic researchers will shortchange the first and last phases of the process and qualitative methods.

A comparison of their norms (expressed in the answers to the suggested questions) to the actual distribution of budgets and time by the same researchers could further test our proposition. We expect it to show that actual projects are even more empiristic than the norms of their directors. The reasons for this tendency, if found, may be explained—and the explanatory statements themselves verified—if we examine the granting arrangements.

The existing granting arrangements, we suggest, tend to penalize the analyst and favor the collector of data and the semi-processor. This could be demonstrated by comparing these groupings in terms of their incomes (including summer salaries), the funds allotted for overseas travel and attendance at professional meetings, and the amount of money granted for secretarial help and research assistance. In short, we suggest, empiristics are significantly more rewarded than other researchers, and are given greater access to the facilities they require and greater freedom from other work which may hamper their research.

Moreover, the granting arrangements of the federal agencies and the major foundations tend to generate pressure on the empiristically minded to conduct more empiristic work than even they favor. This could be tested by asking a sample of project directors: how many research projects have you conducted over the last ten years? And of those, in how many did you have what you considered ample time for collection of data? For preliminary analysis? For final analysis? For writing of reports? Which of these aspects was the most shortchanged? The same questions may be repeated regarding a shortage of funds for the satisfactory completion of the various stages.

The research reports of these various projects could be scrutinized by a panel of, let us say, three experienced social scientists, acting as independent judges, to categorize the extent to which the data have been fully analyzed. The underlying reasons for insufficient analysis could be ascertained by interviews with heads of research centers and informal interviews with some project directors and research assistants. Those seem to include the fact that in the United States—unlike most West European countries—full-time academic research is not a fully established career. Researchers cannot readily obtain tenure, obtain the title of "professor," and be voting members of a university faculty. Moreover, the continued payment of their salaries requires, in the majority of the cases and institutions, gaining a new grant as soon as the old one runs out, or in the very near future. As the lead time of a new grant is about a year, the last period of an old grant—when analysis should take place—is the one preoccupied in part by proposal-writing, fund-raising, and psychological reorientation to the next project.

Probably much more significant is the fact that in most projects the first and middle phases run for a longer time and cost more than initially was planned for or approved by the granting agency. The period in which time and funds run out is, again, that in which analysis of the data should occur.

It seems fairly clear that there are in our environment cultural, organizational, and economic pressures toward the empiristic approach. Thus it does not seem that such an elaborate testing of this proposition is necessary. A few interviews with the heads of research centers or an examination of their products should suffice. Our main concern is with finding the sources of empiristic tendencies (for which the studies suggested above would be helpful; for instance, they suggest that the attitudes of researchers as well as economic considerations are involved) with an eye to suggesting remedial actions.

Assuming that it is established that analysis is lagging severely behind the collection of information, the following measures may be taken to correct the imbalance. They differ in costs, expected productivity, and the extent to which they themselves require research.

A study of proposals should be made to see if (a) analytic proposals are more likely to be rejected than data-collection ones; (b) budget reductions usually entail a proportionally larger decrease in the funds allocated to analysis; (c) project directors expect it to be more difficult to gain approval for analytic proposals and items and, hence, cut them in anticipation. If the answer to these questions is in the affirmative, special funds for analysis should be set aside, granting officers should be instructed not to reduce budget items allotted for analysis, and steps should be taken so that funds budgeted for analysis will not be used otherwise. Timetables should allow for a proper period for analysis and writing of the final report. Research centers should be given grants to finance in-between periods—that is, between projects—to allow for proposal writing for new projects without depriving the old ones. A center which supported our work in an earlier period and with which we are familiar invites researchers from other centers for a "writing" year, getting many more books per ten thousand dollars than other centers. This procedure has some merit in that it provides for analysis where it is lacking, but it deprives the centers where the work was originally conducted of part of the credit. Also, it is limited in scope; most researchers cannot get such a "writing year"; those who do get it cannot count on it since such funding is particularly susceptible to revision and withdrawal; and the facilities given are mainly restricted to a year's salary, which in effect precludes many kinds of analysis.

Granting agencies' staffs may be asked to answer the same questionnaire offered to researchers; if they tend to be empiristic, steps may be taken to alter such an orientation or to circumvent it. While in the natural sciences teamwork is more widely established, in many social sciences the norm of earlier humanistic research still has a strong hold: one scholar is responsible for the product. While he may be assisted and consulted, the title role is infrequently shared. Research may be conducted to see if those best at organizing the collection of data are also the best analysts, and especially if those best at analyzing data are much less effective at *arranging* for its collection. (Collection itself is already frequently delegated.) Furthermore, in those cases in which projects had two directors who differed in terms of relative empirical and reflective tendencies, was the final product significantly improved in terms of the balance between these two elements?

This may suggest a *sequential team approach,* with two project directors for large projects—both working out the design, one in charge of the collection data and of the preliminary processing, the other in charge of the final processing and the actual writing of the report, each acting continually as a consultant for the other. This arrangement, it should be stressed, assumes not simply division of labor, but division of labor between persons who differ in their skills along the lines indicated. If such arrangements are demonstrated to be productive, this may help make them more acceptable. Still, many studies will be conducted by one director, often empiristically oriented. Here it would be best if after a given period following completion of a project, the data were released (unless the project director specifically requests otherwise) so that other researchers—specialists in analysis—could work with them.

A special substudy should be devoted to semi-processing to check that our contention is valid, that most studies stop here because they run out of funds, time, and motivation, and to determine what accounts for the small subset of studies which get through to final analysis. Also, this would help to test our proposition that most semi-processing is "detached," using prefabricated categories not relevant to the final analysis and which can be used as "stand-ins" for relevant ones only at a *great* loss of accuracy: that is, that much semi-processing is more damaging than useful.

If our propositions, as presented so far, are verified, it follows that there .are now in the United States large amounts of unanalyzed, under-analyzed, and semi-analyzed data where additional analysis could be productively carried out. Moreover, as analysis is less costly than data-collection, the additional analysis could proceed at a lower cost per finding. Hence, more funds should be made available for:

1. "Analysis and writing years" for project directors who "completed" one or more studies. Some documentation of the potential value of data to be further analyzed is to be expected, either on the basis of partial analysis already carried out or the quality and integrity of the man.

2. Secondary analysis by others than the original researchers, for those stored data which are promising (to be tested, as above) where the original

researchers provide a release or are willing to participate in "secondary" analysis with others whose specialty is analysis. (All funding agencies should demand a written commitment from recipients of funds that X years after a recipient of public funds ceased to work with a body of data—unless a special case is made that he intends to work with it again—it becomes public domain and a copy is filed in a central archive, such as the Williamsburg archives.) After all, even the copyright to one's own work, unsupported by public funds, is exhausted after a given period. (This will also allow studies to be rerun and help to maintain standards which may be slipping, a topic· we do not pursue here.)

3. If most studies do not adequately analyze their own data, rare indeed is the study which systematically relates its findings to those of others, although perfunctory references are quite common. The *codification* of the findings of several studies, often essential for the transition from facts to knowledge, is obviously not the job of primary research. It requires skills and facilities very similar to those of secondary analysis, as outlined above. Hence, the need for such codification constitutes one more mission for, and another reason why, support should be granted to reflective units and men specializing in analysis.

4. *Special training for secondary analysis* and, more generally, for analysis is needed. We suggest, as a testable proposition, that much more time is devoted in methods courses to collection of data than to analysis and much of the time that is devoted to analysis is used to reinforce the questionable procedures of detached semi-processing. Hence, there is a need to support the teaching of final analysis by the codification of teaching material, seminars for faculties, and other means.

Second, secondary analysis and codification have some special methodological problems which arise out of their need to use data which are already collected, and often have been collected for purposes other than those of the secondary analysis. Matters such as "correction" of the data by return to primary study of a subsample, by the use of "global" qualitative data, the limits of tolerability of error, and the issues raised by finding in secondary analysis that the primary one was invalid, all deserve more systematic and collective-professional attention.

Science is always an unfinished enterprise. Yesterday's accepted theories are challenged today. Findings are tentative; and applicable mainly to this sample or "that population." And thus, on this ground alone, there is endless questioning. For instance, the birth control pill, up to a certain point in 1970, was very widely considered safe by the public as well as by doctors and most medical researchers. However, suddenly, a flurry of reports appeared indicating that, even though the pill had been used by millions of people, there was no conclusive evidence available as to its effects, and a whole new set of questions about the safety of the pill arose. Thus, it is not surprising that despite the existence of some 400-odd studies on ITV, the conclusions, on strictly technical grounds, are far from conclusive, nor that the effectiveness of methadone is still questioned despite the existence of half a dozen major studies and replications, all of which seem very incomplete. (Let us recall that one of the key variables of the proposition concerning the utility of methadone has not been tested, *i.e.,* that it has a blocking effect with regard to heroin. *It follows that the scientific input into the policy-making processes on these questions is inevitably tentative and always given to revision from internal scientific sources.* No wonder the politicians and the public are reluctant to rely strongly on this source of information.

Another source of difficulty within the scientific information production process itself is the fact that the United States is in an era of the mass production of science, and thus many completed studies are not conducted by qualified people. This lack of research qualifications is due to many things. Medical research, for instance, is frequently carried out by people trained in medicine but not in research techniques. They often have little familiarity with research design, sample sizes, formal theorizing, or statistics of analysis.

Secondly, even when research is conducted by people who are formally qualified, in the sense that they have a degree and training in the appropriate area, their training may have been accomplished at an institution of low educational quality or their talents or skills are below average.

Furthermore, and here the external structure intrudes, the rewards available for conducting a study, any study—independent of its quality and the validity of its results—are quite high. Successful operators can get, especially in the easier environment of previous years, research funds year after year to collect data, and, as long as they publish something, someplace, they are very likely to continue to get funds even if their studies have relatively small samples, poor designs, and other obvious failings. Basically the equalitarian approach to science in the U.S.A. mitigates against the allocation of research funds only to the high quality researchers and institutions; the pressure over the years is toward greater equality in the allocation of research support, not less so. This is most clearly visible in the case of the ITV evaluative research. Practically all the methodological reviews of existing studies agree that the majority of the studies are of low quality and full of methodological deficiencies.[66] Such studies clutter up the evaluation

---

[66] Wilbur Schramm, "What We Know About Learning From Instructional Television," *Educational Television: The Next Ten Years* (Stanford: The Institute for Communication Research, 1962), pp. 52–76; D. W. Stickells, "A Critical Review of the Methodology and

processes and make it difficult to review the field without first having to plow through hundreds of studies in order to locate those which are comparatively adequate. This is another reason why the picture generated by scientific research is unclear.

A third source of difficulty is the concentration of scholarly activity, especially in the United States, in analytic disciplines, such as psychology or economics or chemistry, with little emphasis on preparation in applied, synthesizing, or interdisciplinary work. As a result, researchers are qualified to deal with isolated slices of reality but not with relationships to the other slices (*i.e.*, multifaceted applied problems) and are more interested in enriching science than in studying ongoing systems. Thus, there are extremely few experts in the area of gun control, while there are many more people willing to write about the psychology of violence. There are many students of chemistry, but very few people are willing to make highway safety their research topic, especially if they are qualified. Of course some very important and good work is done in these areas; off the campuses, in the applied bureaus and research corporations, both for profit and not for profit, and also in research facilities attached to the government. But they cannot fill the existing gap, both because of the low prestige attached to these research units, which pushes researchers to seek academic affiliation if they are of high quality and because of the unstable, unpredictable funding of these units, which are dependent on fashions in public concern and governmental and foundation whims.

Then there is the matter of communicating the findings to the users. The typical research report—of which we reviewed hundreds—tends to be published in esoteric language, relying heavily on tables, and often in a journal inaccessible to most, such as the *New England Medical Journal*. Longer reports are frequently not published but either put on microfilm or in stenciled reports. A conservative estimate would suggest that 99.5 percent of these never reach the appropriate decision-makers or even their "gate-keepers." One of the intrinsic reasons for difficulty in communicating scientific knowledge to decision-makers is that science, by necessity, proceeds in terms of probability statements and very rarely can deal with specific events. The policy-makers and the gate-keepers are often legally trained and they are looking for clear definitions, without loopholes. Hence, when the scientific data is presented to them, they are leery of it because of the risk involved; they are not trained to think in terms of relative risk models. This was to some degree eased by the increased popularity, for a while, of the cost-effectiveness approach which implied probabilities; however this

Results of Research Comparing Television and Face-to-Face Instruction." Unpublished Ph.D. dissertation, Pennsylvania State University, 1963.

approach is no longer fashionable. Accordingly, it takes some special extra effort to communicate the findings to the decision-makers before they are available to affect policy. Bruce L. Smith provided a good illustration of how this is achieved in his study of how RAND "sold" its findings to the Air Force who had supported their study.[67] It proved to be a long process, involving hundreds of briefings, during which RAND personnel tried to convince people of various ranks in the Air Force to reexamine their assumptions because of the findings of the study. Similarly, Herman Kahn, director of the Hudson Institute, has engaged in a large number of briefings and press conferences, while attempting to get his conclusions across. Most researchers are not willing to do this and thus, often their findings simply do not reach the appropriate authorities (as for instance seems to be the case with much of the recent work on antabuse). Or, when decision-makers have a prejudice against a proposed remedy because of a previous bad experience with such propositions they will not be helped to overcome it by the researchers.

In this context, it is useful to contrast what has happened to methadone and to antabuse. In Dole, one finds more of the public fighter. This was important both initially when attempts were made to prevent him from doing his research, and later, when he had his findings in hand. Dole deliberately turned to the popular media, giving interviews to the *New Yorker,* having books written about him, being very accessible to newsmen, and making many non-technical statements which attracted public attention to his work. One of the authors of this volume was preparing an article for *The Public Interest,* in 1968. When he telephoned Dr. Dole and said that he and Bernard Barber, who had just published the book *Drugs and Society,* wanted to come and talk to him about his methadone project, Dole was quite willing. They went down to Rockefeller Institute and had lunch with Dole. Initially he was very cautious, until he established that they were not hostile to methadone. Once this was established, he opened his laboratories to the visitors, allowed them to interview his patients, to see the urine tests, and to discuss at great length his findings. They spent several hours there. As a consequence the author included a rather favorable discussion of methadone in *The Public Interest* article, and, as he also happened to meet a few days later with Fred Hayes, who was at that time director of the Bureau of the Budget of New York City, told him about methadone. All this seems not to be the case for Dr. Ruth Fox and the antabuse studies, and may be one reason antabuse has not received similar attention, although of course, there are also other reasons. Drug addiction is more in the public eye than al-

---

[67] Bruce L. Smith, *The Rand Corporation: A Case Study of a Nonprofit Advisory Corporation* (Cambridge: Harvard University Press, 1966).

coholism, and because of drug addiction's association with crime, workable remedies are in greater demand. Also, the Dole-Nyswander studies seem somewhat more complete than those of Fox, but we don't believe the difference is as great as would be suggested by the public reaction to the two remedial drugs or by that of the policy-makers.

Overall, we see numerous difficulties within the knowledge-production process itself. An entire additional set of difficulties is specifically associated with evaluations of remedial programs. Garth L. Magnum has discussed the information needed to evaluate a program properly, and has suggested that the following steps facilitate such evaluations:

1. The practical objectives must be stated clearly;
2. The extent to which those objectives are being achieved must be determined;
3. A measurement must be established of all the direct and indirect costs;
4. "A measure must be developed of all direct and indirect benefits, recognizing the nonquantifiable nature of many of the latter, yet guarding against the tendency to use the nonquantifiable as a justification for any difference between costs and benefits."[68]

The principle methodological problems have been in specifying and defining the various elements mentioned. As was mentioned earlier, few if any programs meet these criteria and hence evaluation becomes extremely difficult. Program objectives are frequently not clear—does methadone aim to rehabilitate in the sense of getting people to work—or help them toward psychological well being? Do gun laws in the United States aim at greater public safety, domestic disarmament, or at appeasing influential parts of the electorate? On what basis can one specifically identify "all" the costs?

The preceding discussion assumes that both the observer and the actor have a capacity to evaluate decision-making strategies and to determine which is the more effective. Incrementalists, however, argue that since values cannot be scaled and summarized, "good" decisions cannot be defined and, hence, evaluation is not possible. In contrast, it is reasonable to expect that the decision-makers, as well as the observers, can summarize their values and rank them, at least in an ordinal scale.

For example, many societal projects have one primary goal such as increasing birth control, economically desalting sea water, or reducing price inflation by one-half over a two-year period. Other goals which are also served are secondary, *e.g.*, increasing the country's R and D sector by investing in desalting. The actor, hence, may deal with the degree to which the *primary* goal was realized and make this the central evaluative measure

---

[68] Garth L. Magnum, "Determining the Results of Manpower and Antipoverty Programs," *op. cit.*, Vol. 3, p. 1172.

for a "good" policy, while noting its effects on secondary goals. When he compares projects in these terms, he, in effect, weighs the primary goal as several times as important as all the secondary goals combined. This procedure amounts to saying, "As I care very much about one goal and little about others, if the project does not serve the first goal, it is no good and I do not have to worry about measuring and totaling up whatever other gains it may be providing for my secondary values."

When there are two or even three primary goals (*e.g.,* teaching, therapy, and research in a university hospital), the actor can still compare projects in terms of the extent to which they realize each primary goal. He can establish that project X is good for research but not for teaching, while project Y is very good for teaching but not as good for research, etc., without having to raise the additional difficulties of combining the effectiveness measures into one numerical index. In effect, he proceeds as if they had identical weights.

Finally, an informal scaling of values is not as difficult as the incrementalists imagine. Most actors are able to rank their goals to some extent (*e.g.,* faculty is more concerned about the quality of research than the quality of teaching).

> One of the most imaginative attempts to evaluate the effectiveness of programs with hard-to-assess objectives is a method devised by David Osborn, Deputy Assistant Secretary of State for Educational and Cultural Affairs. . . . Osborn recommends a scheme of cross-multiplying the costs of the activities with a number representing the rank of its objectives on a scale. For instance, the exchange of Fulbright professors may contribute to "cultural prestige and mutual respect," "educational development," and gaining "entree," which might be given scale numbers such as 8, 6, and 5, respectively. These numbers are then multiplied with the costs of the program, and the resulting figure is in turn multiplied with an ingenious figure called a "country number." The latter is an attempt to get a rough measure of the importance to the U.S. of the countries with which we have cultural relations. It is arrived at by putting together in complicated ways certain key data, weighed to reflect cultural and educational matters, such as the country's population, Gross National Product, number of college students, rate of illiteracy, and so forth. The resulting numbers are then revised in the light of working experience, as when, because of its high per capita income, a certain tiny middle-eastern country turns out to be more important to the U.S. than a large eastern European one. At this point, country numbers are revised on the basis of judgment and experience, as are other numbers at other points. But those who make such revisions have a basic framework to start with, a set of numbers arranged on the basis of many factors, rather than single arbitrary guesses.[69]

---

[69] Virginia Held, "PPBS Comes to Washington," *The Public Interest,* No. 4 (Summer, 1966), pp. 102–115, quotation from pp. 112–113.

Thus, in evaluation as in decision-making itself, while full detailed rationalism may well be impossible, truncated reviews are feasible, and this approach may be expected to be more effective in terms of the actors' goals than "muddling through."

In addition to these intrinsic restraints on evaluation programs there are a host of extrinsic ones, including:

1. Administrative constraints: The "practitioners are extremely reluctant to give the experimenter enough power."[70] Thus, the evaluative experimenter often has significant limitations on the amount of manipulation that he can perform.

2. Scarcity of potential subjects: There exist in the literature on evaluational studies examples of well-designed studies that could not recruit enough volunteers for either experimental or control groups.

3. Misinterpretation or obstruction by interested agencies: Rossi cites the case of an evaluational study on the flow of birth control information to lower-class persons which was ruined by the actions of the city agencies. At the same time as the study was occurring the city set up birth control clinics in the areas designated as controls by the evaluation researchers.

4. Inadequacy of the practitioner's data collection: A problem is presented by the practitioner's lack of adherence to the canons of research; this results in slipshod data collection as well as lack of rigor in establishing control groups.[71]

Rossi concludes that: "In sum, it is not easy either to get the freedom to undertake properly controlled experiments or to do them when that consent is obtained."[72]

He further has suggested a strategy for evaluation research. One of the prime components of this strategy is the need of those involved in the study to be fully committed to the accuracy and validity of the research. The researcher has the responsibility to "impress on the practitioner that in most cases results are slight and that there is more than an off-chance that they will be unfavorable."[73] The practitioner for his part should be willing to accept the results. Another part of the strategy suggests that ways of using controlled experiments in evaluation should be devised. Also needed are

---

[70] Peter Rossi, "The Study of Man: Evaluating Social Action Programs," *Trans-action* (June, 1967), p. 52.

[71] This difficulty and several other problems in evaluational research are discussed in a seminar paper prepared by Sally T. Hillsman and Carol Weiss, "Problems in the Evaluation of Mental Health Projects" (Proceedings of a Seminar at the Bureau of Applied Social Research, February 24, 1970), p. 2.

[72] Rossi, *op. cit.*, p. 52.

[73] *Ibid.*

specialized studies which would give more comparative information than a single gross evaluation. For example, if one wanted to evaluate the effectiveness of the Job Corps program, one could evaluate several types of Job Corps camps, comparing them with one another. A third part of the strategy consists of applying "soft" evaluational techniques. Soft techniques can be as adequate as more subtle and precise ones if one desires to ascertain only massive effects. The evaluation of birth control methods is a case in point:

> If a birth control method is judged effective only if all chance of conception is eliminated, then the research design can be very simple. All that needs to be done is administer the technique and then check for any births (or conceptions) thereafter.[74]

Whatever techniques the researchers choose, severe problems are posed by the psychological resistance of the programs' administrators. The administrators want to believe that their programs are effective, and as long as the researchers' results are positive, a satisfactory working relationship exists between the researchers and the practitioners. However, the practitioners "never seriously consider the possibility that results might come out negative or insignificant," and negative evaluations of program success are often greeted with open hostility. In terms of the cases cited by Rossi, the negative evaluations had little effect on the organization's procedures.

Finally there are the more obvious political forces, which are separate from questions of the merit of the technology, but which still very much affect decisions concerning its utilization. Such forces affect not only the decisions as to whether ITV or IUD is to be considered effective and is to be used, but also the degree to which funds are available for research, for development, for experimentation, and hence ultimately for allowing us to attempt to make a decision whether a procedure works or not. These forces include contextual influences such as the general atmosphere encouraging or discouraging basic research, applied research, higher education, or innovations in general. Between 1950 and 1968 research in the United States experienced a great rise in support. After 1968 there has been some constriction of support, but also greater interest in applied and policy research. All this affects the development of the issues at hand, not in any direct fashion, but by providing the evaluative background for the selection and direction of programs.

In addition, there are very powerful interests directly involved in each of these social problem areas. With regard to methadone, there are at least three major competing approaches to the treatment of heroin addiction. The punitive approach is earnestly pursued by the Federal Bureau of Nar-

---

[74] *Ibid.*

cotics. Group treatment as well as psychotherapy has been embraced by Commissioner Efrem Ramirez of New York City, and by Synanon, the Phoenix Houses, and a number of other such therapeutically oriented organizations. And finally, there are the people who believe in chemical therapy like Dole and Nyswander. When methadone first came to public attention, both New York City and New York State recommended on the one hand that the punitive approach be pursued by setting up detention centers for addicts, and on the other hand that the group and psychiatric treatment approach also be pursued, with the New York City Commissioner of Narcotics being a psychiatrist. Dole was an individual medical researcher who had in effect little or no support. There is some reason to believe that, if he had not been working at the prestigious Rockefeller Institute and had not at one point mobilized the support of the Governor, he would have been prevented from continuing his work by the Federal Bureau of Narcotics, which at that time defined methadone as a dangerous narcotic and tried to prevent any research on it. Thus, initially there was a relatively weak proponent of one approach facing two other powerful forces. And indeed, they did considerably delay both the research on and the application of methadone. When methadone became widely used in 1969 and 1970, it was done, not as an operational "treatment" system, but very frequently as an expansion of the "experimental" program because it had not received federal approval as a treatment drug. However, expanded experimentation with methadone was allowed up to the point where, in effect, it did serve as an operational drug.

The influence of the political situation is even clearer in the case of gun control. Here the forces at play are extremely powerful, well organized, and highly mobilized. There is on the one hand opposed to gun control the gun lobby which includes highly mobilized and organized, well financed, nationwide organizations, with nationally distributed publications, and legislative lobbyists. On the other hand, most legislators, almost all concerned experts, and the majority of the public recognize that gun control is desirable. As is often the case when a strongly vocal minority which feels very intensely about a subject gets organized and opposes the majority of the public and the legislators who do not have such a strong interest in the subject, the minority has prevailed. This is particularly so, as the gun lobby has been able to draw upon fear of a possible communist take-over or invasion and some widely held beliefs about constitutional protection of the right to bear arms. This holds true not only for extensive gun control legislation but also for large-scale experimentation and studies of the subject, so again we know much less about the effectiveness of gun control than we would know if there was less politically powerful opposition to such research.

In the case of ITV, the forces at work include the fears of the teachers about the possibility of losing their jobs, their rights to the expression of their ideas, and protection from tight supervision.[75] The administrators of academia are relatively weak compared to the faculty, and hence it is not surprising that they frequently lose out in the battle as they try to introduce ITV. To the degree that ITV has been tried, it was often due to the provision of special support by foundations which financed experiments and the purchase of equipment which lay unused when the foundation support ran out. Ronald Gross observed:

> With the soaring of school and college enrollments after World War II, educators seized upon instructional technology as the panacea for the problems of mass education. In the early fifties television was introduced as a way of bringing the best teachers to millions of students, despite the exigencies of geography and economics. Later in the fifties came the teaching machines. "Every teacher who can be replaced by a machine," proclaimed B. F. Skinner of Harvard, "deserves to be." Most recently, the godsend has been the computer, which purportedly can diagnose each student's needs, provide him with a sequence of multi-media lessons, constantly respond and adjust the instruction to match his performance.
>
> In each of these cases the powers that be in education smiled on the notion—the Ford Foundation and the Carnegie Corporation financed televised teaching and programmed instruction; the Federal Government indicated that it would be a likely source of funds for a computer-based "systems approach" to education. The most recent result has been the so-called "Education Industry," formed by major electronics and computer companies, like R.C.A. and I.B.M., merging with publishers like Random House and Science Research Associates, in the hopes of matching hardware and software to create a workable technology of instruction.
>
> Despite this support, each of the prospective "revolutions in education" has come a cropper.[76]

One of the reasons why one cannot adequately document the full benefits of ITV, aside from the reasons already mentioned, is that many of its most useful features require large-scale repetitive use, which so far has been largely boxed in by the interests and sentiments opposed to the use of ITV.

While this discussion may leave the impression that data, evidence, and experts' knowledge play no role in the evaluation and selection of remedial programs and technology, this is not the case. A careful examination in any of these areas shows that information is one significant vector in the picture. For example, methadone has succeeded in moving out from its

---

[75] James W. Thornton, Jr. and James W. Brown (eds.), *New Media and College Teachings* (American Association of Higher Education, 1968), p. 42, *Seminar Abstracts*, No. 24 (Pennsylvania State University, June 10, 1968).

[76] Ronald Gross, *New York Times Book Review* (September 14, 1969).

quarantined, suspect, persecuted status to one of semi-popularity, as these lines are written. (However we remain cautious in this regard because we expect a reaction against methadone to set in by the time these lines are published.) This development was due largely to the fact that the methadone maintenance procedure which was originally viewed as a pet project of Dr. Dole and his wife, Dr. Nyswander, succeeded in being replicated independently by other students of the area and then their own data was subjected to several largely independent evaluations. The evaluation studies have serious limitations and the replications may be far from complete, but the very fact that they did generally reaffirm the conclusions of the Dole-Nyswander reports did lead to public acceptance of methadone despite the resistance. Of course, another contributing factor was the fact that the competing methods hardly worked at all.

One can imagine a vectogram suggesting the general distribution of influences under which a potential technological innovation can be researched and developed up to the point at which a decision about its large-scale use can be reasonably made. The vectogram would include representations, not only of the orientation and influence of the various interest groups and public sentiments relating to the proposed innovation, but also an indication of the degree to which evidence relating to the efficacy of the innovation can be accumulated. Since the actual, as opposed to potential, collection of relevant information would be apt to influence the field of forces the model would be interactive, with a third, symbolically temporal, dimension. That is, the degree to which information can be collected depends in part on the extent to which interests are arrayed against the particular innovation, and, conversely, the interests for and against an innovation, and experimentation with it, are affected by the production of information.

However, the vectors are only partially interrelated; there is a certain amount of leeway or "play." There are some effectively independent individuals, and some independent research funds, as in the case of methadone in the Rockefeller Institute. When they can succeed in pushing an innovation far enough forward that it becomes sufficiently supportable and publicly visible, it may take off even when the majority of the interests are against it, although, as we see in the cases of gun control and ITV, this is far from a foregone conclusion. We refer here primarily to gun control and ITV rather than to antabuse because antabuse research may not have reached the take-off stage yet. We would consider IUD and the Breath Test as both having taken off scientifically. IUD has received public and official endorsement in the United States as the traffic safety device also has in Britain, but not yet in the United States.

Surprisingly, the development and acceptance of technological innovations is affected by fashions. There are fashions not only in the application of the technologies, but even in the early studies, development, and experimentation with proposed innovation. While this might seem to be a superficial factor, nevertheless it is our impression that the investigations as well as the application of all the innovations we have examined have followed a general pattern. This pattern includes a period of early experimentation during which something goes wrong and the innovation comes to be viewed with disapproval by the established community of professionals and the policy-makers who rely on them. This happened to the IUD in the late 1920s and early 1930s and to antabuse in the late 1950s. This is followed by a long period of experimentation under resistance. When and if the research and development take off despite the hostile context, the innovation proceeds to gain a measure of popularity, as IUD did in the 1960s, ITV in the mid-60s, and methadone in 1970. The innovation becomes fashionable. This is usually followed by a reaction, when the shortcomings of what is so often initially over-enthusiastically adopted as a cure become known, and at that point a more realistic perspective sets in. Thus, early hopes are followed by long latency, breakthroughs, fashionability, and then a realistic adaptation—for those innovations which complete the cycle. Also, usually at this stage the innovation is beginning to be considered no longer a new and original topic and it again becomes difficult to get research funds and to experiment, even though at this point this sort of work is often most needed. For instance, by 1970, IUD had lost much of its fashionability as a research topic, and ITV even more so. The only exception to this pattern is gun control—which has received a total high-powered resistance all the way; possibly it should be considered as simply not yet having taken off in this country. It is much more held back, even as a "disapproved" research topic, than were the others.

Thus overall, there is an extensive range of factors complicating and hampering the acquisition and use of information on the effectiveness of proposed technological remedies.

Science and Engineering

The technologies we are dealing with are all clearly in the applied area. There is a widely subscribed-to myth that technological innovations arise from basic scientific principles and are then incorporated in the development of extensive new technical systems (*e.g.,* new principles in physics "led" to the atomic bomb). As we see it, while there is such a flow from basic research, from science to applied systems, the relationship is much less close, much less one-directional than is often implied. On the contrary, research on applied systems has a discipline and life of its own. Both in the sense that much of the information and many of the principles used in applied research cannot be traced to an analytic discipline and in the sense that breakthroughs in applied areas lead to major developments in science, as in the development of computer technology, microscopes, and, previously, telescopes. (This topic will be discussed in greater detail below in the context of governmental support of research.) *In principle, therefore, it seems more accurate to view applied research and basic research as two semi-autonomous activities which interact with each other.*

The preceding is one of the deeper reasons why we frequently do not understand why a remedial procedure of technology "works," but, of course, we do not hesitate to draw on it. This is not to suggest that it is unnecessary or undesirable to find out why a system works. On the contrary, when the reasons for the effectiveness of a technique are not known, the application of the technology entails accepting fundamentally unascertainable risks. We do not really know what we are doing; we only know that one of the immediate, overt results is desirable and presumably justifies accepting the risks. So for pragmatic, not just scientific, reasons fully understanding a system is important. But, as the technologies at hand illustrate, such understanding may frequently, in part, follow the development of the system.

While we observe that methadone "works" (within the terms of discourse established earlier), it is, at this point, extremely unclear why it works. The explanations differ, from the physiological (the fact that it is introduced orally rather than intravenously; or it may give a different "high" than heroin and, hence, the dosage can be stabilized) to psychological and social (*e.g.*, the change in the social definition of the person using it). Much the same can be said about antabuse.

The Dole explanation that the heroin addiction is a result of a physiological imbalance in the body and that methadone makes up for the deficiency somewhat like a vitamin is not endorsed by any other source that we came across and is doubted by everybody we discussed this matter with, including members of Dole's own staff. At the same time there is mounting indication from other sources about physiological sources of other addictions. For instance, Dr. B. D. Ehagat of St. Louis University has reported to the Federation of American Societies for Experimental Biology in its April 1970 meeting in Atlantic City that there is a physical basis for the cigarette habit. The basis is a result of the effect of nicotine on NoreTine Thrine (NE). NE is a regulatory hormone of the brain and other nervous system tissues. Nicotine increases both its production and its utilization. As a result, the smoker's brain is kept in a state of abnormal excitement. Once the body becomes accustomed to this increase in the production and use of NE, any withdrawal of nicotine results in depression. Thus the body begins to depend on nicotine. Therefore the smoker must smoke to "dose" himself with nicotine in order to keep the production of NE at the elevated level.

Another report refers to the relationship between smoking cessation and obesity. Dr. Stanley C. Glauser, from Temple University School of Medicine, reports that the metabolism of smokers differs from that of non-smokers, and this affects their weight. For instance, he reports that the mean oxygen consumption of smokers was 283 milliliters a minute, but after they stopped smoking it dropped to 260 milliliters a minute. Their heart rate dropped from 60 to 57 beats a minute, which adds up to more than 4,800 beats a day. He reports other metabolic changes such as a decrease in the protein-bound iodine and in the calcium in the blood. The smokers he studied gained an average of 6.5 pounds after they ceased smoking. According to the observations made, only one of those ate more; the rest is attributed by Dr. Glauser to the change in the metabolic processes.

With regard to ITV, in a sense the opposite situation prevails. There is nothing to "know" here. What is being applied here are quite well-known principles of teaching, all without any great scientific mystery or technical refinement. The value of the system lies precisely in the greatly increased use of these well-known principles that is made possible by a new technology which previously was unavailable. Excellent examples of this are the acclaimed National Educational Television's shows "Sesame Street" and "The Electric Company."[77]

A similar statement may be made about gun control. While there is considerable controversy about the extent to which gun control would be effective, there is very little doubt as to why it works to the extent that it does.

The IUD is similar to methadone and antabuse. We knew it "worked" long before the medical processes involved were perceived and as far as we can tell, they are far from completely understood at present.

It follows that we do not fully share in the somewhat self-serving myth of the scientific community that the most direct way to enrich a society's capacity to solve its problems is by enriching its basic research. While basic research should, of course, be supported for its own sake and to some extent because it does provide input for applied systems, equally significant is the need to invest in applied work directly aimed at evolving workable systems.

Here it might be useful to apply the kind of research and development approach used in the creation of missiles to the development of new socially useful technologies. There is an inclination in the latter area to jump from the drawing boards to full-grown systems. Thus, for instance, Title I (in support of schooling for the disadvantaged) was in existence for four years at the level of $1.2 billion a year before the first significant study testing the assumptions on which the system was based was available, the Coleman

---

[77] For evaluative data, see Samuel Ball and Gerry A. Bogatz, *The First Year of Sesame Street* (Princeton, N.J.: Educational Testing Service, 1970).

Report. The report is widely understood to imply that the Title I system was either unnecessary or unworkable.

This contrasts sharply with the way in which the negative income tax was first experimented with on several hundred families in New Jersey all before the enacting legislation was completed. While this procedure was not entirely due to superior wisdom (in part, it was caused by the unwillingness of Congress to legislate the negative income tax), still, a more careful staging, including operational experimentation, was usefully employed here before the system was considered for nationwide application.

Methadone also was used slowly on ever-larger groupings, with the first experiments conducted under highly controlled conditions, *i.e.*, the patients initially lived in an experimental hospital ward; and somewhat later the patients were living in the community and coming in to the hospital for their medication. This sequence allowed precisely that which was necessary at this stage, a very sharp reduction in the administrative costs of the program; and at the same time, it allowed debugging of some of the difficulties involved in the application of the system, particularly the simplification of valid urine tests. Antabuse has not reached this stage. IUD has followed roughly the same principle stages. ITV has had a large number of both small-scale experiments and a fair number of large operational experiments, but none of these seem to be cumulative or part of a systematic attempt to exploit the full potential of the system. It would be appropriate now for a state university system such as that in California or in New York to introduce the system on a really large scale.

THE DIFFERENTIATION OF SHORTCUTS: MECHANISMS AND MIXING

As was suggested above, there is a need to understand the mechanisms by which the various technologies work. On the one hand, this is a theoretical need; we seek to understand the processes which affect our lives. We have a curiosity. On the other hand, there are pragmatic considerations here. Initially, if we understand the mechanisms, it may be easier to come up with parallel interventions when we have analogous problems. For instance, if we understood how methadone works we might be more successful in developing blocking and/or counter drugs for alcoholism and smoking. Additionally, many of the specifications appropriate to mass application of the technologies as well as the assessment of long-run effects depend on the knowledge of the mechanisms involved. Thus, for instance, if any of these technologies works only or chiefly because of the Hawthorne effect (*i.e.*, simply because attention is being accorded the individuals), then their efficacy must be expected to decline over the longer run, unless special efforts are made to design a continued expression of interest, and concern into the procedures. Or, if methadone works primarily because it is taken orally rather than intravenously, we would have to be concerned with the possibility that methadone might be given to the addicts to take in unsupervised conditions and they might then take the drug intravenously.

We also need to understand the technologies' operative mechanisms in order to resolve the question of the value of mixing human and technical elements. Whether or not the technologies can be applied purely or must be mixed with other non-technological treatments is a vital question for the costs of mass use. Methadone can be given both with or without psychotherapy, and with or without systematic attempts to find employment opportunities for the patients. This is also true of antabuse. ITV can be introduced by itself or together with various kinds of live teaching, especially discussion groups following televised instruction. IUD can be given with or without attempts to change peoples' preferences about family size. Gun control can be introduced with or without attempts to reduce the causes of criminality by rehabilitation efforts. The most important reason why we must answer the question of the necessity and value of mixing is that the costs of "human" additions to a technological system are very high both absolutely, and per unit result. For instance, seat belts may save a life at a cost of $87, while driver education may cost as much as $88,000 per life saved.[78] Thus, the question arises—how much education is necessary to make people wear seat belts? Or, would it be better to have only cars which do not start unless the seat belt is in place?

The data is not conclusive on this point precisely because the mechanisms involved are often not known or only known in part. It is our impression that often a significant part of the problem can be handled by pure technological systems. This seems particularly appropriate for those groups of people who are already motivated or socially situated so as to be able to solve their problems by themselves once they overcome their particular "hang up." Thus, a subpopulation of heroin addicts seems capable of a socially normal and productive life once they are able to break their heroin habit with the help of methadone, even if they are not given any other kind of assistance. The same holds true for alcoholism and antabuse. This relationship is particularly clear in the case of IUD. It is not a central question here whether people have very clear and set family size preferences. Rather their desire for birth control may be seen to be affected by the availability of a cheap, easy-to-use technique which can be introduced at one point in time and need not be taken every day or each time they engage in inter-

---

[78] Elizabeth B. Drew, "HEW Grapples with PPBS," *Readings on Modern Organizations,* Amitai Etzioni, ed. (Englewood Cliffs, N.J.: Prentice-Hall, Inc., 1969), p. 178.

course and thus has to be continually faced in terms of the practical, moral, and religious questions involved. That is, the significant fact that IUD can be taken once and then "forgotten" does generate a sizable subpopulation which will use and benefit from this technology—but not other more demanding birth control devices—without any making changes in their family size preferences. Similarly, the very introduction of a breath-testing device on the highways will reduce the drinking-before-driving of some subpopulation for whom the very existence of such a test would be sufficient deterrent.

It is, hence, misleading to ask whether the technology can work without the addition of a "human" input. The answer to this question would have to be both yes and no. The more appropriate question seems to us to be for what segment of the population, and for what segment of the problem can the technology work without additional human inputs. (The segment of the population refers simply to the number of heroin addicts, for example, out of the total population of addicts who could benefit from methadone alone.) The segment of the problem is measured differently. For example, assuming that there are *"x"* million smokers, it is not enough to say that 20 percent of them could stop smoking with Nicoban without any additional inputs. They may represent less than one-fifth of that population injured by smoking because they may include mainly the light smokers. Similarly, many heroin addicts who volunteer for treatment may be less hooked than those who do not. And those drivers turned away from drinking by the existence of the breath test may be mainly social drinkers, who constitute the easier part of the problem.

It seems likely that *while the technologies can be used by themselves effectively for some subpopulations, usually these are the people for whom "treatment" is easiest.* This is not to say, though, that pure technological treatment is ineffective or insignificant. It simply means that one has to know which subpopulations are the most amenable to this treatment. They may still be as large as two-thirds of the population and as much as one-third of the problem. By treating those "purely" we help to save the resources necessary for the provision of mixed systems for the others.

In this context there is a tendency to talk critically about "creaming," referring to the process of taking off the easiest part of a problem first. Although the motivation for such a procedure is to produce cheap and easy successes, in principle there is nothing wrong with "creaming." It simply means that one focuses on the subpopulation where one can get the largest results for the resources available. "Creaming" is wrong only when one expects to treat with the same means and at the same cost the parts of the population and of the problem which are left behind.

There seems likely to be significant subpopulations for which mixed systems are necessary. Some of the heroin addicts seem to need special assistance if they are to find work and if they are not to return to a life of heroin addiction and criminality. Many of the serious crimes which occur among friends or relatives in hot blood may literally disappear if weapons are not available. However, hardened criminals may well need rehabilitation or jailing. Some of the subjects to be taught on ITV may well require discussion groups and some of the students may particularly need them, especially the less motivated ones. The last example allows us to provide a general principle which may serve to explain what segments of the population and of the problem need mixed systems above and beyond the principle that they are those individuals most deeply affected by the particular problem.

One of the issues involved in the problem of matching a pure or mixed technological system with a segmented target population is specifying what it takes to change a person or a social group, and hence ultimately a society. Thus, for instance, if certain people are alcoholics, the question is do we have to change their personalities or their social environment before they can overcome their illness. The answer to this is far from clear, even on sheer theoretical grounds; interpretations vary all the way from those social analysts who believe that the issue is a matter of definition—that by ceasing to call alcoholics alcoholics, and by viewing them as "people who drink," we could eliminate most, if not all, of the problem—up to people who believe that the causes of such problems are inherited genetically, or are so deep in the personality structure that nothing can be done about it through drugs or other remedies. An intermediate position would suggest the probable utility of long deep psychoanalysis, or group therapy, or a change in basic social structure in order to make life less tension-provoking.

To further differentiate the issue, the answer may vary for different social problems. Thus, for instance, it might be almost impossible for a person who is a homosexual or who is obese (as distinct from overweight) or who is a lifelong alcoholic, to be cured, except when a total change in his social environment occurs such as when an individual is integrated successfully into such therapeutic communities as Alcoholics Anonymous or Synanon. Unfortunately there seem to be some reasons why the capacity to create such groups is limited to very small subpopulations of the total and why these groups can only be helped to develop to a limited extent. Basically such communities seem to be the result of "natural" development. Hence they do not provide a likely avenue for organized societal change, both because they are limited in their scope, and because they cannot be guided.

We have already noted that subpopulations differ from the viewpoint of the depth of the difficulty. The difference may be that the behavior alteration that we are after entails either only an instrumental skill change or a personality change. For instance, it seems likely that there would be varying degrees of difficulty if you tried to get a person to change his dressing habits as opposed to his drinking habits. Quite probably, one set of habits is more deeply ingrained than the other. With regard to instruction, we can differentiate between subjects which require only instrumental information, and subjects which entail some alteration in basic values or the acquisition of aesthetic tastes. Hence, it makes a considerable difference whether one attempts to teach people typing and cooking or poetry and civics. This distinction is not completely accurate because one could teach civics (or poetry) as if it were primarily instrumental information, primarily teaching technical and specific points about governmental institutions, such as the number of members of Congress and the year the Supreme Court was created. And conversely, one could conceivably use the teaching of typing to try to communicate middle-class values about neatness and accuracy. Thus the real differentiating factor would be not the formal nature of the subject of instruction, although this may be correlated with the issue at hand, but the degree to which instrumental as against expressive communication is involved; the extent to which we seek to communicate information or skills as against communicating our values and bringing about basic character changes. Now in general you would expect the humanities to contain more of the latter while much of the natural sciences would fall into the former category; primary school education to be more expressive and graduate education more instrumental, with the other years of high school and college falling into their place in the sequence. We would expect that the more instrumental subjects could be more easily communicated by the use of pure technology, while the more expressive material would require a greater "mixing." The evidence supporting this proposition is so far rather weak. However, the main reason for this may be that the question was never asked quite in this particular form. The studies we are aware of have only approximated it in one way or another. Our grounds for making these suggestions are thus mainly theoretical. It seems likely that changes of information are more easy to achieve than normative changes.

Assuming for a moment that additional studies would show that this differentiation holds empirically, this would suggest the conditions in which rehabilitation and psychotherapy would be necessary in conjunction with drug therapy and gun control and under what conditions they would not be necessary. When people are functioning relatively well, or when all we seek to communicate is information (*e.g.,* the danger of drug overdosage), relatively pure systems could accomplish the desired goals. When what we seek is character change, mixed systems would have to be used and the human input would have to be larger.

Finally, one should definitely not treat the question of human input into the human-technological mix as a dichotomous issue. Different proportions should be used for different needs, up to making the system mainly human with the technology being only an assisting factor.

THE GOVERNMENTAL AND MORAL CONTEXT

The Federal Scene[79]

Which areas of domestic applied research and development receive attention is to a very large degree determined by the federal government as most funds for such work are derived from federal sources. Accordingly we should consider the effect federal procedures have on the development of domestic technology. The technological needs of our domestic programs are now being served by research and development efforts dispersed widely among federal agencies as well as outside the government in universities, research corporations, and private industry. To some extent this arrangement is both inevitable and desirable. Most agencies have some specific research needs of their own that they themselves can probably best serve. The existence of a multiplicity of R & D centers in the private sector helps to insure that a given approach will not monopolize the funds and prematurely drive out others which may prove to be more productive in the long run. However, the existing system of R & D centers serving the government does suffer from several deficiencies that may be corrected by a proposed agency that is to specialize in domestic technological development, the Agency for Technological Development (ATD).

1. In many federal agencies, the technological division is an administrative stepchild. Only rarely are its special needs adequately understood either by the agency heads, whose backgrounds and training tend to be neither in research nor in technical development, or by the civil servants who stand between the technological division and the agency heads. It is important to note that these technological environments are not accidental; they are a result of the fact that the development of new technologies is neither the primary mission of these agencies nor the primary means of fulfilling their major missions. Thus, it is not surprising, nor is it a phenomenon limited to this country, that government agencies, staffed by civil servants, lawyers, and economists, find it difficult to provide an environment hospitable to laboratories and testing grounds, to engineers and applied psychologists. It is unreasonable to expect that a directive by a Secretary or the enunciation of a new policy will change such "structural" features. In-

---

[79] This section draws on a previously published article: Amitai Etzioni, "Agency for Technical Development for Domestic Programs," *Science,* Vol. 164 (April 4, 1969), pp. 43–50.

stitutionalization of a protechnological environment seems necessary if effective service of technological missions is to be possible—that is, establishment of an agency which will have technological development as its prime mission and which will be organized and staffed accordingly.

2. The budgets of most of the existing governmental domestic R & D units constitute small fractions of the total budgets of the agencies to which these units are attached (see Table 1), and only part of this budget is used for technological development.

Of the total R & D obligations, most of the funds are used for non-domestic missions; it is estimated that $13.8 billion have been obligated to the Department of Defense, NASA, and the Atomic Energy Commission and $2.1 billions to the other 27 agencies. The situation in some of the key domestic agencies is shown in Table 1.

Table 1. Estimated Obligations for Fiscal Year 1966

Agency	Total R & D obligations (in millions of dollars)	Percentage of total agency budget
Department of Agriculture	243.7	3
Department of Commerce	88.9	8
Department of Labor	11.8	2
Department of State	14.6	4
Office of Economic Opportunity	60.0	4

Source: Federal Funds for Research, Development and Other Scientific Activities, Fiscal Year 1965, 1966, 1967 (Washington D.C.: U.S. Government Printing Office), pp. 30 ff.

Obviously these obligations for R & D reflect neither a high national priority nor, it seems, the potential value of the work involved. For the Departments of Interior and HEW, the percentages of the budgets allocated to R & D were higher, although not high—10 and 12 percent, respectively. In Interior, R & D expenditures are concentrated largely in a few highly technological subagencies, such as the Bureau of Mines; whether or not other bureaus could benefit from larger R & D expenditures remains in doubt. The 12 percent of the budget spent on R & D by HEW is spent largely for the research (R) and not for technology (D). Actually, out of every four dollars obligated, only one dollar is obligated for development,[80] which is, of course, the more expensive part of the R & D process.

---

[80] *Federal Funds for Research, Development and Other Scientific Activities, Fiscal Year 1965, 1966, 1967* (Washington, D.C.: U.S. Government Printing Office), p. 31.

The small and politically weak Office of Science and Technology in the White House seems unable to campaign effectively for these various R & D units, and the National Science Foundation's mission is, by and large, limited to research, primarily of a basic nature, although NSF has been paying some attention recently to matters involving transfer of technology, engineering, and so on. It is likely that only the combination of all, or at least some, of these units and their elevation to the level of an agency will bring new technologies for domestic missions the needed support, as only then will domestic R & D be able to compete effectively in the federal give-and-take for funds.

3. The fact that many of the numerous agencies active in the domestic areas now develop their own technological facilities seems to lead to some waste and to a measure of duplication. While some of these facilities are area-specific, others—such as computer centers and testing grounds—could be combined. Establishment of a federal R & D agency specializing in domestic missions would seem more economical than support of R & D in each of the numerous agencies and subagencies with a domestic mission.

4. A significant proportion of the national R & D is, and surely will continue to be, carried on "out-of-house," in the private sector—in universities, research corporations, and private industry. However, the universities tend—quite properly—to focus on research at the expense of development, and on basic research at the expense of applied research. The forces are many and powerful which underlie this tendency of university research to be remote from practical needs. They include the prestige attached to research as compared to technological development, and to basic research as compared to applied research. Career advancement is often tied to achievement in basic research and, furthermore, scientists are often reluctant to accept the outside guidance that is found more frequently, and in greater detail, in applied and developmental work than in basic research.[81]

Also many members of academia firmly believe that the best way to solve a practical problem is to invest in basic research; research funds are to be cast upon the oceans of science in the hope that the "answers" to specific problems will someday be washed ashore. Experience, as well as the empirical testing of this belief, seems to suggest otherwise.

The first atom bombs were produced in a concentrated effort specifically designed to result in such a product (Project Manhattan). Polio vaccine was developed by Salk and Sabin task forces. The use of high dosages of methadone as a means of handling heroin addiction was discovered during a

---

[81] H. Orlans, ed., *Science, Policy and the University* (Washington, D.C.: The Brookings Institution, 1968).

deliberate effort to find an effective medical approach to heroin addiction. A manual lunar landing was achieved as a result of the deliberate efforts of Project Apollo. A study by Jacob Schmookler shows that significantly more results are produced in those areas in which there are significantly greater R & D efforts (as measured by investments).[82] A study by the Department of Defense (Project Hindsight), which sought to establish the ways in which the systems most useful to defense were evolved, lends further support to this conclusion: of the 556 "events" which led to the evolution of the desired system, 92 percent were technological.[83] The study has been criticized[84] for focusing on technological payoffs (only weapons were studied as payoffs) and neglecting scientific inputs (by not tracing the "events" farther back). In addition, a study of the sources of new findings in chemistry has been used to counter Hindsight's insights.[85]

The questions about the relative importance and independence of scientific and technological inputs need not be resolved before the arguments in favor of a new technological agency can be examined. The following statements seem to summarize a kind of consensus of experts which is evolving:

1. Investment in basic research must be continued because ultimately it is the foundation on which much of the later, more applied work builds; Hindsight findings exaggerate the importance of technological development.

2. Investment in technological development is needed because a) there is no "automatic" route from scientific findings to useful technologies (and the costs of technological developments are 15 to 60 times those of the initial research), and b) some developments are intrinsically technological and cannot be traced back to scientific findings—that is, the scientists' belief in the dependence of technological development on scientific research underestimates the need for investment in technologies per se.

3. Technological developments are more "guidable" than research, especially basic research. Hence, if the goal is to increase the capacity to

---

[82] Jacob Schmookler, *Invention and Economic Growth* (Cambridge, Mass.: Harvard University Press, 1966); R. Nelson, "The Economics of Intervention: A Survey of the Literature," *Journal of Business* 32, 101–127 (1959).

[83] "First Report of Project Hindsight" (Department of Defense Publication, Washington, D.C.: U.S. Government Printing Office, 1969).

[84] D. S. Greenberg, *The Politics of Pure Science* (New York: New American Library, 1967), pp. 32–33. The Illinois Institute of Technology is reported to be completing a study with more "depth" reporting and heavier emphasis on nontechnical elements (private communication).

[85] Greenberg, *op. cit.;* also *Chemistry: Opportunities and Needs* (Washington, D.C.: National Academy of Sciences–National Research Council, 1965).

treat domestic problems, the payoffs from direct investment in technological development will be greater than those from research, as the former will be more "on target."

4. While universities—with the significant exceptions of some engineering schools, university-affiliated laboratories, and a few other units—are oriented toward basic research, private industry and some research corporations are quite willing and able to work on specific technologies under the guidance of the government.

An agency specializing in technological development for domestic missions would, thus, increase the "weight" of these missions both in the federal give-and-take and in the private sector.

Another reason why an Agency for Technological Development might be more effective than the existing multiple technological units within the scores of federal agencies and bureaus entrusted with domestic missions is that such an agency would be concerned with relations among technologies, a matter to which the present dispersed system cannot give much attention. New transportation systems, for example, are often designed without sufficient regard for housing problems, housing projects are designed without recognition of the problems of crime control, and so on.[86] Another example of this approach is the effort to use new technology in education. In February of 1970, the Commission on Instructional Technology reported to President Nixon and the Congress: "Technology, we believe, can carry out its full potential for education only insofar as educators embrace instructional technology as a system and integrate a range of human and nonhuman resources into the total educational process."[87] Administratively, it would be necessary to include new technologies within an expanded organizational framework. To the extent that various specialized efforts are placed under one administrative roof, the likelihood will be increased that both the negative and the positive "side effects" of new technologies and their place in domestic programs will be more fully taken into account. Even within one agency there are barriers to such coordination, and these barriers are almost insurmountable between agencies.

There are exceptions: interagency cooperation between the Atomic Energy Commission and the Department of Interior on desalination and reduction of pollution is a case in point. But such collaboration is not common, and it is difficult to conceive, in view of the fragmenting forces at work,

---

[86] "University Units of Urban Study Hit as Failures," *Chronicle of Higher Education* 3, No. 6 (1968), p. 1.

[87] Ian E. McNett, "Technology Deserves Much Larger Place in Education, Federal Commission Says," *Chronicle of Higher Education* (February 16, 1970).

how it could become the norm. Dael Wolfle, addressing himself to this point, wrote:

> Many of the large problems that confront us . . . differ from those of the space program in focusing on people rather than on rockets and space vehicles. . . . But the social programs, like the space program, call for management structures linking government, industry, and universities. The new program will involve research, planning, coordination, and testing. And they will be bothered by multiple divisions of responsibility, conflicting ambitions and interests, decisions to use existing facilities or to assemble new ones, multiple channels of communication and authority, and the problems of building up and of phasing down as priorities shift to new targets or as new opportunities open up.[88]

Hence, we agree here with Wolfle that NASA provides a more effective administrative model.

In short, there seem to be several significant reasons for favoring an agency for domestic technological development. Many of the objections to such an agency seem to revolve around the issue of political feasibility.

When we prepared a previous version of this material we sent it "for comments" to a number of acquaintances in government agencies, on congressional committees, and in research corporations. Of the eighteen who responded, all but one live in the Washington area. Such "feedback" is quite useful even in working on a regular academic paper, as it is very difficult for most writers to anticipate all the questions that the exposition of a concept or a finding may raise. Seeking such response becomes almost inescapable when one is dealing with policy proposals. Here, it is most useful to take into account the viewpoints of those who would be affected if the proposal were to be implemented, and of those highly familiar with the political constraints which the proposal will confront.

It was the consensus of the respondents that greater technological development would indeed be helpful in handling many of our domestic problems. And almost all of them agreed that such development would entail heavy investment in the technologies themselves and not just in basic or applied research. However, practically all of the respondents questioned the political feasibility of creating an agency devoted to the advancement of technology. It was repeatedly stated, with considerable force and conviction, that the existing agencies, Congress and its committees, and industry would oppose such a plan.

Speed of Payoffs and Congress. Among those whose profession is turning blueprints into social instruments or programs, and among those who work on developing new technologies, it is commonplace to expect a period of

---

[88] Dael Wolfle, *Science,* Vol. 162 (1968), p. 753.

significant modifications and "de-bugging." It seems impossible to anticipate, on the drawing boards or in tests with small-scale models, all, or even
most, of the difficulties a functioning, full-scale model will encounter. (The
same holds for the routine production of what was developed as a prototype.) Hence, considerable effort and investment are needed precisely in this
phase—that is, in evolving the first "prototypes" and setting up routine
"production." The more "de-bugged" these phases are, the less likely it is
that revisions will be necessary once mass production is under way. An analogous situation would be the correction of a stencil before it is run off instead
of editing all the finished copies.

Occasionally, the temptation to skip preliminary testing is not resisted.
For instance, it was reported that construction of the landing gear for the
lunar spacecraft was being advanced while close pictures of the surface of
the moon were still being sought. While the following impression cannot
be documented, it seems likely, as was noted earlier, that, by and large, the
tendency to "jump" into the field, to skip preliminary testing and de-bugging, is much stronger in the domestic area than in the areas of defense and
space, and that this situation is most likely to occur in regard to new social
programs (for example, computer-assisted teaching). One of the surprising
experiences in interviewing officials in federal agencies and members of Congress is to discover how often they are not fully aware of the effort, time,
and costs involved in turning an idea, already fully "researched," into a
smoothly functioning system.

The degree of "tolerance" for prolonged and repeated preliminary
testing or the inclination to skip stages are not abstract character traits, some
people being cautious types and others hotheads. The orientation toward
preliminary testing is greatly affected by budgetary considerations (preliminary testing often costs more than the original research); by the fact that
application in the field is often paid for by a body other than that which
conducted the R & D effort; by political considerations (adequate preliminary testing may carry the payoff of a program launched by one administration into the lifetime of the next one); and even by international considerations (How are the Russians progressing?). Many of the domestic programs
launched between 1965 and 1968 had been insufficiently tested, while others,
not tested at all, resulted in frequent costly reorganizations *after* the programs had been launched, or in programs that failed to take off.[89]

In discussions of this approach, the argument that a program which
does not promise quick results will not be tolerated by Congress is often
raised. A new, more candid approach may have to be tried. Instead of over-

---

[89] Daniel P. Moynihan, "Professors and the Poor," *Commentary,* Vol. 46 (August, 1968),
pp. 19–28.

selling a program in terms of its yield and speed, perhaps it should be stated openly that the program will be innovative and experimental, and that, even if only one of every five projects were to yield a major new technology, the money would have been well spent. Also, by keeping testing "in-house," the reactions to initial inevitable failures may be more limited.

The concern of the respondents was with both the "producers" and the "consumers" of new technologies. On the producers' side, it was pointed out that many agencies already have R & D units which they would, for the most part, be quite reluctant to relinquish. These agencies can be expected to be supported by the congressional committees charged with overseeing their work—committees which would tend to oppose a reduction in the missions (and funds) they oversee. Finally, private industry, it was stated, is also working with agencies and subagencies, specific industries having built relations with those government agencies that deal with "their" technologies. Hence, industries would tend to object to a reorganization which would make "their" units disappear into a much larger technological agency, over which they would have less sway. Thus, for instance, the railroad industry would much prefer to deal with the Department of Transportation than with the envisioned Agency for Technological Development (ATD). The same holds for other groups, especially professional associations. For example, the American Medical Association would much rather be involved, it was stated, with the Dangerous Drug Division of the Department of Justice than with the new ATD.

It may be expected that the suggested ATD would encounter less resistance than earlier suggestions to concentrate science and technology in one department have met with, since neither science nor military and space technology (the non-domestic major "development" items) would be included. Some of the domestic agencies (for example, HUD) are at the very beginning of developing their R & D units and seem to be less committed to their own units than agencies in which the R & D units are well established. Still, there can be little doubt that the formation of an agency specializing in domestic, mainly urban, technological problems will encounter considerable opposition from existing domestic agencies.[90] Still, the proposal deserves some attention on the following grounds. First, like economists' models of free competition, it serves to point up the "dis-economies" generated by the existing system and their estimated size and location. Second, it points out that, even if only the R & D units of some of the numerous domestic agencies could be combined, part of the dis-economy would be reduced. (NASA never "internalized" all the space work; important seg-

---

[90] J. L. Sunquist, *Politics and Policy: The Eisenhower, Kennedy, and Johnson Years* (Washington, D.C.: The Brookings Institution, 1968).

ments were, and still are, effected by the Air Force, and through the combined efforts of NASA and the Air Force.)

Finally, such a reorganization may be introduced by a powerful President, one ready to withstand the counter-pressures in order to gain what may be a significantly more effective arrangement. This is not completely without precedent; when NASA was first created, R & D units were transferred to it from the Armed Services. While this move was initially not well received by the Air Force, the Army, and some members of Congress, the reorganization was carried out nonetheless. Similarly, in recent years several reorganizations of HEW did make some parts of the Department somewhat more immune to external pressures and more responsive to the Secretary's direction. All this is to say that a measure of administrative reform is possible despite counter-pressures.

One line of approach would be to concentrate first on the R & D work of the agencies in which these divisions are still relatively small or in which the division suffers more from being in an agency alien to technological missions. Among the agencies my respondents listed as qualifying on one or both of these counts were Justice, Interior, Commerce, and Labor, as well as some parts of HEW (especially the Office of Education).

On the other hand, where technological development and the major agency mission are as intimately linked as they are in the Department of Transportation and in some parts of HEW (especially the health services), attempts to separate the two and to transfer the technological component to a new agency were considered both politically impractical and of questionable value. Among the areas most often cited as areas in which full-fledged attention to technological development has not yet evolved were education (despite the recent rise of educational laboratories), job training, crime prevention, and housing. Reduction of pollution and weather control were listed by some as suitable candidates, while others held them to be more "advanced," in terms of R & D work by existing agencies, than the other four areas cited.

This list of units "more suitable" for transfer led to consideration of a second, closely related but still analytically autonomous, issue.

Relations with the Consumers of New Technologies. Two schemes for the relations between a new technological agency and the agencies which would abandon their own technological work can be envisioned. The first, which comes to mind most readily, seems to be the less practical. The second, under prevailing conditions, seems the more feasible.

A student of "pure" administration, undiluted with politics, may envision a technological agency that would serve the regular agencies, which would draw on it for their "hardware," somewhat as the three Armed Forces draw on the Joint Ordnance Service. In the language of organizational

specialists, the ATD would be a "functional" service for the "line" operations carried out by implementing agencies. The latter would order the
specific technologies they need, and perhaps even pay for them.

However, any scheme which assumes tight interagency cooperation
seems, according to the respondents, to be about as realistic as ignoring
gravity. Each federal agency is, to a considerable extent, an independent
entity (often with quite autonomous subentities), and previous attempts to
rely on close interagency cooperation such as the envisioned arrangement
would require have been, as a rule, quite unsuccessful. Several respondents
reported experiences as members of an interagency board or committee that
did not "work," or told about a "system" that was developed by one agency
and ignored by another because it was alien to the latter's conception, needs,
interests, or ambitions. "The President can gain interagency cooperation
but you cannot appeal to him too often, and even he cannot get such cooperation all the time," one veteran of the Washington scene observed. Two
attempts to create "comprehensive" domestic agencies (the Office of Economic Opportunity and Housing and Urban Development), which were
supposed to combine their efforts in specific sectors—poverty and urban
problems, respectively—with the relevant work of other agencies, have not
yielded much interagency coordination thus far. Above all, it was indicated,
one cannot expect one agency to evolve a program and another to pay for it.
"And who will pay for the new technologies if not the federal government?"

Consideration of this financial question points to a second view of the
potential place of an ATD in the federal and general political-administrative
mesh. Here, it is essential to take into account one feature of the domestic
environment. In the fields of space and defense the federal government is
both the main source of funds for R & D and the customer for most of the
products—whether it be a weapon or a spacecraft. In the domestic sphere,
on the other hand, often the customer is not the funding agency or any
other federal agency but, rather, the states, the cities, or various corporate
bodies (for example, hospitals and universities). For reasons outlined below,
these bodies are in a very different relationship to a potential "earth NASA"
than the federal agencies are.

About 160 American cities have experienced one or more of the "standard" domestic crises. It is inconceivable that each city, or even each of the
fifty states, will set up its own technological agency. Most of them do not
have the necessary funds, and the skills needed are so rare that, even if all
the specialists now living in America were recruited for these missions, they
would not suffice to staff more than the technological divisions of a few cities
or states.

Moreover, it must be noted that major technological breakthroughs
have been made by a few talented men or by a concentration of high-quality

manpower. Thus, even if each city could hire, let us say, two urban sociologists (the total number is more like several score than several hundred), only a few of these would have sufficient talent to actually benefit the cities.

Finally, if the solution to each problem—for example, the discovery of an inexpensive method of water depollution—had to be "reinvented" in fifty states or 160 cities, this would result in an extreme duplication of effort. And no one state or city can be expected to be the technological agency for the rest of the country. Hence, a national service for local authorities may be more politically feasible than one for other federal agencies.

At the same time, local autonomy will have to be preserved. The local governments could be best served, it seems, if the ATD were to institute a kind of "cafeteria"-style presentation of its new techniques, with states and cities able to choose whatever systems they wished to acquire and install. Thus, no strings would be attached to the program; a city or state seeking to build a new transportation, school, or housing system could acquire tested blueprints, specifications, and technical assistance (in the form of teams of engineers, city planners, and so on) from the federal agency and apply them where and when it wished.

So we return to the question of who will bear the costs of the implementation of the programs, once a prototype has been developed. It is very widely held in Washington that the agency promoting an innovation must pay for implementation: HUD for new housing, the Department of Transportation for new trains, the Office of Education for new teaching technologies, and so on. Most cities and states are impoverished. While it is difficult to raise federal taxes, especially to pay for the expansion of domestic programs, this is considered easier than to raise local taxes.[91]

The implication for the issue at hand is that the agency which will pay for the implementation of a specific innovation—for example, a new type of housing—will also seek to be the one to evolve the relevant technology. Hence, it is argued, there is no place for an ATD.

This argument may well be somewhat extreme. If an agency were to develop a highly effective new technology—new computers, for instance—would not other agencies with similar requirements adopt it?

Possibly, the creation of an intercity (and interstate) technological dissemination system might be a necessary federal investment, the costs of such a system would not be too large for ATD to handle, nor would it require extensive collaboration with other agencies.

Finally, if the cities or states are unable or unwilling to pay for utilization of the new technologies, federal agencies in the near future are also

---

[91] J. Spivak, *Wall Street Journal* (December 11, 1968).

unlikely to be able to finance mass programs, even if the new technologies are their own. (The reasons for this statement are discussed above.) In the longer run, all indications are that an increased amount of federal revenue will be channeled to states and cities; that is, the latter will have more "disposable" money to buy innovations and will not have to adopt the concepts of HUD or the Office of Economic Opportunity or the Office of Education but can absorb mainly those compatible with their own conceptions and needs (within some federal constraints, such as the requirement for desegregation). Hence, ultimately, the question of the value of the ATD is clearly linked to the nature and size of our future domestic drives. Whether these are going to be funded largely in the New Deal style, by way of federal agencies set up for specific problem areas, or whether funds are going to be spent increasingly by cities and states, with the federal agencies providing technical and other assistance, has yet to be decided. We expect that the tendency will be to turn over more funds to states and cities, and we see within this pattern a place for an Agency for Technological Development. It can assist local bodies in handling their problems, and the localities will pay for the technologies, even if it is the federal revenues that put the needed funds in their pockets.

The Moral Aspects of a New Technology; the Case of Sex Control[92]

We cannot close our discussion without exploring the moral issues involved. Although science may be abstracted from daily life and its normative complications are often concealed, technology is part of everyday life and its normative ramifications are ever pressing.

We deal here with a different example than those studied in the preceding chapters since it helps to highlight these issues; however the discussion applies to the previously discussed "shortcuts" as well as to the topic at hand, a procedure presently being developed for sex (not birth) control.

Using various techniques developed as a result of fertility research, scientists are experimenting with the possibility of controlling whether a newborn infant will be a male or a female. So far, they have reported considerable success in their experiments with frogs and rabbits, whereas the success of experiments with human sperm appears to be quite limited, and the few optimistic reports seem to be unconfirmed. Still, work is progressing. While differential centrifugation seemed to provide one major approach to sex control, Emil Witschi, among others, noted that the force used in centrifugation may well damage the sperm, thus making this particular

---

[92] This section is based on a previously published article: Amitai Etzioni, "Sex Control: Science and Society," *Science,* Vol. 161 (December 13, 1968), pp. 1107–1112.

method of control especially undesirable.[93] The electrophoresis of spermatozoa has been carried out successfully over a period of years, but its application has been limited to animals.[94] The length of time needed to develop sex control of animals is difficult to ascertain; particularly in the case of human beings, sex control still seems to rest in the future. Despite the indefiniteness of the onset of sex control, both professional forecasters of the future and leading scientists see sex control as a mass practice in the foreseeable future. Herman Kahn and A. J. Wiener, in their discussion of the year 2000, suggest that one of the "one hundred technical innovations likely in the next thirty-three years" is the "capability to choose the sex of unborn children."[95] H. J. Muller has taken a similar stand about gene control in general.[96]

Sex control would satisfy the desire of many couples to be able to determine the sex of their children. Since there are differential cultural values attached to the sex of a child, many couples have more children than they wanted while trying to achieve an altered sex composition. Sex control by medication is expected to be more widely practiced than the present means of sex control, which involves conceiving more children and gambling on what their sex will be. The societal consequences of sex control are partially predictable from already existing studies of societies with skewed sex ratios.

In light of the serious effects on the social structure that this technological innovation can cause, scientists should consider the moral implications of such a technology before the methods are made available to the public. The possible consequences of the introduction of these methods should be seriously weighed before the methods are made available to the public.

Societal Consequences. In exploring what the societal consequences may be, we again need not rely on the speculation of what such a society would be like; we have much experience and some data on societies whose sex ratio was thrown off balance by war or immigration. For example, in 1960 New York City had 343,470 more females than males, a surplus of 68,366 in the twenty to thirty-four age category alone.[97]

We note, first, that most forms of social behavior are sex-correlated, and hence that changes in sex composition are very likely to affect most aspects

---

[93] Emil Witschi, personal communication.

[94] P. E. Lindahl, *Nature,* Vol. 181 (1958), p. 784; V. N. Schroder and N. K. Koltsov, *Nature,* Vol. 131 (1933), p. 329; M. J. Gordon, *Scientific American,* Vol. 199 (1958), pp. 87–97.

[95] Herman Kahn and A. J. Wiener, *The Year 2000: A Framework for Speculation on the Next Thirty-Three Years* (New York: Macmillan, 1967), p. 53.

[96] H. J. Muller, *Science,* Vol. 134 (1961), p. 643.

[97] Calculated from C. Winkler, ed., *Statistical Guide 1965 for New York City* (Department of Commerce and Industrial Development, New York, 1965), p. 17.

of social life. For instance, women read more books, see more plays, and in general consume more culture than men in the contemporary United States. Also, women attend church more often and are typically charged with the moral education of children. Males, by contrast, account for a much higher proportion of crime than females. A significant and cumulative male surplus will thus produce a society with some of the rougher features of a frontier town. And, it should be noted, the diminution of the number of agents of moral education and the increase in the number of criminals would accentuate already existing tendencies which point in these directions, thus magnifying social problems already overburdening our society.

Interracial and interclass tensions are likely to be intensified because some groups, lower classes and minorities specifically,[98] seem to be more male-oriented than the rest of the society. Hence while the sex imbalance in a society-wide average may be only a few percentage points, that of some groups is likely to be much higher. This may produce an especially high boy-surplus in lower status groups. These extra boys would seek girls in higher status groups (or in some other religious group than their own)[99] in which boys will be scarce.

On the lighter side, men vote systematically and significantly more Democratic than women; as the Republican party has been losing consistently in the number of supporters over the last generation anyhow, another five-point loss could undermine the two-party system to a point where Democratic control would be uninterrupted. (It is already the norm, with Republicans having occupied the White House for fourteen years over the last thirty-six. Other forms of imbalance which cannot be predicted are to be expected. "All social life is affected by the proportions of the sexes. Wherever there exists a considerable predominance of one sex over the other, in point of numbers, there is less prospect of a well-ordered social life." "Unbalanced numbers inexorably produce unbalanced behavior."[100]

Society would be very unlikely to collapse even if the sex ratio were to be much more seriously imbalanced than we expect. Societies are surpris-

---

[98] S. Winston suggests the opposite but he refers to sex control produced through birth control which is more widely practiced in higher classes, especially in the period in which his study was conducted, more than a generation ago. "Birth Control and the Sex Ratio at Birth," *American Journal of Sociology*, 38 (1932), pp. 225–231.

[99] C. F. Westoff, "The social-psychological structure of fertility," *International Population Conference* (International Union for Scientific Study of Population, Vienna, 1959).

[100] Quoted in J. H. Greenberg, *Numerical Sex Disproportion: A Study in Demographic Determinism* (Boulder: University of Colorado Press, 1950), p. 1. The sources indicated are A. F. Weber, *The Growth of Cities in the Nineteenth Century, Studies in History, Economics, and Public Law*, Vol. 11, p. 85; and H. von Hentig, *Crime: Causes and Conditions* (New York: McGraw-Hill, 1947), p. 121.

ingly flexible and adaptive entities. When asked what would be expected to happen if sex control were available on a mass basis, Kingsley Davis, the well-known demographer, stated that some delay in the age of marriage of the male, some rise in prostitution and in homosexuality, and some increase in the number of males who will never marry are likely to result. Thus, all of the "costs" that would be generated by sex control will probably not be charged against one societal sector, that is, would not entail only, let us say, a sharp rise in prostitution, but would be distributed among several sectors and would therefore be more readily absorbed. An informal examination of the situation in the USSR and Germany after World War II (sex ratio was 77:7 in the latter) as well as Israel in early immigration periods, support Davis' non-alarmist position. We must ask, though, are the costs justified? The dangers are not apocalyptical; but are they worth the gains to be made?

A Balance of Values. We deliberately chose a low-key example of the effects of science on society. One can provide much more dramatic ones; for example, the invention of new "psychedelic" drugs whose damage to genes will become known only much later (LSD was reported to have such effects), drugs which cripple the fetus (which has already occurred with the marketing of thalidomide), and the attempts to control birth with devices which may produce cancer (early versions of the intrauterine device were held to have such an effect). Additionally while methadone is reported to have no seriously harmful effects on those who use it, if, as presently seems possible, large numbers of people come to use the drug in heavy doses over most of their lives, a condition of considerable sensitivity and potential danger will exist for a number of years until the consequences of long-term maintenance on the drug can be more adequately established. But let us stay with a finding which generates only relatively small amounts of human misery, relatively well distributed among various sectors, so as not to severely undermine society but only add, maybe only marginally, to the considerable social problems we already face. Let us assume that we only add to the unhappiness of seven out of every hundred born (what we consider minimum imbalance to be generated), who will not find mates and will have to avail themselves of prostitution, homosexuality, or be condemned to enforced bachelorhood. (If you know someone who is desperate to be married but cannot find a mate, this discussion will be less abstract for you; now multiply this by 357,234 per annum.) Actually, to be fair, one must subtract from the unhappiness that sex control almost surely will produce, the joy it will bring to parents who will be able to order the sex of their children; but as of now, this is not, for most, an intensely felt need, and it seems a much smaller joy compared to the sorrows of the unmateable individuals.

We already recognize some rights of human guinea pigs. Their safety and privacy are not to be violated even if this means delaying the progress of science. The "rest" of the society, those who are not the subjects of research, and who are nowadays as much affected as those in the laboratory, have been accorded fewer rights. Theoretically, new knowledge, the basis of new devices and drugs, is not supposed to leave the inner circles of science before its safety has been tested on animals or volunteers, and in some instances approved by a government agency, mainly the Federal Drug Administration. But as the case of lysergic acid diethylamide (LSD) shows, the trip from reporting a discovery in a scientific journal to the drug's appearance in the bloodstream of thousands of citizens may be an extremely short one. The transition did take quite a number of years, from the days in 1943 when Albert Hofmann, one of the two men who synthesized LSD–25 at Sandoz Research Laboratories, first felt its hallucinogenic effect, until the early 1960s, when it "spilled" into illicit campus use. (The trip from legitimate research, its use at Harvard, to illicit unsupervised use was much shorter.) The point is that no additional technologies had to be developed; the distance from the chemical formula to illicit composition required in effect no additional steps.

More generally, Western civilization, ever since the invention of the steam engine, has proceeded on the assumption that society must adjust to new technologies. This is a central meaning of what we refer to when we speak about an industrial revolution; we think about a society being transformed and not just a new technology being introduced into a society which continues to sustain its prior values and institutions. Although the results are not an unmixed blessing (for instance, pollution and traffic casualties), on balance the benefits in terms of gains in standards of living and life expectancy much outweigh the costs. [Whether the same gains could be made with fewer costs if society would more effectively guide its transformation and technology inputs is a question less often discussed.][101] Nevertheless we must ask, especially with the advent of nuclear arms, if we can expect such a favorable balance in the future. We are aware that single innovations may literally blow up societies or civilization; we must also realize that the rate of social changes required by the accelerating stream of technological innovations, each less dramatic by itself, may supersede the rate at which society can absorb them. Could we not regulate to some extent the pace and impact of the technological inputs and select among them without, by every such act, killing the goose that lays the golden eggs?

Scientists often retort with two arguments. Science is in the business of searching for truths, not that of manufacturing technologies. The applica-

---

[101] For one of the best discussions, see E. F. Morison, *Men, Machines and Modern Times* (Cambridge, Mass.: M.I.T. Press, 1966). See also A. Etzioni, *The Active Society: A Theory of Societal and Political Processes* (New York: Free Press, 1968), Chapters 1 and 21.

tions of scientific findings are not determined by the scientists, but by society, politicians, corporations, and the citizens. Two scientists discovered the formula which led to the composition of LSD, but chemists do not determine whether it is used to accelerate psychotherapy or to create psychoses, or, indeed, whether it is used at all, or whether, like thousands of other studies and formulas, it is ignored. Scientists split the atom, but they did not decide whether particles would be used to produce energy to water deserts or super-bombs.

Second, the course of science is unpredictable, and any new lead, if followed, may produce unexpected bounties; to curb some lines of inquiry —because they may have dangerous outcomes—may well force us to forego some major payoffs; for example, if one were to forbid the study of sex control one might retard the study of birth control. Moreover, leads which seem "safe" may have dangerous outcomes. Hence, ultimately, only if science were stopped altogether might findings which are potentially dangerous be avoided.

These arguments are often presented as if they themselves were empirically verified or logically true statements. Actually they are a formula which enables the scientific community to protect itself from external intervention and control. An empirical study of the matter may well show that science does thrive in societies where scientists are given less freedom than the preceding model implies science must have, for example, in the Soviet Union. Even in the West in science some limitations on work are recognized and the freedom to study is not always seen as the ultimate value. Whereas some scientists are irritated when the health or privacy of their subject curbs the progress of their work, most scientists seem to recognize the priority of these other considerations. (Normative considerations also much affect the areas studied; compare, for instance, the high concern with a cancer cure to the almost complete unwillingness of sociologists, since 1954, to retest the finding that separate but equal education is not feasible.)

One may suggest that the society at large deserves the same protection as human subjects do from research. That is, the scientific community cannot be excused from the responsibility of asking what effects its endeavors have on the community. On the contrary, only an extension of the existing codes and mechanisms of self-control will ultimately protect science from a societal backlash and the heavy hands of external regulation. The intensification of the debate over the scientists' responsibilities with regard to the impacts of their findings is by itself one way of exercising it, because it alerts more scientists to the fact that the areas they choose to study, the ways they communicate their findings (to each other and to the community), the alliances they form or avoid with corporate and governmental interests—all these affect the use to which their work is put. It is simply not true that a scientist working on cancer research and one working on biological warfare are equally likely to come up with a new weapon and a new vaccine. Leads are not that random, and applications are not that readily transferable from one area of application to another.

Additional research on the societal impact of various kinds of research may help to clarify the issues. Such research even has some regulatory impact. For instance, frequently when a drug is shown to have been released prematurely, standards governing release of experimental drugs to mass production are tightened,[102] which in effect means fewer, more carefully supervised technological inputs into society; at least society does not have to cope with dubious findings. Additional progress may be achieved by studying empirically the effects that various mechanisms of self-regulation actually have on the work of scientists. For example, urging the scientific community to limit its study of some topics and focus on others may not retard science; for instance, sociology is unlikely to suffer from being now much more reluctant to concern itself with how the U.S. Army may stabilize or undermine foreign governments than it was before the blowup of Project Camelot.[103]

In this context, it may be noted that the systematic attempt to bridge the "two cultures" and to popularize science has undesirable side effects which aggravate the problem at hand. Mathematical formulas, Greek or Latin terminology, and jargon were major filters which allowed scientists in the past to discuss findings with each other without the nonprofessionals listening in. Now, often even preliminary findings are reported in the mass media and lead to policy adaptations, mass use, even legislation,[104] long before scientists have had a chance to double-check the findings themselves and their implications. True, even in the days when science was much more esoteric, one could find someone who could translate its findings into lay language and abuse it; but the process is much accelerated by well-meaning

---

[102] See reports in the *New York Times:* "Tranquilizer Is Put Under U.S. Curbs: Side Effects Noted," December 6, 1967; "F.D.A. Is Studying Reported Reactions To Arthritis Drug," March 19, 1967; "F.D.A. Adds Two Drugs To Birth Defect List," January 3, 1967. On May 24, 1966, Dr. S. F. Yolles, director of the National Institute of Mental Health, predicted in testimony before a Senate subcommittee: "The next 5 to 10 years . . . will see a hundredfold increase in the number and types of drugs capable of affecting the mind."

[103] I. L. Horowitz, *The Rise and Fall of Project Camelot* (Cambridge, Mass.: M.I.T. Press, 1967).

[104] For a detailed report, see testimony by J. D. Cooper, on February 28, 1967, before the Subcommittee on Government Research of the Committee on Government Operations, United States Senate, 90th Congress (First Session on Biomedical Development, Evaluation of Existing Federal Institutions), pp. 46–61.

men (and foundations) who feel that although science ought to be isolated from society, society should keep up with science as much as possible. Perhaps the public relations efforts on behalf of science ought to be reviewed and regulated so that science may remain free.

A system of regulation which builds on the difference between science and technology, with some kind of limitations on the technocrats serving to protect societies coupled with little curbing of scientists themselves, may turn out to be much more crucial. The societal application of most new scientific findings and principles advances through a sequence of steps, sometimes referred to as the R & D process. An abstract finding or insight frequently must be translated into a technique, procedure, or hardware, which in turn must be developed, tested, and mass-produced, before it affects society. While in some instances, like that of LSD, the process is extremely short in that it requires few if any steps in terms of further development of the idea, tool, and procedures, in most instances the process is long and expensive. It took, for instance, about $2 billion and several thousand applied scientists and technicians to make the first atomic weapons after the basic principles of atomic fission were discovered. Moreover, technologies often have a life of their own; for example, the intrauterine device did not spring out of any application of a new finding in fertility research but grew out of the evolution of earlier technologies.

The significance of the distinction between the basic research ("real" science) and later stages of research is that, first, the damage caused (if any) seems usually to be caused by the technologies and not by the science applied in their development. Hence if there were ways to curb damaging technologies, scientific research could maintain its almost absolute, follow-any-lead autonomy and society would be protected.

Second, and most important, the norms to which applied researchers and technicians subscribe and the supervisory practices which already prevail are very different than those which guide basic research. Applied research and technological work are already intensively guided by societal, even political, preferences. Thus, while about $2 billion a year of R & D money are spent on basic research more or less in ways the scientists see fit, the other $13 billion or so are spent on projects specifically ordered, often in great detail, by government authorities (for example, the development of a later version of a missile or a "spiced-up" tear gas). Studies of R & D corporations—in which much of this work is carried out, using thousands of professionals organized in supervised teams which are given specific assignments—pointed out that wide freedom of research simply does not exist here. A team assigned to cover a nose cone with many different alloys and to test which is the most heat-resistant is currently unlikely to stumble upon, let us say, a new heart pump, and if it were to come upon almost any other lead, the boss would refuse to allow the team to pursue the lead, using the corporation's time and funds specifically contracted for other purposes.

Not only are applied research and technological developments guided by economic and political considerations but also there is no evidence that they suffer from such guidance. Of course, one can overdirect any human activity, even the carrying of logs, and thus undermine morale, satisfaction of the workers, and their productivity, but such tight direction is usually not exercised in R & D work nor is it required for our purposes. So far guidance has been largely to direct efforts toward specific goals, and it has been largely corporate, in the sense that the goals have been chiefly set by the industry (for example, building flatter TV sets) or mission-oriented government agencies (for instance, land on the moon before the Russians). Some "preventive" control, like the suppression of run-proof nylon stockings, is believed to have taken place and to have been quite effective.

We are not suggesting that the direction given to technology by society has been a wise one. Frankly, it seems desirable that there be much less concern with military hardware and outer space and much more investment in domestic matters; less in developing new consumer gadgets and more in advancing the technologies of the public sector (education, welfare, and health); less concern with nature and more with society. The point though is that, for good or bad, technology is largely already socially guided, and hence the argument that its undesirable effects cannot be curbed because it cannot take guidance and survive is a false one.

What may have to be considered now is a more preventive and more national effective guidance, one that would discourage the development of those technologies which, studies would suggest, are likely to cause significantly more damage than benefit. Special bodies, preferably to be set up and controlled by the scientific community itself, could be charged with such regulation, although their decrees might have to be as enforceable as those of the Federal Drug Administration. (The Federal Drug Administration, which itself is overworked and understaffed, deals mainly with medical and not societal effects of new technologies.) Such bodies could rule, for instance, that whereas fertility research ought to go on uncurbed, sex-control procedures for human beings are not to be developed. One cannot be sure that such bodies would come up with the right decisions. But they would have several features which make it likely that they would come up with better decisions than the present system for the following reasons:

1. They would be responsible for protecting society, a responsibility which so far is not institutionalized.

2. If they act irresponsibly, the staff might be replaced, let us say by a

vote of the appropriate scientific associations. However, governmental involvement in such decision-making has been suggested.

3. Finally, such bodies could draw on data as to the societal effects of new (or anticipated) technologies, in part to be generated at their initiative (at present, to the extent such supervisory decisions are made at all, they are frequently based on folk knowledge).

> Selections among alternative technologies require that choices be made among competing and conflicting interests and values. To the extent that those choices are made and enforced collectively rather than individually, they are essentially political in character and must therefore be the responsibility of the politically responsive branches of government and of those publicly accountable bodies that are specifically entrusted with regulatory responsibilities in narrowly circumscribed areas. The making of such choices is, in principle, indistinguishable from the resolution of many other conflicts that beset society.[105]

Most of us recoil at any such notion of regulating science, if only at the implementation (or technological) end of it, which actually is not science at all. We are inclined to see in such control an opening wedge which may lead to deeper and deeper penetration of society into the scientific activity. Actually, one may hold the opposite view—that unless societal costs are diminished by some acts of self-regulation at the stage in the R & D process where it hurts least, the society may "backlash" and with a much heavier hand slap on much more encompassing and throttling controls.

The efficacy of increased education of scientists to their responsibilities, of strengthening the barriers between intrascientific communications and the community at large, and of self-imposed, late-phase controls may not suffice. Full solution requires considerable international cooperation, at least among the top technology-producing countries. The various lines of approach to protecting society discussed here may be unacceptable to the reader. The problem must be faced, and it requires greater attention as we are affected by an accelerating technological output with ever-increasing societal ramifications, which jointly may overload society's capacity to adapt and cause more unhappiness than any group of men has a right to inflict on others, however noble their intentions.

---

[105] "Technology Assessment: NAS Panel Asks New Federal Mechanisms," *Science,* Vol. 165 (September 5, 1969).

INDEX